The Quality of Democracy in Post-Communist Europe

The countries of the former Eastern Bloc and Soviet Union have exhibited remarkable diversity in their post-communist regime paths. Whereas some states have become demonstrably more democratic and have moved, in the space of fifteen years, from the periphery to the centre of European politics, in others the political and economic climates seem hardly to be better, and their societies no more free, than in the final years of the Cold War.

Assessing progress towards democracy in the former Eastern Bloc – or the lack of it – requires a qualitative examination of post-communist polities. This collection of articles brings together a number of perspectives, both macro- and micro-analytical, on the 'quality' of democracy in post-communist Europe.

This volume was previously published as a special issue of *The Journal of Communist Studies and Transition Politics*.

Derek S. Hutcheson will be a Lecturer in Comparative Politics at University College Dublin, Ireland, from January 2006. He was previously a British Academy Postdoctoral Fellow in the Department of Politics, University of Glasgow.

Elena A. Korosteleva, formerly a British Academy Postdoctoral Fellow at the University of Glasgow, is now a Lecturer at the Department of International Politics at the University of Wales, Aberystwyth.

The Quality of Democracy in Post-Communist Europe

Edited by
Derek S. Hutcheson & Elena A. Korosteleva

Routledge
Taylor & Francis Group

LONDON AND NEW YORK

First published 2006 by Routledge
2 Park Square, Milton Park, Abingdon, Oxon OX14 4RN

Simultaneously published in the USA and Canada
by Routledge
270 Madison Avenue, New York, NY 10016

Routledge is an imprint of the Taylor & Francis Group

© 2006 Taylor & Francis Group Ltd

Typeset in Times by Techset Composition Limited
Printed and bound in Great Britain by Antony Rowe Ltd, Chippenham, Wiltshire

British Library Cataloguing in Publication Data
A catalogue record for this book is available from the British Library

Library of Congress Cataloging in Publication Data
A catalog record for this book has been requested

ISBN 0-415-34807-2

Contents

Notes on Contributors

Leonardo Morlino is Professor of Political Science at the University of Florence, Italy. He is the author of more than a hundred articles and books focusing on authoritarianism and democratic theory. His recent publications include *Democracy Between Consolidation and Crisis: Parties, Groups, and Citizens in Southern Europe*, 2nd edn. (2003) and *Democrazie e Democratizzazioni* (2003).

Dirk Berg-Schlosser is Professor of Political Science at Philipps University, Marburg, Germany. His recent publications include *Authoritarianism and Democracy in Europe 1919–39* (2002, co-authored with Jeremy Mitchell), *Poverty and Democracy* (2002, co-authored with Norbert Kersting) and *Democratization in Comparative Perspective* (2004).

Clare McManus-Czubińska is Lecturer in the Department of Central and East European Studies, University of Glasgow; **William L. Miller** is Edward Caird Professor of Politics, University of Glasgow; **Radosław Markowski** is Director and Principal Investigator of the Polish National Election Survey Programme, Polish Academy of Sciences; **Jacek Wasilewski** is Head of the Unit of Elite and Political Behaviour Research, Polish Academy of Sciences.

Stephen White is Professor of International Politics at the University of Glasgow; and **Ian McAllister** is Director of the Research School of Social Sciences at the Australian National University, Canberra. They acknowledge the assistance of the UK Economic and Social Research Council under grant L213252007 to Stephen White, Margot Light and John Löwenhardt.

Derek S. Hutcheson will be a Lecturer in Comparative Politics at University College Dublin, Ireland, from January 2006. He was previously a British Academy Postdoctoral Fellow in the Department of Politics, University of Glasgow. His research focuses on the 'quality of democracy' in post-communist Europe, particularly in Russia and Eastern Germany, and he is the author of *Political Parties in the Russian Regions* (London/New York: RoutledgeCurzon, 2003). He wishes to acknowledge the financial support of the British Academy and UACES.

Elena A. Korosteleva, formerly a British Academy Postdoctoral Fellow at the University of Glasgow, is now Lecturer at the Department of International Politics at the University of Wales, Aberystwyth. Her recent publications include a special issue of the *Journal of Communist Studies and Transition Politics* on 'The Quality of Democracy in Post-Communist Europe' (Vol. 20, No. 1, 2004, edited with Derek Hutcheson) and *Postcommunist Belarus* (Rowman & Littlefield, 2004, edited with Stephen White and John Löwenhardt).

Lucan A. Way is Assistant Professor of Political Science at Temple University, USA. He is writing a book with Steven Levitsky (Harvard University) on hybrid regimes in Africa, the Americas, Asia and post-Communist Eurasia. He is also working on a book focusing on the obstacles to authoritarian consolidation in the former Soviet Union.

Paul G. Lewis is Reader in Central and East European Politics at the Open University, where he has taught many courses in comparative politics, European studies and international relations. Major recent research topics have been the development of parties in post-communist Europe and the process of EU enlargement. Recent publications include *Political Parties in Post-Communist Eastern Europe* (2000) and *Pan-European Perspectives on Party Politics* (2003, with Paul Webb).

Preface

DEREK S. HUTCHESON and
ELENA A. KOROSTELEVA

From the Second World War until the late 1980s, Europe was divided by a military 'Iron Curtain' – an 'Eastern Bloc' of communist-ruled, Soviet-oriented countries offset by a Western half allied to the North Atlantic Treaty Organization (NATO). Nowhere was this more clearly embodied than in Germany, where the presence of the Berlin Wall provided a stark reminder of the partition of the continent into Soviet and Western spheres of influence.

Just as its construction in 1961 had symbolized a further entrenchment in the division of Europe, images of the fall of the Wall in November 1989 epitomized the wider collapse of one-party rule in Eastern Europe. One by one, revolutions swept across the Eastern Bloc, as the communist parties, having ruled for some 40 years, lost their hold on power in the space of a few short months. The disintegration of the Soviet Union itself two years later led at least one philosopher to hypothesize 'the end of history'. The Cold War was over; liberal democracy, it appeared, had won.[1]

Fifteen years on from the collapse of the Wall, Europe is a very different place. Berlin is today the vibrant capital of reunited Germany, with little trace of the Wall remaining. The Czech Republic, Hungary and Poland, all former signatories to the Warsaw Pact, were admitted to NATO in 1999. May 2004 saw the enlargement of the European Union to embrace ten new member states, eight of which – the Czech Republic, Estonia, Hungary, Latvia, Lithuania, Poland, the Slovak Republic and Slovenia – were communist-ruled less than two decades ago. In most of the above-mentioned countries there have now been several rounds of free elections, and power has alternated between different ideological groupings.

Yet the optimism of the early 1990s has not translated into smooth progress towards democracy throughout the region. As will be seen in some of the contributions to this collection, problems still remain even in those countries generally considered to be at the forefront of democratization. Moreover, it is no longer possible to speak of 'Eastern Europe' as a homogeneous group of states. The countries of the former Eastern Bloc and the former Soviet Union have exhibited remarkable diversity in their post-communist regime paths. Whereas some states have become demonstrably more democratic and have moved in the space of 15 years from the periphery to the centre of European politics, in others the political and economic climates seem hardly to be better, and their societies no more free, than in the final years of the Cold War.

Assessing progress towards democracy in the former Eastern Bloc – or the lack of it – requires a qualitative examination of post-communist polities. The present collection of articles brings together a number of perspectives – both macro- and micro-analytical – on the 'quality' of democracy in post-communist Europe, a decade-and-a-half on from the start of the transition process. Different types of regime are emerging in post-communist Europe. At one extreme, a number of countries in Central Europe appear to be making good progress towards the consolidation of democratic government. At the other, the experiences of the post-Soviet states of Russia, Ukraine and, particularly, Belarus, may lead us to question whether there is necessarily an inevitable democratic 'end point' to transition, or whether it is possible for post-communist states to settle into what the authors in this collection variously term 'demagogical democracy' or 'competitive authoritarianism' – in other words, consolidated regimes that are neither fully democratic nor completely authoritarian.

Leonardo Morlino begins this discussion with a re-examination of various theories of democracy. In order to assess the quality of democracy in post-communist Europe, it is first of all necessary to define the criteria by which a 'good' or 'quality' democracy may be measured. Morlino examines the procedural dimensions of democratic government – the rule of law and accountability – and the ways in which the outcomes of these may be assessed. He also introduces a number of factors (many of which have relevance to contemporary post-communist Europe) that can be considered 'subversive' and lead to democratically deficient regimes.

Dirk Berg-Schlosser continues the theme of defining and measuring effective democratic governance. Using a variety of quantitative data, including various indices of democracy and recent socio-economic data, he highlights the diverse nature of contemporary Europe. He examines the entire area of continental Europe, from Portugal in the west to Russia in the east. This analysis highlights once again the mixed progress made towards democracy in post-communist Europe, and also some manifestations of increasingly regressive tendencies even among the more established regimes of long-standing EU member states.

The remaining chapters focus on a number of themes relating to the 'quality' of democracy in individual countries or groups of countries in post-communist Europe. Clare McManus-Czubińska, William L. Miller, Radosław Markowski and Jacek Wasilewski focus on Central Europe and on the key issue in the region at the present time: the above-mentioned

EU accession process. The fact that these countries stand on the threshold of EU membership just 15 years after they were one-party states shows how much progress has been made in a comparatively short time. Yet McManus-Czubińska and her collaborators, through a focus on the accession referendums held in these countries in the summer and autumn of 2003 (and in particular on the June 2003 referendum in Poland), suggest that Central European voters were not as enthusiastic about joining the EU as the high numbers voting in favour of the accession treaty might imply. They suggest that the referendums provided voters with constrained choices imposed by elites, and did not allow electorates to express their true views. Moreover, they question the appropriateness of using referendums to provide clear choices among a subtle range of options. The implications for 'democracy' of this constrained choice and unsuitable use of institutional tools form a central theme in their article.

Stephen White and Ian McAllister's contribution focuses on different aspects of political engagement and disengagement in Russia, Ukraine and Belarus – the three Slavic post-Soviet states and the central axis of the former USSR. White and McAllister examine voters' trust and confidence in the institutions of the state more than a decade on from the collapse of the Soviet Union. They find low levels of political efficacy – the electorate actually considers itself to have less influence over politics than under one-party rule! – and low levels of trust in many of the institutions of democracy, such as parliaments and parties. They also examine patterns of engagement and disengagement and seek to provide explanations for these.

Remaining on the theme of engagement and looking at the case study of Russia, Derek Hutcheson focuses on a neglected aspect of Russian electoral politics – voting 'against all' as a means of registering political protest, as an alternative to simple abstention. He analyses the patterns and bases of electoral protest over the past decade. Preliminary indications suggest that abstainers and protesters are in fact two quite distinct groups of voters, with the latter consciously casting a 'positive negative' ballot rather than simply disengaging from politics altogether.

Elena Korosteleva focuses on the quality of democracy in Belarus and Ukraine, corroborating the findings of White and McAllister and of Lucan Way. Combining Aristotle with observations and empirical data in these two post-Soviet states, she concludes that both fulfil Aristotle's criteria for a 'demagogical democracy': the citizens display little understanding of their rights and responsibilities, allowing for manipulation and dictate by their governments.

Lucan Way also uses Ukraine as a case study, comparing it with similar regimes around the world. His conclusion is broadly similar, even if it approaches the question from the other side: rather than 'demagogical democracy', he suggests, Ukraine is an example of 'competitive authoritarianism'. Both Korosteleva and Way highlight the fact that former Soviet states are not necessarily heading towards liberal democracy, but instead contain elements of both: authoritarian tendencies tempered by regular, but not always free and fair, elections.

Paul Lewis provides a short concluding note to the collection. He picks up a number of themes that feature elsewhere, giving an overview of developments in Eastern and Central Europe in the post-communist period. He points out the growing dichotomy between those countries at the vanguard of democratization, and the others which are increasingly faced by problems that may be insurmountable.

The articles presented here offer a diverse range of perspectives on a diverse range of countries. They show that the path to democracy is not always a smooth or a linear one. Many problems remain to be surmounted, but, 15 years after the collapse of one-party rule in Eastern and Central Europe, it is a timely moment to reflect on the quality of the polities that have emerged from the post-communist transitions.

NOTE

1. Francis Fukuyama, *The End of History and the Last Man* (London: Penguin, 1992).

'Good' and 'Bad' Democracies: How to Conduct Research into the Quality of Democracy

LEONARDO MORLINO

Defining Democracy

What is a 'Good' Democracy?

The analysis of the quality of democracy – that is, an empirical scrutiny of what 'good' democracy is about – requires not only that we have a definition of democracy, but also that we establish a clear notion of quality.

The minimal definition of democracy[1] suggests that such a regime has at least universal, adult suffrage; recurring, free, competitive and fair elections; more than one political party; and more than one source of information. In addition, democratic institutions, existing rights and also the decision making process should not be constrained by non-elected elites or external powers.[2] Among the countries that meet these minimal criteria, further empirical analysis is still necessary to detect the degree to which they have achieved the two main objectives of an ideal democracy: freedom and equality.

Thus, the analysis of a 'good democracy' should theoretically set alongside those regimes that are to varying degrees deficient in principal democratic features. Amongst them are *hybrid regimes*,[3] whose failure to ensure free and fair electoral competition and a minimum level of civil rights keeps them below the minimum threshold to be classified as democratic. Likewise, the *defective democracies*[4] should also be left out of the analysis. This category includes 'exclusive' democracies, which offer only limited guarantees for political rights; 'dominated' democracies, in which powerful groups use their influence to condition and limit the autonomy of elected leaders; and 'illiberal' democracies, which offer only partial guarantees of civil rights. In reality, the last three models may also be seen as institutional hybrids, and thus fall short of the minimum threshold specified above.

Deficient democracy is a recurrent expression used to depict East European regimes, but it often bears a different meaning. These are regimes that have just overcome the minimal democratic threshold, but still experience problems of consolidation. By displaying minimal requirements for democracy, they differ from hybrid regimes (see above) and can be included in the analysis here.

Delegative democracy, sometimes referred to as *populist democracy*, also falls well within the scope of this analysis, having overcome the necessary threshold. These regimes are usually based on a majority system, and host relatively 'clean' elections; parties, parliament and the press are usually free to express their criticisms, and the courts block unconstitutional policies.[5] In practice, however, citizens of these democracies, which O'Donnell finds in Latin America, for example, 'delegate others to make decisions on their behalf', such that they no longer have the opportunity to check and evaluate the performance of their officials once they are elected. Other bodies of government, even those meant for this purpose, neglect or fail to carry out their watchdog functions, and consequently the rule of law is only partially or minimally respected.[6]

The second step in evaluating 'good' and 'bad' democracies requires a clear definition of 'quality'. The use of the term in the industrial and marketing sectors suggests three different meanings of quality. First, quality is defined by the established procedural aspects associated with each product – a 'quality' product is the result of an exact, controlled process carried out according to precise, recurring methods and timing: here the emphasis is on the *procedure*. Second, quality consists of the structural characteristics of a product, be it the design, materials or functioning of the good, or other details that it features: here the emphasis is on the *contents*. Finally, the quality of a product or service is indirectly derived from the satisfaction expressed by the customer, by their requesting again the same product or service, regardless of either how it is produced or what the actual contents are, or how the consumer goes about acquiring the product or service: such an interpretation suggests that the quality is based simply on *result*.

The three different notions of quality are thus grounded in either procedures, contents or results. Each has different implications for the empirical research. Importantly, even with all the adjustments demanded by the complexity of the 'object' under examination – namely, democracy – it is still necessary to keep these conceptualizations of quality in mind as we elaborate definitions and models of democratic quality.

Moving from these premises, a definition of democratic quality will be suggested in the following section. Furthermore, the principal dimensions of democratic quality will be evaluated with a particular emphasis on the betrayal and circumvention of quality goals. In the final section a comparative conclusion will be drawn and a few issues will be pointed out for further discussion.

What is the 'Quality' of Democracy?

Starting from the definition above, and from the prevailing notions of quality, a quality or 'good' democracy may be considered to be one presenting *a stable institutional structure that realizes the liberty and equality of citizens through the legitimate and correct functioning of its institutions and mechanisms.* A good democracy is thus first and foremost a broadly legitimated regime that completely satisfies citizens ('quality' in terms of 'result'). When institutions have the full backing of civil society, they can pursue the values of the democratic regime. If, in contrast, the institutions must postpone their objectives and expend energy and resources on consolidating and maintaining their legitimacy, crossing even the minimum threshold for democracy becomes a remarkable feat. Second, a good democracy is one in which the citizens, associations and communities enjoy liberty and equality ('quality' in terms of 'content'). Third, in a good democracy the citizens themselves have the power to check and evaluate whether the government pursues the objectives of liberty and equality according to the rule of law. They monitor the efficiency of the application of the laws in force, the efficacy of the decisions made by government, and the political responsibility and accountability of elected officials in relation to the demands expressed by civil society ('quality' in terms of 'procedure').

With the above in mind, five possible dimensions can be indicated here, along which good democracies may vary. The first two are procedural dimensions. Although related to the contents, these dimensions mainly concern the rules. The first procedural dimension is the rule of law; the second is accountability.[7] The third dimension concerns the responsiveness or correspondence of the political decisions to the desires of the citizens and civil society in general. The final two dimensions are substantive in nature: the penultimate one refers to civil rights expanded through the achievement of certain freedoms; and the final one refers the progressive implementation of greater political, social and economic equality. These five dimensions will be further elaborated in three sections below. Before undertaking this, several general considerations will be emphasized.

The analytical framework proposed here differs somewhat from other studies on the quality of democracy, such as those of Altman and Perez-Linan[8] and of Lijphart.[9] Both of these develop a quantitative comparative strategy. Here we stress the virtuous combination of qualitative and quantitative measures in the empirical analysis of the phenomenon. The differences also emerge in the definition of a good democracy, the dimensions of variation and related indicators of quality proposed above. Altman and Perez-Linan draw on Dahl's concept of polyarchy (civil rights, participation and competition) and may fit into the first substantive dimension indicated above as well as into the procedural dimensions. Conversely, Lijphart's inclusion into the analysis of the quality of democracy of such dimensions as female representation, electoral participation, satisfaction with the democracy, and corruption, coincide closely with the five dimensions mentioned.

The institutions and mechanisms of representative democracies are the main objects of the analysis of the quality of democracy. This is not to ignore direct democracy as the highest expression of democratic quality, but to acknowledge the secular experience of representative democracies and their actual potential for improvement. If the analysis has to be focused on representative democracies, then accountability – a core feature in the experience of representative democracy – becomes a truly central dimension in so far as it grants citizens and civil society in general an effective means of control over political institutions. This feature attenuates the difficulties that exist objectively when there is a shift from direct to representative democracy.

Accountability is implicitly based on two assumptions from the liberal tradition that highlight the interconnected nature of all of the dimensions explained above. The first assumption is that, if citizens are genuinely given the opportunity to evaluate the responsibility of government in terms of the satisfaction of their own needs and requests, they are in fact capable of doing so, possessing above all a relatively accurate perception of their own needs. The second assumption is that citizens, either alone or as part of a group, are the only possible judges of their own needs: no third party can decide those needs. To leave these assumptions unmentioned is mistaken; they should instead be stated and taken into account from the outset. It is also erroneous to consider each of them as a mere ideological choice. It is instead important to acknowledge that Western democracies have followed a liberal-democratic trajectory and that any concrete analysis of the quality of democracy must take this into account, and also the shift in a direction marked by more egalitarian choices. Those assumptions refer only to vertical accountability, however, and will be further examined in the next section.

Freedom and equality, however they are understood, are necessarily linked to accountability and responsiveness. Indeed, a higher implementation of freedom and equality for citizens and civil society lies in the sphere of representative mechanisms. In addition, effective rule of law is also indispensable for a good democracy. The rule of law is intertwined with freedom in the respect for all those laws that directly or indirectly sanction those rights and their concrete realization. As the next section will explain, freedom, equality and even accountability are actually unobtainable if respect for law is ineffective or the government and the administration do not grant decisional efficacy. These are fundamental preconditions necessary for deciding and carrying out policies to achieve a better democratic quality.

The main subjects of such a democracy are the citizen-individuals, the territorial communities, and the various formal and informal associations with common values, traditions or aims. In this sense, the possibility of good democracy exists not only in the case of a defined territory with a specific population controlled by state institutions under a democratic government, but also of broader entities such as the European Union. The main point is that the above-named subjects are at the heart of a democracy in which the most important processes are those that work 'bottom-up' rather than 'top-down'. In this way, the transfer of analytical dimensions from the national level to the supranational level – although not uncomplicated and without difficulty – is possible. The key is to hold constant the same elements characteristic of each dimension.

The necessity of capturing the empirical complexity of the notion of 'quality' democracy motivates the employment of the five dimensions elaborated above. This elaboration pinpoints two aspects of each dimension: each might vary from the others in terms of a form and of a degree of development. That being the case, the analysis calls for indicators, certain measures that reveal how and to what degree each dimension is present not only in different countries, but also in various models of good democracy. These empirical data should also enable the eventual tracking of the growth of quality democracies.

Moreover, such a multidimensional analysis is also justified by the possibility of accepting in this way a pluralist notion of quality. That is, the contents, the procedure and the result also correspond to three different conceptions of quality. And each conception has its own ground in terms of values and ideals. In other words, if the notion of democratic quality is to come out of the realm of utopia and become a legitimate topic of empirical research, then multidimensionality is essential to capture it empirically, as is the related acknowledgement that different, equally possible, notions of quality are likewise necessary in order to proceed in that direction. The different policy implications of such pluralism should not be ignored.

The Procedural Dimensions

Rule of Law

The line of reasoning set out above brings us to a closer analysis of the constituent dimensions of democratic quality, the essential conditions for their existence, and the numerous and related problems associated with the empirical study. The procedural dimensions are considered in this section. The first procedural dimension encompasses decisional output and its implementation, and is constituted by the rule of law. The second concerns the relationship between input and output and refers to accountability. A large body of literature already exists that discusses these two dimensions.[10] Here, each dimension will be analysed with reference to four aspects: the empirical definition, the main indicators, the attempts and practice of its subversion, and the central condition or conditions.

The *rule of law* is not only the enforcement of legal norms. Rather, it connotes the principle of the supremacy of law, and entails at least the capacity, even if limited, to make the authorities respect the laws, and to have laws that are not retroactive, and are available to the public, universal, stable and unambiguous.[11] These characteristics are fundamental for any civil order and constitute a primary requirement for democratic consolidation,[12] along with other basic qualities such as civilian control over the military.

With regard to the rule of law and its enforcement we can identify a number of key features for a 'good democracy'. These include the following:

- the equal enforcement of law towards everyone, including all state officials: that is to say, all individuals are equal under the law and no one is above the law, also at supranational level;
- the supremacy of the legal state, meaning that no areas are dominated by organized crime, even at a local level;
- no corruption in the political, administrative and judicial branches;
- the existence of a local, centralized civil bureaucracy that competently, efficiently and universally applies the laws and assumes responsibility in the event of an error;
- the existence of an efficient police force that respects the individual rights and freedoms guaranteed by law;
- equal, unhindered access of citizens to the judicial system in case of lawsuits between private citizens or between private citizens and public institutions;
- reasonably swift resolution of criminal inquiries and of civil and administrative lawsuits;
- independence of the judiciary from any political influence;
- ability of the courts to have their rulings enforced;
- supremacy of the Constitution, interpreted and defended by a Constitutional Court.

All the above concern the effective implementation of the law and the fair resolution of lawsuits within the legal system. Various indicators can represent each one and the relevant data can be analysed on a case-by-case basis using both qualitative and quantitative techniques. The main characteristics, and the degree to which the rule of law is respected, can be reconstructed for each case in each country.[13]

It should be emphasized, even if only in passing, that the analysis implicitly proposed here would be extremely expensive and practically impossible to apply to a high number of cases. The level of detail and thoroughness built into the investigation is meant for a limited number of cases, yielding the best results for a project aimed at examining few countries. Additional cases would require a reduction in the number of variables and the elimination of some dimensions. Those that should necessarily be kept in the empirical analysis, even in a quantitative analysis involving many cases, include the detection of (i) the possible presence of mafias that become a territorial limitation to the rule of law; (ii) the civilian control of military and police; (iii) the level of corruption, with whatever data are available on the phenomenon; (iv) the access of citizens to the court system; and finally (v) the duration of legal proceedings using the pertinent judiciary statistics.

It is clear, however, that these indicators can provide only an incomplete illustration of the phenomenon.

A closer look at the specific problems of implementation should be accompanied by certain awareness of some opposing forces, which here can be defined as forces *subverting* the quality of democracy. Within a well-established democratic regime none would dare to challenge the democratic dimensions openly, but the political elite and other actors may try to circumvent, betray or subvert these dimensions or their aspects.

Thus, a rigorous application of laws, or, in certain cases, the relationship with a superficially efficient bureaucracy, can have particularly negative consequences for socially weak and vulnerable members of society.[14] Then, there is the possible use of the law as a genuine 'political weapon'.[15] Here we see a persistent temptation for politicians to use the law against their adversaries. Politicians are also tempted to use judicial acts to reinforce their own positions against the opposition. In other cases, when there is collusion among politicians, the judges themselves, with the support of the media, are tempted to turn to the judiciary in retaliation for certain political decisions that they consider unacceptable. On a different level, there is also a growing tendency among individual citizens or economic groups to resort to the law to assert their own interests: some scholars label this phenomenon a 'juridification' of contemporary democracy. Finally, and not altogether different, is the popular cultural attitude that interprets the law as a severe impediment to realizing one's own interests that should be circumvented in any way possible. This attitude, common in various countries throughout the world, from Southern Europe to Latin America and also Eastern Europe, extends from the popular to the entrepreneurial classes. The Italians often say *'fatta la legge, trovato l'inganno'* suggesting that 'fraud goes hand in hand with law'.

In summary, the empirical analysis of the democratic rule of law should be done carefully, with attention to the attempts and practice of its subversion that powerfully work against its actual realization. Rule of law remains an essential feature of democratic quality, and it plays a very important role for the existence and development of the other dimensions. What, then, are the fundamental conditions that allow for at least a moderate development of the rule of law? Research on various dimensions of this theme suggests that the diffusion of liberal and democratic values among both the people and, especially, the elite, complemented by the existence of the bureaucratic traditions and by the legislative and economic means essential for its full implementation, are the necessary conditions for the democratic rule of law.

However, these conditions exist in very few countries, and they are very difficult to create. Consequently, it is also difficult to cultivate this dimension of democratic quality. The most reasonable strategy would be to proceed incrementally, following the lines and objectives that have been set out above. This strategy is inherently critical of Putnam's conclusion that the institutional contours of a specific democratic regime are fixed in the oldest civic traditions of that country, and that national institutions change slowly.[16]

Accountability

The second dimension of democratic quality is the obligation of elected political leaders to answer for their political decisions when asked by citizen-electors or other constitutional bodies. Schedler suggests that accountability has three main features: information, justification, and punishment or compensation.[17] The first element – information on a political act or series of acts by a politician or political body (the government, parliament and so on) – is indispensable for attributing responsibility. The second – justification – refers to the reasons furnished by the governing leaders for their actions and decisions. The third, punishment or compensation, is the consequence drawn by the elector or some other person or body following an evaluation of the information, justifications and other aspects and interests behind the political act. All three of these elements require the existence of a public dimension characterized by pluralism and independence and the real participation of a range of individual and collective actors.

Accountability can be either vertical or horizontal.[18] Vertical accountability is when electors can make their elected official responsible for their actions. This first type of accountability has a periodic nature, and is dependent on the various national, local and (if they exist) supranational election dates. The voter decides and either awards the incumbent candidate or slate of candidates with a vote in their favour, or else punishes them by voting for another candidate, abstaining from the vote, or spoiling the ballot. The actors involved in vertical accountability are the governors and the governed, and thus they are politically unequal. This dimension of democratic quality can become less intermittent only if one considers the various electoral occasions at the local, national and, for European citizens, supranational levels. Continuity is also supported when citizens can vote in referendums on issues regarding activity of the central government.

Horizontal accountability holds when governors are responsible to other institutions or collective actors that possess the expertise and power to control the behaviour of the governors. In contrast to vertical accountability, the actors are for the most part political equals. Horizontal accountability is relatively continuous, being formally or substantially formalized by law. In practice, it is usually manifest in the monitoring exercised by the governmental opposition in parliament, by the various assessments and rulings emitted by the court system, if activated, and by constitutional courts, agencies of auditing, central banks and other bodies of a similar purpose that exist in democracies. Political parties outside parliament also exercise this kind of control, as do the media and other intermediary associations, such as unions and employers' associations.[19]

Certain underlying conditions must exist to ensure that the two forms of accountability can be fully claimed. For vertical accountability, political competition and the distribution of power must at least be fair enough to allow for genuine electoral alternatives at the various levels of government. Altman and Perez-Linan's focus on competition and their development of an indicator that measures the 'balanced presence of opposition in parliament' should be mentioned here. This indicator has a negative value when the governing party dominates the legislature in terms of seats or when the opposition is so strong that it poses problems for the decision-making efficacy of the government. The absence of alternation and bipolarism between two parties, or between party lines or coalitions, diminishes the importance and force of vertical accountability. If it exists, it is relevant only at the level of individual candidates.

The presence of horizontal accountability instead hinges on a legal system that, as mentioned above, provides for the exertion of checks and balances by other public entities that are independent of the government, and not competing as an alternative to it. This form of accountability demands strong and well-established intermediary structures (such as parties); a responsible, vigilant political opposition; independent media that are conscious of their civil function; and a well-developed network of active, informed organizations and associations that share democratic values.

Given the opacity and complexity of political processes, politicians have ample opportunity to manipulate their contexts in such a way as to absolve themselves of any tangible responsibility. Subversion of accountability can become a frequent practice of established democracies. In this vein, accountability frequently becomes a catchphrase more connected to the image of a politician than to any decisions he or she may have made or results he or she may have achieved. Negative outcomes are easily justified by making reference to unforeseen events, or by taking advantage of favoured press to influence public opinion. At the same time, good results obtained by careful leadership may have negative or punitive consequences for the incumbent leader at the time of the next elections if either uncertainties of the moment or better management of image by the competing political elite become dominant aspects of the electoral campaign.

The very action, often ideological and instrumental, of parties or other components of the political opposition, or even of media actors that are in a position to conduct public processes, sometimes on inconsistent grounds, again confirms the difficulty of implementing accountability. The lack of clear distinctions between incumbent leaders and party leaders – the head of government often also controls the governing party – means that parties, be they of the opposition or of the majority, are hindered in carrying out their role as watchdogs for their constituents. At the parliamentary level, party discipline is considered more important than accountability towards the electors and, in practice, the parliamentary majority supports the government without controlling it. Furthermore, there should also be a clear distinction between the responsible leader, either of the government or of the opposition, and the intermediate layers of party actors that range from militants to sympathizers. The latter should trigger a bottom-up process that gives direction for how parties should control the government or organize their opposition. Recent research on party organization in some advanced democracies[20] indicates the existence of an opposite trend characterized by strong, oligarchic leaders who act in collusion – rather than in competition – with other parties. The most extreme hypothesis related to this phenomenon is that parties, supported by public financing, shape what are in fact 'cartels'.

As Maravall[21] has elaborated, the ways in which government leaders can avoid accountability are numerous. At the same time, if the horizontal accountability is lacking or extremely weak, vertical accountability remains the only instrument for guaranteeing this dimension of quality democracy. The opportunities to exercise vertical accountability are only periodic, however, and in some cases citizens must wait several years before the next elections. The result is that we obtain a sort of 'delegative democracy'[22] – a democracy of poor quality in which the citizen casts his or her vote and is subsequently ignored until the next election. Citizens are left without any means of controlling corruption and poorly performing government, and there are no other institutions really capable of guaranteeing horizontal accountability.

The central conditions for ensuring accountability are fairly obvious, and are already more or less clear from the above discussion. A few, however, should be explicitly mentioned. First of all, in addition to genuine electoral alternatives and bipolarism among political parties, for one form of accountability to exist to any effective degree, the other must be present as well, with each thereby reinforcing the other. Second, judiciary and other public institutions that are independent of the executive and legislature and capable of concretely exercising the checks provided for by law are also necessary. Third, it is also essential that interested, educated and informed citizens who have internalized the fundamental values of democracy remain involved in the political process. A key, basic element for effective accountability, be it vertical or even horizontal, is a good level of citizen participation. The fourth condition is the presence of independent sources of information – a requirement that is in many ways related to the previous one. Last but not least, vertical and horizontal accountability are both supported when a range of active intermediary actors of various dimensions, such as parties and associations, are organizationally rooted in civil society.

The Outcome

Responsiveness

In analysing democratic quality, it is fairly common to refer to the responsiveness of government, that is, the capacity to satisfy the governed by executing the policies that correspond to their demands. This dimension is analytically related to accountability. Indeed, judgements on responsibility imply that there is some awareness of the actual demands, and that the evaluation of the government's response is related to how its actions either conform to or diverge from the interests of its electors. Responsiveness, therefore, should be treated in connection with accountability.[23]

This dimension of democratic quality is not particularly difficult to define. Eulau and Karps[24] in their work demonstrate how responsiveness is connected to representation 'in action'. They also show how this dimension is manifested through four main components in relation to (i) the policies at the centre of public interest; (ii) the services that are guaranteed to the individuals and groups represented by the government; (iii) the distribution of material goods to their constituents through the public administration and other entities; and finally (iv) the extension of symbolic goods that create, reinforce or reproduce a sense of loyalty and support towards the government.

The empirical study of responsiveness, however, is more complicated. In fact, the idea that even educated, informed and politically engaged citizens always know their own needs and desires is at best an assumption, which is especially tenuous in situations when citizens are just learning how to attend to their needs. Empirical measures of citizens' satisfaction, as an outcome of perceived responsiveness, can be found in the surveys that have been regularly conducted for many years, especially in the United States and Western Europe, but also in Latin America, Eastern Europe and other countries around the world.[25] Some scholars have also indirectly obtained a second measure of responsiveness by gauging the distance between the governors and the governed on certain policies, and not just in terms of left-right divisions.[26]

Perhaps the most effective method for measuring the responsiveness dimension is to examine the legitimacy of government – that is, the citizens' *perception* of responsiveness, rather than the reality. This brings us back to the process of democratic consolidation,[27] but from a slightly different perspective. In fact, certain dynamics that open the door for democratic consolidation in many countries, such as uncritical acceptance of the institutions in place, simple obedience for a lack of better alternatives, or negative memories of the past, may no longer be relevant for measuring legitimacy but are relevant for analysing responsiveness.

Here, the key element is the support for democratic institutions, and the belief that these institutions are the only real guarantors of freedom and equality, and that this understanding reaches every societal level, from the most restricted elite to the general masses.[28] The diffusion of attitudes favourable to the existing democratic institutions and the approval of their activities would suggest satisfaction and, indirectly, that civil society perceives a certain level of responsiveness. In countries associated with high levels of legitimacy, one should also see a full range of interests and forms of political participation.

Analyses of this type, however, bring to light a number of problems and limitations. The end of the twentieth century was accompanied by various challenges to legitimacy. These challenges prompted Kaase and Newton[29] to speak of the 'crisis of democracy', with particular reference, for example, to the distancing of citizens from political parties, the emergence of anti-party attitudes, and the growing incidence of more general dissatisfaction and anti-establishment attitudes. In their analysis, Pharr and Putnam[30] do not hesitate to use the term 'dissatisfied democracy', and they, together with Dalton,[31] emphasize the decline of 'the capacity of political actors to act according to the interests and desires of citizens' that in this analysis indicates a decline in responsiveness. On the whole, the three authors observe a decline of confidence in public institutions. Newton and Norris corroborate this with a specific reference to parliament, the legal system, the armed and police forces, and public administration.[32] In her analysis of corruption, Della Porta also notes the growing lack of confidence in government, the scanty application of law and, more related to this author's perspective, the resulting inadequate responsiveness.[33] Moreover, one can see the connection between the rule of law (or the lack of it), weak accountability and the incapacity of governments to respond to the demands of their citizens, for whom the guarantee of law takes precedence over other needs.[34]

There are at least two directions of the objective limits of responsiveness. First of all, elected leaders do not always seek to understand and respond to the perceptions and positions of the citizens. They instead work to maximize their own autonomy and influence citizens' perceptions and understandings of what the most important issues are. Politicians take advantage of the complexity of problems and, evidently, of the shifts in political priority that occur over the course of their governance.

The resources which government has available to respond to the needs of civil society shape the second direction of limits. Poor resources and economic constraints on public spending affect the responsiveness of even the wealthiest countries. For example, a population cannot enjoy increasing revenues of pensions and health care when government is burdened with budgetary limitations. Likewise, the persistent problems posed by unemployment and immigration are also illustrative of the difficulty of finding satisfactory, legitimate and responsive solutions in contemporary democracies. Indeed, the situation now becomes associated more with discontent, dissatisfaction, fear of poverty and general democratic malaise. Such conditions contribute to a de-legitimization of democratic systems and encourage the type of populism mentioned by Korosteleva elsewhere in this collection when referring to demagogical democracies.

The contextual conditions that favour responsiveness are similar to those that support accountability. They include well-established, independent, informed and engaged civil society, with the concurrent presence of strong and active intermediary structures. It is fairly obvious why these factors are essential. Civil society and intermediary organizations are crucial for explaining at least one facet of responsiveness – the perception of needs. Government output, or the actual response of government to its electors, is the other facet of responsiveness. The potential for this form of responsiveness is only possible – with all of the difficulties mentioned above – in richer and more developed democracies and societies. In summary, the economic factor, so central to the explanation of democratic consolidation, also plays an important role in the capacity of governments to respond to the needs of their citizens and general populations.

At this point, one can draw at least three partial conclusions from the above discussions on the rule of law, accountability and responsiveness. From the empirical definitions of each dimension, one can deduce the reciprocal relationships that exist among them. While the various aspects of the rule of law provide the grounds for citizens' and other entities' demands for accountability, the presence of genuine accountability promotes improvements in the legal system and in respect for law. The rule of law is also an essential premise for responsiveness that, in turn, can be an important condition for evaluating accountability. Besides, the implementation of some accountability helps very much in having a stronger responsiveness, which may bring about a better implementation of the rule of law. The actions of these three dimensions compose a sort of triangle, with each side bearing different weight and meaning. Figure 1 illustrates the relationships among these dimensions of democratic quality. This analysis brings one to address openly another question. That is, are the connections between those three dimensions so strong that the two notions of quality in terms of

FIGURE 1
DEMOCRATIC QUALITY: CONNECTIONS BETWEEN PROCEDURAL DIMENSIONS
AND RESULT

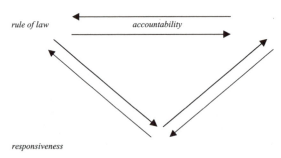

procedure and of result are not alternative, but rather, in the best case, complementary?

If not for all of the issues raised above, one could construct a fairly optimistic scenario for the future implementation of these three dimensions. Solutions to some of these problems have emerged, but other elements, ranging from international and supranational events to the transformation and weakening of party structures, continue to pose further obstacles to the full development of the rule of law, accountability and responsiveness.

Finally, a reflection on the chief dynamics surrounding these dimensions indicates that the bulk of responsibility for achieving them now falls on democratic, participatory civil society, assumed to be gifted with rich cultural and economic resources. This same civil society, however, might feel threatened by a number of new phenomena such as immigration and the associated presence of profoundly different cultures. This, in turn, might lead to greater pressure for self-protective measures that limit the rights of non-citizens, thereby placing the substantive dimensions of democratic quality in jeopardy as well.[35]

The Content

Freedom and Equality

These are the two main recurrent democratic ideals. Consequently, they are central to a normative definition of quality democracy. About the second democratic value, equality, a specification is in order: for a lot of people, and scholars, equality has to be seen as solidarity rather as equality in its more literal meaning. It is the social solidarity that has to be seen in a society, rather than an utopian equality that raises several problems even in its different meaning.[36] Dahl, Marshall and numerous other scholars have provided a number of suggestions as to how essential rights should be promoted within a democracy to achieve freedom and equality/solidarity.[37] Chiefly, these rights can be grouped under political rights, civil rights and social rights.

Political rights include the right to vote, the right for political leaders to compete for electoral support, and the right to be elected to public office ('passive electorate'). But in a good democracy, the political right *par excellence*, that is, the right to vote, can be strengthened and extended if the electoral mechanisms are such that the voter gains the possibility or right to elect the government either directly (elections for head of state or prime minister who also fills the office of the head of government), or else *de facto* (when the leader of the winning party or coalition in a bipolar context is elected prime minister). An even richer version of this right is achieved when citizens can influence or choose the electoral candidates in intra-party or primary elections. One problem to resolve on this theme is the extension of political citizenship to adult residents in a given territory so that immigrants can also participate in this part of the political process.

Essential civil rights include personal liberty; the right to legal defence; the right to privacy; the freedom to choose one's place of residence; freedom of movement and residence; the right to expatriate or emigrate; freedom and secrecy of correspondence; freedom of thought and expression; the right to information and a free press; and the freedoms of assembly, association and organization, including political organizations unrelated to trade unions. In addition, from the broader category of civil rights the so-called civil-economic rights should receive their own mention. Elaborated by Giddens,[38] these include not only the rights to private property and entrepreneurship, constrained as they are within the social limits fixed by law, but also the rights associated with employment and connected with how the work is carried out, the right to fair pay and time off, and the right to collective bargaining.

As the overwhelming majority of democratic legal systems have established this collection of civil rights, there are two primary dimensions that appear to be important for a good democracy. The first pertains to the capacity to enrich the legacy of rights and freedoms enjoyed by citizens without limiting or damaging others. The second concerns the actual procedures by which these rights are granted to all residents in a certain area. This latter takes us back to the issues of efficiency that were raised in the discussion on the rule of law. As stated in the preceding section, for example, the right to a legal defence entails the right to due process, to a speedy trial, and to legal assistance regardless of one's economic means. Although the overlapping of such rights appears messy and less than elegant from a theoretical point of view, this is inevitable if one wishes to demonstrate how rights and freedoms are the 'contents' of democracy.

Equality or solidarity has been realistically achieved through the implementation of social rights. In a democracy these include the right to health or to mental and physical well-being; the right to assistance and social security; the right to work; the right to human dignity; the right to strike; the right to study and to an education; the right to healthy surroundings and, more generally, to the protection of the environment; and the right to housing. There is not much variation on these rights from country to country, though all face obstacles to full realization and all can have greater potential for improvement than do political or civil rights.

The greatest problem associated with the social rights resides in the cost that they impose on the community. Consequently, there have been several attempts to redesign policies that support social rights in a way either to alleviate the economic burden they place on society or to change the allocation of that burden. It is also well known, however, that a broad application of social rights is the best available path for diminishing inequality and, therefore, at least partially attaining the other democratic ideal. Despite this, many democratic countries demonstrate serious deficiencies in social rights, which are often more precarious than civil or political rights.

The main prerequisites for the further consolidation of social rights, therefore, (beyond political will) include sufficient affluence of society to furnish the means for the realization of the policies of cohesion for less well-to-do individuals, and, at the same time, unified, organized unions that represent a broad range of employees and are capable of obtaining the recognition and eventual expansion of those rights.[39]

The implementation of equality is closer to utopian objectives, and is not always advocated by all supporters of democracy. In this sense one can distinguish at least two phases in affirmation of this value. The first is widely accepted and concerns formal equality. It infers both equality before the law, and the prohibition of discrimination on the basis of sex, race, language, religion, opinions and social and personal conditions.[40] The second is more problematic, and pertains to the pursuit of substantive equality. It concerns the lifting of barriers that limit social and economic equality, and therefore 'the full development of the human person and the effective participation of all workers in the political, economic, and social organization of a country'.[41] In a culture with a dominant Catholic component, the second notion of equality has been translated into solidarity and the related actions for guaranteeing to everyone at least minimal social rights.

It is necessary to underline how the problem of legitimacy has to be recast. In terms of democratic consolidation, legitimacy concerns the acceptance and support of democratic rules and institutions.[42] In terms of responsiveness, legitimacy is related to the presence of attitudes and behaviours that confirm satisfaction with the existing democracy. For the substantive dimensions of democratic quality, legitimacy connotes broad support for a regime that implements the values indicated above. In effect, this happens in extremely rare cases in some European countries, since the aspect of efficiency or even of accountability is deeply entrenched in various conceptualizations of democracy; but in the best of cases, one sees an affirmation of freedom limited only to basic rights, and an affirmation of equality incorporated only in the most important social rights.[43] In this sense, the concrete assurance of these values meets with resistance and opposition for reasons unrelated to economic constraints that many people see as perfectly justifiable. The explanation, then, for the diffusion of these political conceptions, that largely or partially mute equality, can easily be traced back to the cultural traditions of a country as well as individual choices.

The numerous, thick relationships between the dimensions of quality democracy in terms of procedure, result and contents should by now be quite evident. One recalls again how the affirmation of the democratic values emerges through their transformation into formalized rules, institutions, or at least routines or recurring patterns, which then become elements of the legal system and of the rule of law. But the assessment of the accountability is based on the values of those who make the assessment and the related political decisions can – and should – be assessed in relation to how successfully they implement those beliefs. The substantive dimensions would not make sense without the procedural dimensions: this is a well-known principle of democratic regimes. For quality democracy, however, the substantive dimensions are even more important than the procedural dimensions. As will be shown in the next section, differences remain in how the various dimensions are implemented in relation to the specific conditions found in each country.

'Bad' Democracies and Tools of Subversion

The two procedural dimensions, the result dimension, and the two substantive ones complement each other to produce various possibilities of quality democracy. The procedural dimensions are mainly substantiated in the efficient application of the legal system, in the fair resolution of legal disputes, and in the political responsibility demanded by the voters, intermediary structures, associations and other organs that make up a democratic regime. The responsiveness is related to the actual largely perceived satisfaction of civil society. The two substantive dimensions identify the extent to which freedom and equality are implemented.

Democracies can thus vary according to the greater or lesser realization of each of the main dimensions, sometimes driven by various combinations of choices and concrete opportunities. The variation across regimes resides mainly in the major or minor presence of each dimension, with obvious, ample possibilities for diverse combinations. For example, a more effective democracy might be the result of real guarantees of freedom, and when the implementation of equality closely adheres to the strong rule of law.

A more *responsible* democracy is one that is also characterized by levels of freedom and equality that meet the minimum threshold, but that also exhibits a comprehensive respect for accountability. A fully responsive democracy is characterized by the strong and diffuse support of a satisfied society that provides firm testimony to that regime's responsiveness. Free or egalitarian democracies might vary in terms of their procedural characteristics, but each exhibits a strong affirmation of one of the two values. It could also be hypothesized that a full-fledged democracy is such regime, in which all the above dimensions are present to a very high degree. Moreover, the expression 'to a very high degree' draws attention to the partial empirical indeterminacy of each dimension. Leaders and citizens with different values can differently understand the meaning of each dimension, and such an understanding can vary over time.

The problem of democratic quality can also be handled in a different way. In fact, despite the connections mentioned above and in the previous section, two clearly different models of quality democracy can be sketched among the different dimensions. They are *effective democracy* and *responsive democracy*, which cover two basically different visions of democracy. In the first, rule of law and accountability are *a priori* guarantees of quality; in the second, the citizens are able to assess how the regime actually works on the basis of its results. In the effective democracy the core aspects lie in the rules and the possibility that those rules are capable of making the governing leaders politically responsible for their actions; in the responsive democracy, the assessment of the citizens is what counts. The former is in the final analysis a vision from above of a quality democracy; the latter is a vision from below. But the key point is to understand empirically which one of these two models can be implemented to a greater extent, and better empirically analysed as well. For the reasons implicit in the descriptions both of the related dimensions and of the two models, the *effective democracy* may be a quality democracy with lower possibility of subversion.

In fact, the actual inquiry should address the question, 'How possible would it be to avoid some of the recurrent tools of subversion for each dimension?' Here, it may be useful to sum up the main tools of subversion that are recurrent in the various dimensions of the quality of democracy. They are presented in Figure 2, and major dangers of subversion of the responsiveness can immediately be singled out.

Figure 2 indirectly suggests how one might define a *democracy with lower or without quality*: that is, a democratic regime where subversion is frequently practised, even up to the point of developing de-legitimation and related problems of consolidation.[44] Within this perspective a 'bad' democracy can be particularly inadequate in each one of the dimensions analysed above. Thus, such a democracy can be characterized by legal systems that do not conform to democratic values where there is widespread corruption or

FIGURE 2
RECURRENT TOOLS OF QUALITY SUBVERSION

- Rule of law
  - Law as a political weapon
  - Law as a tool to carry out economic interests
  - Law as a set of rules to circumvent
  - Limits in rule implementation
- Accountability
  - Strongly majoritarian institutional design (low competition)
  - Weak parties or party discipline in oligarchic parties
  - Salience of image and role of information
  - Supranational level and blame shift
- Responsiveness
  - Manipulative role of elites and of information
  - Complexity of actual problems
- Freedom and equality
  - Specific ways of acknowledgement and implementation of rights
  - Allocation of the costs of rights (especially, social rights)

organized crime; limited independence of the judiciary; lengthy delays in the resolution of legal disputes; and expensive (and thus exclusive) access to the court system. O'Donnell's concept of delegative democracies would correspond to such a democracy, with widespread corruption, the absence of horizontal accountability, and weakness of vertical accountability.[45] In some analyses, populist democracies are party-less regimes in which the fragmentation of political identities and both ideological and organizational confusion characterizes the decline of representative mechanisms.[46] Consequently, these regimes see weaker enforcement of accountability and a greater presence of movements and the 'masses' in direct relation with political leaders.[47]

Moreover, a 'bad' democracy can be characterized by the absence of electoral alternatives, little competition among the dominant political forces and weak intermediary structures.

A third kind of 'bad' quality democracy is distinguished by the degree of legitimacy or illegitimacy of diffuse discontent. Such a democracy often experiences multiple challenges to its institutions by organized groups that launch protests, strikes and demonstrations on a more or less regular basis. The result is that governments, in reaction to these challenges, often defend themselves by cracking down on other freedoms. The experience with terrorist movements in Italy and Germany, and the reactions of these countries' respective democratic regimes, are very good examples of this dynamic. The new legislation approved in the United States after the terrorist attack of 11 September 2001 tends in the same direction.

There is a 'bad' democracy when civil rights are barely guaranteed, and the political right *par excellence* – the vote – is limited to *diktat* by the oligarchy. In such a hypothesis a single media mogul – or the state – may monopolize information, with the expected results in terms of exaggerated influence over public opinion and restricted alternatives for other forms and sources of information.

There is another kind of 'bad' democracy where social and economic differences are particularly accentuated. It may emerge in the presence of deep economic problems, when the economic policies pursued by the government are rooted in strong conceptions of the market and competition, but are not attenuated by the presence of welfare institutions to create forms of solidarity and social justice. In addition, high levels of immigration of individuals who have no means of subsistence and are willing to take any job can also contribute to the development of this type of regime. In these democracies, social and economic distances between sub-groups of the population steadily increase, rather than decline.

Finally, one could think of a 'bad' democracy characterized by all problems illustrated above with regard to the lack of rule of law, accountability, responsiveness, freedom and equality, where most of the tools of subversion in the different dimensions are often used.

Unsolved Problems; Open Questions

These introductory remarks have aimed at shaping a research strategy to develop a better analysis and understanding of democratic quality in old and especially new democracies. These may be applied to East European countries and to any other country in the world, although no explicit case was illustrated here.[48]

Unsolved problems and open questions for conducting research into the quality of democracy are plentiful. Some of them can be summarized in conclusion as a way of highlighting the key aspects, which will be addressed in the remaining contributions to this collection.

First, what are the explanations and the consequences of the different dimensions of democratic quality? In particular, what are the explanations and the consequences of such dimensions as political participation associated with public withdrawal from politics and low levels of public awareness in post-communist Europe?

Second, to what degree are different levels and facets of public distrust for democratic institutions relevant to the government responsiveness and, consequently, how could this improve or subvert the quality of democracy in post-communist Europe?

Finally, how and in what ways do low levels of social capital and weak civil society impinge upon the quality of democracy, or some aspects of it?

These and other questions are the challenges for the authors of this issue, as well as for every scholar who follows the general direction of this research.

NOTES

1. See Robert Dahl, *Polyarchy: Participation and Opposition* (New Haven, CT: Yale University Press, 1971).
2. Philippe Schmitter and Terry Karl, 'What Democracy Is ... and Is Not', in Larry Diamond and Marc Plattner (eds.), *The Global Resurgence of Democracy* (Baltimore, MD: Johns Hopkins University Press, 1993), pp.39–52 (pp.45–6).
3. Larry Diamond, 'Thinking About Hybrid Regimes', *Journal of Democracy*, Vol.13, No.2 (2002), pp.21–35.
4. Wolfgang Merkel and Aurel Croissant, 'Formal Institutions and Informal Rules of Defective Democracies', *Central European Political Science Review*, Vol.1, No.2 (2000), pp.31–47.
5. Guillermo O'Donnell, 'Delegative Democracy', *Journal of Democracy*, Vol.5, No.1 (1994), pp.55–69.
6. Ibid., pp.60–62.
7. Kitschelt and his associates consider 'accountability' to be a 'procedural' dimension: see Herbert Kitschelt, Zdenka Mansfeldova, Radosław Markowski and Gábor Tóka, *Post-Communist Party Systems: Competition, Representation and Inter-Party Cooperation* (Cambridge: Cambridge University Press, 1999).
8. David Altman and Anibal Perez-Linan, 'Assessing the Quality of Democracy: Freedom, Competitiveness, and Participation in 18 Latin American Countries', *Democratization*, Vol.9, No.2 (2002), pp.85–100.
9. Arend Lijphart, *Patterns of Democracy: Government Forms and Performance in Thirty-Six Countries* (New Haven, CT: Yale University Press, 1999).
10. See, for example, Juan Mendez, Guillermo O'Donnell and Paulo Sergio Pinheiro (eds.), *The Rule of Law and the Underprivileged in Latin America* (Notre Dame, IN: University of Notre Dame Press, 1999); Jose Maravall and Adam Przeworski (eds.), *Democracy and the Rule of Law* (Cambridge: Cambridge University Press, 2002); Andreas Schedler, Larry Diamond and Marc Plattner (eds.), *The Self-Restraining State: Power and Accountability in New Democracies* (Boulder, CO: Lynne Rienner, 1999); Mark Bowens, *The Quest for Responsibility: Accountability and Citizenship in Complex Organizations* (Cambridge: Cambridge University Press, 1998).
11. The minimal definition of the rule of law, suggested by Maravall, refers to the implementation of laws that (i) were enacted and approved following pre-established procedures; (ii) that are not retroactive ... but general, stable, clear, and hierarchically ordered; and (iii) applied to particular cases by courts free from political influence and accessible to all, the decisions of which follow procedural requirements, and that establish guilt through ordinary means. See Maravall and Przeworski, *Democracy and the Rule of Law*, p.2.
12. See Leonardo Morlino, *Democracy Between Consolidation and Crisis: Parties, Groups and Citizens in Southern Europe* (Oxford: Oxford University Press, 1998).
13. See, for example, the analysis of the Italian case in Donatella Della Porta and Leonardo Morlino, *Rights and the Quality of Democracy in Italy: A Research Report* (Stockholm: IDEA, 2001).
14. Guillermo O'Donnell, 'Polyarchies and the (Un)rule of Law in Latin America', in Mendez, O'Donnell and Pinheiro, *The Rule of Law*, pp.303–38 (pp.312–13).
15. See Maravall and Przeworski, *Democracy and the Rule of Law*.
16. See Putnam's conclusion in Robert Putnam, *Making Democracy Work: Civic Traditions in Modern Italy* (Princeton, NJ: Princeton University Press, 1993), pp.163–85.
17. Andreas Schedler, 'Conceptualizing Accountability', in Schedler, Diamond and Plattner, *The Self-Restraining State*, pp.13–28 (p.17).
18. In addition to this distinction there is another, more traditional one between 'accountability to' and 'accountability for'. Vertical and horizontal accountabilities are the forms of 'accountability to'; the 'accountability for' could overlap with some other dimensions analysed here. Consequently, to accept such a traditional legal distinction and to develop further 'accountability for' would bring us to a conception of democratic quality grounded in the notion of accountability only. This would hinder the pluralist and multidimensional conception that is proposed here.

19. See Guillermo O'Donnell, 'Horizontal Accountability in New Democracies', and Philippe Schmitter, 'The Limits of Horizontal Accountability', in Schedler, Diamond and Plattner, *The Self-Restraining State*, pp.29–52 and 59–62 respectively.

20. Richard Katz and Peter Mair, 'Changing Modes of Party Organization and Party Democracy: The Emergence of the Cartel Party', *Party Politics*, Vol.1, No.1 (1995), pp.5–28.

21. Jose Maravall, *Surviving Accountability*, Jean Monnet Chair Paper (Florence: European University Institute, 1997).

22. See O'Donnell, 'Delegative Democracy'.

23. I will not address the theoretical problems associated with the connection between responsibility and responsiveness, which have been widely discussed within the theory of representative democracy. For more information, see Giovanni Sartori, *The Theory of Democracy Revisited* (Chatham, NJ: Chatham House Publishers, 1987), part II, esp. ch.6, section 9 and n.19.

24. Heinz Eulau and Paul D. Karps, 'The Puzzle of Representation: Specifying Components of Responsiveness', *Legislative Studies Quarterly*, Vol.3, No.2 (1977), pp.233–54.

25. A common question, for example, is 'How satisfied are you with the way in which democracy functions in your country?': see Morlino, *Democracy Between Consolidation and Crisis*, ch.7.

26. See, for example, Lijphart, *Patterns of Democracy*, pp.286–8. There are a number of quantitative studies that analyse this theme, including Heinz Eulau and Kenneth Prewitt, *Labyrinths of Democracy* (New York: Bobbs-Merril, 1973); Eulau and Karps, 'The Puzzle of Representation'; Sidney Verba, Norman Nie and Jae-On Kim, *Participation and Political Equality: A Seven-Nation Comparison* (Cambridge: Cambridge University Press, 1978); more recently, Gary King, 'Electoral Responsiveness and Partisan Bias in Multiparty Democracies', *Legislative Studies Quarterly*, Vol.15, No.2 (1990), p.159ff.; and John Huber and Bingham G. Powell, 'Congruence Between Citizens and Policy Makers in Two Visions of Liberal Democracy', *World Politics*, Vol.46, No.3 (1994), pp.291–326.

27. See Morlino, *Democracy Between Consolidation and Crisis*.

28. Way's and Korosteleva's articles elsewhere in this volume assess the negative consequences of the lack of such understanding and support for democratic values in the new regimes of post-communist Europe.

29. Max Kaase and Kenneth Newton (eds.), *Beliefs in Government* (Oxford: Oxford University Press, 1995), pp.150ff.

30. Susan Pharr and Robert Putnam (eds.), *Disaffected Democracies: What's Troubling the Trilateral Countries?* (Princeton, NJ: Princeton University Press, 2000).

31. Russell Dalton, Susan Pharr and Robert Putnam, 'What's Troubling the Trilateral Democracies?', in Pharr and Putman (eds.), *Disaffected Democracies*, pp.3–31 (p.25).

32. Kenneth Newton and Pippa Norris, 'Confidence in Public Institutions: Fate, Culture, or Performance?', in Pharr and Putnam, *Disaffected Democracies*, pp.52–74.

33. Donatella Della Porta, 'Social Capital, Beliefs in Government and Political Corruption', in Pharr and Putnam, *Disaffected Democracies*, pp.202–29; see also Donatella Della Porta and Yves Meny (eds.), *Democracy and Corruption in Europe* (London and Washington, DC: Pinter, 1997); and Donatella Della Porta and Alberto Vannucci, *Corrupt Exchanges: Actors, Resources and Mechanisms of Political Corruption* (New York: de Gruyter, 1999).

34. Similar analysis of citizens' disengagement from politics in Eastern Europe is presented elsewhere in this volume by White and Hutcheson.

35. The salient issue of non-citizens in the Baltic States can be regarded as a good example, which is mentioned elsewhere in this volume by McManus-Czubińska *et al.*

36. See, for example, Sartori, *The Theory of Democracy Revisited*; Amartya Sen, *Inequality Reexamined* (Oxford: Clarendon Press, 1992); and Luciano Gallino (ed.), *Disuguaglianze ed equità in Europa* (Bari: Laterza, 1993).

37. Dahl, *Polyarchy*; Thomas H. Marshall, *Sociology at the Crossroads* (London: Heinemann, 1963).

38. Anthony Giddens, *The Constitution of Society: Outline of the Theory of Structuration* (Cambridge: Polity, 1984).

39. See Dietrich Rueschemeyer, Evelyne Huber Stephens and John Stephens, *Capitalist Development and Democracy* (Cambridge: Polity, 1992).

40. This equality is also sanctioned by the legal system and is covered in manuals of constitutional rights: see Paolo Caretti, *I diritti fondamentali: libertà e diritti sociali* (Turin: Giappichelli, 2002), ch.5.
41. Part of paragraph 2, article 3 of the Italian Constitution: see Caretti, *I diritti fondamentali*, pp.150–51.
42. See Morlino, *Democracy Between Consolidation and Crisis*, ch.3.
43. For more on the problem of the meaning of democracy at the mass level, see Morlino, *Democracy Between Consolidation and Crisis*.
44. Leonardo Morlino, *Democrazie e Democratizzazioni* (Bologna: Il Mulino, 2003).
45. See O'Donnell, 'Delegative Democracy'.
46. See, for example, Peter Mair, 'Populist Democracy vs. Party Democracy', in Yves Mény and Yves Surel (eds.), *Democracies and the Populist Challenge* (London: Palgrave 2002), pp.81–98.
47. The populist phenomenon, with its placing of 'the people' at the centre of democracy, has recently been analysed as a reaction to tensions, discontent, dissatisfaction and protest – in a word, to the democratic 'malaise' that has surfaced in recent years in Western Europe: see Meny and Surel, *Democracies and the Populist Challenge*.
48. See, for example, Leonardo Morlino, 'What is a "Good" Democracy? Theory and the Case of Italy', *South European Society and Politics*, Vol.8, No.3 (2003), pp.1–32.

The Quality of Democracies in Europe as Measured by Current Indicators of Democratization and Good Governance

DIRK BERG-SCHLOSSER

Introduction

The last decade has witnessed the 'victory' of democracy in many parts of the world. As a legitimate form of government, in a majority of countries it has become 'the only game in town'.[1] Somewhat paradoxically, at the same time in the longer established democracies a certain 'malaise' has been observed, expressed in declining rates of voter turnout, dissatisfaction with major political parties, a number of scandals concerning leading politicians, party financing or both, ineffectiveness in carrying out necessary reforms, and other symptoms of decline.[2]

In Europe, painstaking criteria have been developed (and are being applied) for the acceptance of new members to the European Union, including their 'level of democracy'. Simultaneously, however, the democratic credentials of some of the present member states have been placed in doubt. The most conspicuous example is Berlusconi's Italy, but the temporary inclusion of Haider's populist Freedom Party of Austria in the right-wing coalition of that country, and some other less spectacular instances, raise the question of what criteria for the *quality* of democracy must be applied and maintained in existing and future member states, and in what areas their quality should be further improved.[3] Last but not least, this question also concerns the 'level of democracy' of the European Union itself and the debate about its future constitution.

Such questions have been addressed, of course, by others. In particular, the detailed 'democratic audit' initiated by David Beetham and colleagues,[4] and which is being pursued by institutions such as the International Institute for Democracy and Electoral Assistance (IDEA) on a broader scale,[5] provides an elaborate tool for a differentiated answer to such questions in a specific qualitative sense. It is more difficult, however, to aggregate such information in a more comprehensive way and to provide some ready-made yardsticks for a continuous evaluation of developments.

The purpose of the present contribution, therefore, is more limited. It briefly presents and discusses some of the current general indicators of democratization and good governance in order to assess their respective strengths and weaknesses and to apply them to the situation in practically all present and prospective member states of the European Union. For this purpose, the overall conceptual framework for such an enterprise must first be briefly presented. On this basis, the question will be addressed of how reasonably well-functioning 'liberal democracies' can be identified and distinguished in a minimal sense from other states where these criteria are not (or, at least, not yet) fulfilled. We then turn to a more detailed evaluation of their actual 'governance' and performance in a number of important areas. Finally, the question of how their general quality might be improved in a more demanding normative sense will be discussed. The conclusions in this respect must, of course, remain largely preliminary and, to some extent, speculative. The use of some of our current concepts and tools in political science can be demonstrated in this way, but, as will also become apparent, the indicators presented can serve only in a certain complementary fashion to more detailed qualitative assessments of individual cases. In the future, rather than utilizing purely quantitative and statistical methods, both qualitative and quantitative approaches will have to be more closely related to each other, including better 'macro-qualitative' comparative methods, in order to enhance the *analytic* quality of our endeavours.

The Conceptual Framework

Before we operationalize certain measures and attempt to assess their validity we must have clear definitions of the underlying notions.[6] Here, we must first define the *unit* of analysis – the respective political system or state and its concrete boundaries. This is often taken for granted and left to the 'shadow theory' of democracy,[7] but as the recent examples of the former Yugoslavia and parts of the former Soviet Union demonstrate, such an assumption is not warranted even in present-day Europe, let alone other parts of the world such as Africa, Central Asia and the Middle East. An enduring state formation, therefore, has to precede, conceptually and in political practice, any meaningful democratization.[8] In the European context, this is still painfully evident in Bosnia-Herzegovina and in Kosovo, for example.

If the unit of analysis can be established with relatively undisputed boundaries (and this is an empirical question, not a conceptual one), then the actual political system and its specific 'qualities' come into play. For this purpose we need a sufficiently complex notion of *democracy*, consensual and empirically operationalizable in its basic dimensions, which can adequately capture the differing forms of contemporary appearances of this kind of political system. At the same time, it should be sufficiently distinctive to draw meaningful boundaries with other types of political systems, and sufficiently open to be linked to existing sub-types and possible future developments. We thus need a 'root concept', in the sense identified by Collier and Levitsky, that satisfies these requirements and allows for further differentiation and characterization of present and possible future sub-types ('democracy with adjectives') within the 'ladder of generality'.[9]

Such a root concept is Robert Dahl's notion of 'polyarchy', which has become the most frequently cited framework for empirically oriented democratization studies in recent decades.[10] He explicitly distinguishes two dimensions of this more modest characterization of contemporary democracies: the degree of regular and open competition in a political system; and the extent of different forms of participation in the process of political decision-making by the population of a given society. Implicit in his notion is a third (normative) dimension that concerns basic civil liberties such as freedom of information and organization, and a political order that guarantees and maintains the rule of law to make regular political contestation and participation possible and meaningful. Even though there are some variations in the formulations and interpretations by different authors, these three dimensions of the root concept of democracy, which emphasize the 'input' side of political systems and the necessary institutional and legal framework, have become largely accepted.

To be distinguished from such a definition are the respective historical, economic and cultural bases and conditions of democracy, often seen as 'requisites',[11] and the actual performance and effectiveness of democratic systems which comprise the 'output' side and various distinct policy areas.

The possible interactions between these different aspects can be presented in an overall 'systems' framework (Figure 1), which also indicates the relationships to the major economic, social and cultural sub-systems.[12]

Full details of this framework can be found elsewhere,[13] but it can serve as background to locate the major emphases of the various indicators to be discussed below.

Within such a still relatively abstract framework, which finds different organizational and institutional expressions in existing democracies, a number of functional criteria must be considered that characterize the quality of a democratic political system in its day-to-day operations. Again, we return to Dahl's major dimensions: (i) the extent of participation by all major social groups and strata at the input side of the system; (ii) the open, pluralist contestation by organized, peaceful contenders within the established and generally accepted rules of the game, which is then transmitted by generally 'free and fair' elections into the central political system; this also presupposes (iii) the guarantee of basic civil liberties such as freedom of

FIGURE 1
INTERACTIVE MODEL OF DEMOCRATIC SYSTEM

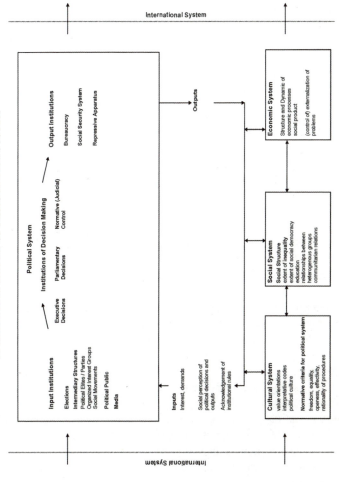

Source: Dirk Berg-Schlosser and Hans Joachim Giegel (eds.), *Perspektiven der Demokratie: Probleme und Chancen im Zeitalter der Globalisierung* (Frankfurt: Campus, 1999), p.21.

expression, information, organization and so on, and their supervision and protection by an independent judiciary and unrestricted organizations of 'civil society'. Taken together, these three dimensions assure the overall 'representativeness' of the democratic system in a functional and limited normative sense.

In addition, other functional criteria must be considered that concern the internal working of the central political system, its efficiency and effectiveness, and the overall performance with regard to essential outputs in the major policy areas. Such criteria may apply, of course, to all kinds of political systems, not just democratic ones. A specific democratic quality, however, concerns the accountability of the executive *vis-à-vis* other democratic institutions and the society at large.[14] Horizontally, this may consist of effective parliamentary and judicial controls, but may also involve some more specialized institutions such as independent auditing offices. Vertically, it refers to the effectiveness of the general feedback mechanisms between the output and the input sides, which is ensured by the perceptions of the political public, independent pluralist media and, eventually, the next elections. Increasingly, perceptions and possibly even controls by the outside world, international public opinion, and regional or global organizations such as the EU or the UN, also may play a role.

Over and above such functional and limited normative criteria that characterize a 'liberal democracy' in a positive sense of the word, some more demanding normative criteria may also be applied. These concern a broader range of participatory activities on the part of the citizens in a 'strong democracy';[15] the fuller inclusion of women, weaker social strata, cultural minority groups and so on;[16] greater equality, not only of political rights, but also of actual social and economic opportunities and living conditions; and a greater measure of solidarity (or 'fraternity', in the sense advanced by the French Revolution) among all members of society – involving mutual trust, tolerance and a high level of 'social capital' and co-operation nationally and, possibly, internationally.[17] The question of the relationship between the economic and the political system of free markets versus public controls, and the possibility of the monopolization of the latter by some dominant actors in the former, also remains a disputed one.

Some of these emphases and debates may seem 'utopian', and there are trade-offs to be considered between possibly diverging goals, but there certainly remain many specific areas for further improvement of the quality of existing democracies in both a functional and a normative sense. Some of the major elements of these qualities at different levels are summarized in Figure 2. Again, this should serve as a background and yardstick for the indicators to be discussed in the following sections.

FIGURE 2

PRINCIPLES OF DEMOCRACY

Level:	micro individual citizens	meso social and political groups and organizations	macro political system, institutions
Principles:			
1. Basic human rights	personal rights, legal protection, freedom of opinion	freedom of organization; protection of minorities	limited state power, independence of judiciary, rule of law
2. Openness of power structure	free access to political communication and political power, rights of control	Organizational pluralism, elite pluralism	separation of powers, limited terms of office, mutual checks and balances
3. Political equality	equality of voting rights, equality of political recruitment	equal opportunity for organizational resources	equal opportunity in the electoral system
4. Transparency and rationality; political efficiency and effectiveness	plurality of sources of information, chances for political education political interest, political participation, civic competence	independence and plurality of media, critical public effective aggregation of interests, mobilization of political support	transparency of decision-making processes, rational discourses, documented bureaucratic procedures effective decision-making rules and institutional balance, sufficient resources

Source: Theo Schiller, 'Prinzipien und Qualifizierungskriterien von Demokratie', in Dirk Berg-Schlosser and Hans Joachim Giegel (eds.), Perspektiven der Demokratie. Probleme und Chancen im Zeitalter der Globalisierung (Frankfurt: Campus, 1999), p.33.

Identifying (Liberal) Democracies and Non-Democracies

With such dimensions and criteria in mind, we can first of all attempt to identify the existence or non-existence of liberal democracies in a minimal sense
among the cases to be considered. In a geographical sense, this investigation
is limited to all 'European' states, that is, all present and possible future
members of the European Union. Since this is also a disputed issue, the
choice is done in a pragmatic way by taking all 15 present member states,
the accession states joining in 2004, and other independent states on the
European continent, some of which may not choose (like Switzerland) or
may not qualify (for example, Belarus or Moldova in their present forms) to
become members. Borderline cases such as Turkey and Russia, which are
not likely to become members in the foreseeable future, are also included
for purposes of comparison. This leaves out only some of the tiny principali-
ties such as San Marino, Liechtenstein and so forth, and the remaining Central
Asian Commonwealth of Independent States (CIS) countries. As has been
mentioned above, the 'statehood' of some of these entities, such as Bosnia-
Herzegovina, also cannot yet be taken for granted.

Among the large number of studies that have developed indicators of
democracy of some kind, we examine only those that have been available
on a long-term and continuous basis.[18] These are the 'index of democracy'
developed by Tatu Vanhanen;[19] the data set compiled by Ted Gurr and his
associates;[20] the annual ratings of 'political rights' and 'civil liberties' by
Freedom House,[21] which, strictly speaking, do not constitute an index of
democracy but which are often taken as a proxy in this respect; and, most
recently, the data on 'voice and accountability' and the 'rule of law' compiled
by the World Bank.[22] Furthermore, in order to include the factor of a certain
minimum level of basic human rights and the absence of more direct forms of
political repression (such as detention without trial for purely political
reasons), a scale of 'gross human rights violations' has been added.[23]

Vanhanen takes as his point of departure the two basic dimensions
considered by Dahl – competitiveness and political participation – and oper-
ationalizes them in a relatively simple, straightforward and more easily
objectifiable manner, taking available electoral data as the base. The
degree of participation (P) is assessed by the voter turnout in consecutive
elections in terms of the share of voting participants as a proportion of the
total population of a country. The competitiveness of elections (C) is
measured by the share of the largest party in national parliamentary elections
subtracted from 100. Both measures are then multiplied by each other and
divided by 100 to result in a scale ranging from 0 to 100 (P*C/100).
A value of 5 on this scale is the minimum threshold for a system to be
considered 'democratic' in his sense.

Gurr and his associates identify three major dimensions of what they call 'institutionalized democracy', referring to the competitiveness of political participation, the openness of executive recruitment, and constraints on the chief executive. On the basis of a variety of sources, in particular the countries' constitutions, they code these dimensions and add them up to create an 11-point scale ranging from 0 to 10. Cases with scores of 8 and above are considered to be fully democratic.

The third continuous (since 1973) and constantly updated source of information is the series of Freedom House surveys of political rights and civil liberties. With the help of an elaborate checklist, they score each country on a scale of 1 to 7, 1 being the best value. They take a threshold of 2.5 on the political rights dimension as the minimum for a liberal democracy.

Since 1996, the World Bank has compiled a wide range of data on 'good governance' from various sources. These include some quantifiable economic and social performance data, and also perception assessments by public, civil society and business sources such as the Economist Intelligence Unit, Standard and Poor's Country Risk Review, the Gallup Millennium Survey and Transparency International. All these sources with their varying coverage in both depth and scope are aggregated into six dimensions by employing an 'unobserved components model'.[24] In this way, an 'index of indices' is created with a wide coverage and a more or less permanent institutional base. Among these six dimensions are two indices of what they call 'voice and accountability' and the 'rule of law', which are arguably essential elements of liberal democracy. These dimensions are scored with a range of -2.5 to $+2.5$, a value of zero representing the threshold for 'democracy'.

Finally, the 'gross human rights violations' or 'political terror scale' measures such violations on a scale of 1 to 5, with 1 the best value. No distinct threshold is given here, but certainly values above 2 must be considered to be insufficient for a liberal democratic regime.

The most recent scores on all these indices are reported in Table 1.

When we compare the actual findings on these scales, it becomes apparent that Vanhanen's measure is the least discriminating. In fact, all countries listed here score above his minimum threshold and even Lukashenko's Belarus passes his test for 'democracy'. It also must be noted that high values on this index do not represent a *better* democracy in any functional or normative sense. Slovakia and Italy actually attain the highest values. This is because his measure of competitiveness, which is an indication of the degree of fragmentation of the party system, cannot be taken as a 'qualitative' standard, but only as a minimum requirement in each case.

The Gurr, Freedom House and World Bank measures identify 30 or 31 cases with a relatively high level of agreement among them. On the human

TABLE 1
DEMOCRATIZATION INDICES

Country	(1)	(2)	(3)	(4)	(5)	(6)	(7)	(8)	(9)	(10)	(11)
Albania	11.97	3	6	3	3	-0.33	-0.04	-0.30	-0.92	2	C
Austria	37.56	10	10	1	1	1.36	1.32	1.88	1.91	1	A
Belarus	7.20	0	0	5	6	-0.97	-1.45	-0.96	-1.12	3	D
Belgium	42.00	10	10	1	1	1.41	1.44	1.57	1.45	2	A
Bosnia-Herzegovina	25.09	–	–	6	4	-1.14	-0.25	-0.18	-0.88	3	D
Bulgaria	24.14	8	8	2	1	0.16	0.56	-0.09	0.05	2	B
Croatia	20.31	0	7	4	2	-0.47	0.46	-0.50	0.11	2	B
Cyprus	31.83	10	10	1	1	1.01	0.94	0.58	0.83	1	A–
Czech Republic	39.20	10	10	1	1	1.01	0.90	0.61	0.74	1	A–
Denmark	41.15	10	10	1	1	1.65	1.72	1.92	1.97	1	A–
Estonia	24.20	7	7	2	1	0.74	1.05	0.33	0.80	1	A–
Finland	41.02	10	10	1	1	1.63	1.70	1.97	1.99	1	A
France	33.39	9	9	1	1	1.43	1.29	1.56	1.33	1	A
Germany	35.40	10	10	1	1	1.48	1.51	1.79	1.73	1	A–
Greece	37.85	10	10	1	1	0.93	1.05	0.74	0.79	1	A–
Hungary	25.19	10	10	1	1	1.01	1.17	0.62	0.90	1	A–
Iceland	38.56	10	10	1	1	1.38	1.52	1.61	2.00	1	A
Ireland	30.11	10	10	1	1	1.42	1.40	1.67	1.72	1	A
Italy	42.77	10	10	1	1	1.05	1.11	0.84	0.82	1	A–
Latvia	27.09	8	8	2	1	0.50	0.91	0.18	0.46	1	A–
Lithuania	24.64	10	10	1	1	0.72	0.89	-0.14	0.48	1	A–
Luxemburg	32.45	10	10	1	1	1.43	1.41	1.69	2.00	1	A
Macedonia	15.46	6	6	4	3	-0.05	-0.29	-0.53	-0.41	2	C
Malta	33.84	–	–	1	1	1.05	1.29	0.04	1.08	1	A
Moldova	21.96	7	8	4	3	-0.19	-0.30	-0.19	-0.49	2	C
Netherlands	38.50	10	10	1	1	1.62	1.63	1.84	1.83	1	A

Country	(1)	(2)	(3)	(4)	(5)	(6)	(7)	(8)	(9)	(10)	(11)
Norway	37.90	10	10	1	1	1.67	1.64	1.99	1.96	1	A
Poland	23.59	9	9	1	1	0.95	1.11	0.44	0.65	1	A–
Portugal	29.64	10	10	1	1	1.25	1.31	1.28	1.30	1	A
Romania	32.11	8	8	4	2	0.03	0.38	−0.27	−0.12	2	B
Russia	29.50	5	7	3	5	−0.34	−0.52	−0.80	−0.78	3	C
Slovakia	43.54	7	9	2	1	0.36	0.92	0.11	0.40	1	A–
Slovenia	31.29	10	10	1	1	0.95	1.10	0.49	1.09	2	A
Spain	39.17	10	10	1	1	1.10	1.24	1.16	1.15	1	A
Sweden	37.47	10	10	1	1	1.62	1.65	1.92	1.92	1	A
Switzerland	18.97	10	10	1	1	1.63	1.63	2.05	2.03	1	A
Turkey	31.85	9	8	5	3	−0.39	−0.47	0.02	0.00	3	C
Ukraine	29.59	7	7	3	4	−0.37	−0.59	−0.64	−0.79	3	D
United Kingdom	30.16	10	10	1	1	1.32	1.47	1.84	1.81	1	A
Yugoslavia (Serbia and Montenegro)	5.85	0	7	6	3	−1.30	−0.20	–	−0.95	4	C

Sources: Tatu Vanhanen, *Prospects of Democracy: A Study of 172 Countries* (London: Routledge, 1997); Tatu Vanhanen, 'Democratization and Power Resources 1850–2000', data file, 2003; Kenneth Jaggers and Ted R. Gurr, *Polity III: Regime Change and Political Authority, 1800–1994*, 2nd edn, (Boulder, CO: ICPSR, 1996); Monty G. Marshall, Keith Jaggers and Ted Robert Gurr, *Polity IV: Political Regime Characteristics and Transitions, 1800–2001* (Maryland, MD: University of Maryland, Integrated Network for Societal Conflict Research, Centre for International Development and Conflict Management, 2001); Freedom House, *Freedom in the World* (New York: Freedom House, 1978–); PIOOM – Interdisciplinary Research Programme on Causes of Human Rights Violations, *World Conflict and Human Rights Map 2001/2002* (Leiden: PIOOM, 2002); Daniel Kaufmann, Aart Kraay and M. Mastruzzi, *Governance Matters III: Governance Indicators for 1996–2002* (Washington, DC: World Bank, 2003).

Key to columns: (1) Vanhanen's Index of Democracy, 1998; (2) Institutionalized Democracy, 1996 (Jaggers and Gurr, *Polity III*); (3) Institutionalized Democracy, 2001 (Marshall, Jaggers and Gurr, *Polity IV*); (4) Political Rights Score, 1996 (Freedom House); (5) Political Rights Score, 2002 (Freedom House); (6) Voice and Accountability Score, 1996 (World Bank); (7) Voice and Accountability Score, 2003 (World Bank); (8) Rule of Law Score, 1996 (World Bank); (9) Rule of Law Score, 2002 (World Bank); (10) Gross Human Rights Violations 2000 (Political Terror Scale, PIOOM); (11) Political System Type.

rights score, only six cases stand out as insufficient. The overall correlations between these measures are given in Table 2.

Despite the insufficiencies and well-grounded criticisms of such measures,[25] it can be contended that, rather than 'reinventing the wheel' repeatedly, a meaningful assessment of the existing political systems in Europe is possible on the basis of this information by looking across these scores and combining them into a simple classificatory scheme (see column 11 in Table 1). Thus, clearly Belarus, Bosnia and Ukraine can be labelled as non-democratic (category D) where there is a high level of agreement among all of the more discriminating indicators, including severe human rights violations. Cases such as Albania, Macedonia, Moldova, Russia, Turkey and Serbia can be classified as purely 'electoral democracies',[26] which achieve somewhat better scores on most measures but fall short of the *threshold* for a 'liberal democracy' *on each indicator* (category C). Among those passing the minimum threshold, cases with restrictions on some measures (for example, a negative 'rule of law' score) such as Bulgaria, Croatia and Romania (category B) can be distinguished from those obtaining fully positive scores (category A).

If, in addition, somewhat higher thresholds (values of +1 and above) are taken on the World Bank data, which are based on the most comprehensive information, a further distinction among the full-fledged and consolidated liberal democracies and some states with lower scores (category 'A−') becomes possible. This category still includes most of the new democracies in Central and Eastern Europe, but also a couple of longer-established ones, such as Italy and Greece, where the scores for the rule of law are below the more demanding threshold. Such a classification, on the face of it, seems to have a high degree of validity, and in future, when these measures are carried forward, some rough 'monitoring' of certain minimum standards of liberal democracies on this basis may be possible.

Some variation over time also becomes apparent when we compare available data for the major indicators for 1996 (the base year of the recent World Bank data set) with the latest scores on these variables (mostly for 2002). While in most cases there is little significant variation during this period, some show a certain improvement. Croatia and Romania, for example, have moved from C to B, in effect crossing the minimum threshold; and Estonia, Latvia and Slovakia (which have moved from B to A−) have joined other more recently consolidated democracies in Central Europe.

Evaluation of 'Good Governance'

As mentioned above, measures indicating the attainment of a certain minimum level of 'liberal democracy' must be distinguished from indices

TABLE 2
PEARSON CORRELATIONS OF DEMOCRACY INDICES

	Political Rights (Freedom House) 2003	Vanhanen's Index of Democracy 1998	Institutionalized Democracy 2001 (Polity IV)	Voice and Accountability 2002 (World Bank)	Gross Human Rights Violations 2000 (Political Terror Scale)
Political Rights 2003 (Freedom House)	1.000	–	–	–	–
Vanhanen's Index of Democracy 1998	−0.573**	1.000	–	–	–
Institutionalized Democracy 2001 (Polity IV)	−0.850**	0.711**	1.000	–	–
Voice and Accountability 2002 (World Bank)	−0.921**	0.661**	0.847**	1.000	–
Gross Human Rights Violations 2000 (Political Terror Scale)	0.838**	−0.561**	−0.670**	−0.848**	1.000

Notes: ** = significant at the $p < 0.01$ level (two-tailed).

assessing the quality of their actual *governance* in a functional sense. The World Bank data are the only ones that cover this aspect more fully. In addition to the 'voice and accountability' and 'rule of law' dimensions already presented, Kaufman and associates list three indices: 'government effectiveness' (the quality of the bureaucracy and public services); 'regulatory burden' (market-unfriendly policies, price and trade controls, and so on); and 'graft' (the exercise of public power for private gain), including various forms of corruption, nepotism or clientelism.[27]

Their 'rule of law' dimension (referring to the independence of the judiciary, respect of basic human rights, the enforceability of contracts, and the like), which has been employed already for assessing some minimal normative requirements of a 'liberal democracy', also overlaps with such characteristics of the central political system. Not all existing democracies are 'well governed' in this sense and there are non-democratic regimes which may be better governed than others – having less corruption, for example, or a certain level of rule of law, like the Prussian state in former times or, possibly, a country such as present-day Singapore. These data are presented in Table 3.

It can be seen that there is a very high level of correspondence between our previous classification of regime types and their quality of governance. All countries classified as D (Belarus, Bosnia, Ukraine) or C (Albania, Macedonia, Moldova, Russia, Serbia, Turkey) have negative scores on all these indicators. But some that pass the threshold (category B), Bulgaria and Romania being examples, also remain below 0 on some of these measures. If we, again, raise the threshold to a level of +1 for the remaining cases in order to obtain some differentiation concerning a higher 'quality', practically the same distinctions as before between our A and A− categories become apparent, all the more recent democracies falling in the A− category, and also Greece and Italy remain below this more demanding level on most indices. The mean values by system type are reported in Table 4.

Government Priorities

Another way to assess a government's orientation and specific 'quality' is to examine the actual fiscal and budgetary policies and the respective priorities given to some major policy areas – for example, expenditures on public health and education, denoting important welfare dimensions; or, conversely, for defence and military purposes.[28] These priorities are listed in Table 5.

If we differentiate these priorities according to our political system types, again some clear-cut characteristics become apparent (see Table 6).

Even though the data are somewhat incomplete for the overall tax share of Gross Domestic Product (GDP) for the less- or non-democratic states,[29]

TABLE 3
INDICATORS OF 'GOOD GOVERNANCE' (WORLD BANK INDICATORS)

Country	(1)	(2)	(3)	(4)	(5)	(6)
Albania	−0.47	−0.37	−0.37	0.08	−0.85	0.05
Austria	1.79	1.55	1.67	1.27	1.85	1.55
Belarus	−1.03	−1.05	−1.67	−0.99	−0.78	−0.86
Belgium	1.85	1.44	1.40	1.10	1.57	1.05
Bosnia-Herzegovina	−0.90	n.a.	−0.93	−1.88	−0.60	n.a.
Bulgaria	−0.06	−0.44	0.62	−0.12	−0.17	−0.62
Croatia	0.19	−0.22	0.19	−0.12	0.23	−0.45
Cyprus	1.00	1.05	1.24	0.63	0.89	1.47
Czech Republic	0.70	0.60	1.12	0.98	0.38	0.55
Denmark	1.99	1.65	1.74	1.38	2.26	2.09
Estonia	0.78	0.45	1.35	1.18	0.66	0.05
Finland	2.01	1.52	1.93	1.26	2.39	2.08
France	1.67	1.41	1.25	0.98	1.45	1.30
Germany	1.76	1.55	1.59	1.29	1.82	1.64
Greece	0.79	0.57	1.13	0.65	0.58	0.35
Hungary	0.78	0.45	1.21	0.47	0.60	0.59
Iceland	1.98	1.19	1.55	0.41	2.19	1.65
Ireland	1.62	1.45	1.64	1.33	1.67	1.72
Italy	0.91	0.68	1.15	0.70	0.80	0.43
Latvia	0.67	−0.02	0.86	0.41	0.09	−0.52
Lithuania	0.61	0.05	0.98	0.27	0.25	−0.12
Luxembourg	2.13	1.90	1.83	1.26	2.00	1.68
Macedonia	−0.39	−0.22	−0.10	−0.19	−0.73	−0.93
Malta	1.16	1.01	1.11	0.14	0.80	0.34
Moldova	−0.63	−0.49	−0.17	0.01	−0.89	−0.19
Netherlands	2.14	1.88	1.87	1.50	2.15	1.99
Norway	1.84	1.77	1.52	1.29	2.00	1.88
Poland	0.61	0.47	0.67	0.34	0.39	0.38
Portugal	1.03	0.87	1.47	1.22	1.33	1.14
Romania	−0.33	−0.53	0.04	−0.43	−0.34	−0.17
Russia	−0.40	−0.48	−0.30	−0.41	−0.90	−0.69
Slovakia	0.40	0.18	0.76	0.18	0.28	0.39
Slovenia	0.82	0.43	0.81	0.38	0.89	0.98
Spain	1.53	1.27	1.41	0.96	1.46	0.72
Sweden	1.84	1.60	1.70	1.22	2.25	2.04
Switzerland	2.26	1.98	1.62	1.18	2.17	1.97
Turkey	−0.20	−0.06	0.08	0.39	−0.38	0.08
Ukraine	−0.74	−0.59	−0.62	−0.57	−0.96	−0.69
United Kingdom	2.03	1.68	1.75	1.54	1.97	1.78
Yugoslavia (Serbia and Montenegro)	−0.73	−0.57	−0.60	−1.09	−0.80	−0.85

Notes: All indicators scored on a scale of −2.5 to +2.5, with positive scores indicating better governance; 'n.a.' means 'not available' or 'missing data'.

Source: Daniel Kaufmann, Aart Kraay and M. Mastruzzi, *Governance Matters III: Governance Indicators for 1996–2002* (Washington, DC: World Bank, 2003).

Key to columns: (1) Government Effectiveness Score, 2002; (2) Government Effectiveness Score, 1996; (3) Regulatory Quality Score, 2002; (4) Regulatory Quality Score, 1996; (5) Control of Corruption, 2002; (6) Control of Corruption, 1996.

TABLE 4
GOOD GOVERNANCE INDICES: MEANS (STANDARD DEVIATIONS)
BY SYSTEM TYPE

Political System	Government Effectiveness (2002)	Regulatory Quality (2002)	Control of Corruption (2002)
Fully consolidated democracy ($N = 18$)	1.75 (0.39)	1.55 (0.28)	1.79 (0.46)
Weakly consolidated democracy ($N = 10$)	0.73 (0.17)	1.05 (0.22)	0.49 (0.26)
Minimal liberal democracy ($N = 3$)	−0.07 (0.26)	0.28 (0.30)	−0.09 (0.29)
Electoral democracy ($N = 6$)	−0.47 (0.19)	−0.24 (0.24)	−0.76 (0.20)
Non-democracy ($N = 3$)	−0.89 (0.15)	−1.07 (0.54)	−0.78 (0.18)
Mean for all cases	0.86 (1.01)	0.89 (0.89)	0.79 (1.09)

Source: As Table 3.

the pattern seems to be clear: the longer-established and fully consolidated democracies use the highest share of GDP for public purposes. This can be taken as an indication of their stronger redistributive and (in this sense, at least) egalitarian tendencies. This impression becomes even more pronounced when we compare the respective public health and education expenditures on the one hand and military expenditure on the other, both expressed as a percentage of GDP. The means for the fully consolidated democracies are clearly the highest for health and education and lowest for the military. Conversely, the less 'democratic' a country has appeared to be on our previous indicators, the less it tends to spend on social welfare and the more on the military. There is, of course, some individual variation among our cases, but the tendency seems to be clear and is also in line with findings from other studies and other regions.[30]

Socio-Economic Performance

These governance characteristics and the resulting policies also shape actual performance significantly. If we assess the changes in GDP per capita (at purchasing power parities), literacy and life expectancy, which are aggregated by UNDP into the composite 'Human Development Index' (HDI) – that is, an arithmetic average score on the above three dimensions– during the period under consideration, similar clear-cut differences can be discerned among the different system types both absolutely and in terms of relative changes. In this way, not only efficiency but also effectiveness and actual outcomes in real terms (increasing life expectancy and so forth), instead of merely financial outputs, can be measured in some important areas. The detailed results are given in Table 7.

TABLE 5
GOVERNMENT PRIORITIES

Country	(1)	(2)	(3)	(4)	(5)	(6)	(7)
Albania	1.2	1.5	2.1	2.5	–	3.1	–
Austria	0.8	0.9	5.6	5.9	5.8	5.7	43.7
Belarus	1.4	1.2	4.7	5.3	6.0	6.1	–
Belgium	1.3	1.6	6.2	6.9	5.9	3.2	45.6
Bosnia-Herzegovina	9.5	–	3.1	–	–	–	–
Bulgaria	2.7	1.8	3.0	3.6	3.4	3.3	–
Croatia	2.6	14.5	8.0	8.5	4.2	5.3	–
Cyprus	3.1	3.4	4.3	–	5.4	–	–
Czech Republic	2.1	1.8	6.6	6.9	4.4	5.4	39.4
Denmark	1.6	1.8	6.8	6.9	8.2	8.2	48.8
Estonia	1.7	1.2	4.7	5.8	7.5	7.3	–
Finland	1.2	1.6	5.0	5.8	6.1	7.6	46.9
France	2.5	3.0	7.2	8.0	5.8	6.1	45.3
Germany	1.5	1.7	8.0	8.1	4.6	4.8	37.9
Greece	4.6	4.5	4.6	4.4	3.8	3.0	37.8
Hungary	1.8	1.6	5.1	4.9	5.0	4.7	39.1
Iceland	0.0	0.0	7.5	6.9	–	5.4	37.3
Ireland	0.7	1.1	5.1	5.2	4.4	5.8	31.1
Italy	2.0	1.9	6.0	5.4	4.5	4.7	42.0
Latvia	1.2	0.8	3.5	4.4	5.9	6.5	–
Lithuania	1.8	0.5	4.3	5.1	6.4	5.6	–
Luxembourg	0.8	0.7	5.3	6.2	3.7	4.1	41.7
Macedonia	7.0	–	5.1	7.4	–	5.6	–
Malta	0.8	0.1	6.0	–	4.9	–	–
Moldova	0.4	0.8	2.9	5.8	4.0	9.7	–
Netherlands	1.6	2.0	5.5	6.8	4.8	5.2	41.4
Norway	1.8	2.3	6.6	6.6	6.8	7.5	40.3
Poland	1.9	2.8	4.2	4.2	5.0	5.2	34.1
Portugal	2.1	2.4	5.8	5.0	5.8	5.5	34.5
Romania	2.5	3.5	1.9	3.6	3.5	3.6	–
Russia	3.8	3.7	3.7	4.3	4.4	4.1	–
Slovakia	1.9	2.3	5.3	6.1	4.2	4.9	35.8
Slovenia	1.4	1.6	6.8	7.1	–	5.8	–
Spain	1.2	1.5	5.4	5.8	4.5	4.9	35.2
Sweden	2.0	1.6	6.5	7.1	7.8	8.3	53.6
Switzerland	1.1	1.5	5.9	6.9	5.5	5.3	35.7
Turkey	4.9	4.3	3.6	2.4	3.5	2.2	33.4
Ukraine	2.7	4.5	2.9	4.9	4.4	7.2	–
United Kingdom	2.5	3.0	5.9	6.9	4.5	5.4	37.4
Yugoslavia (Serbia and Montenegro)	–	–	–	–	–	–	–

Source: United Nations Development Programme (UNDP), *Human Development Report* (New York: UNDP, 1990ff); *OECD Revenue Statistics* (Paris: OSCE, 2002).

Column key: All indicators expressed as a percentage of GDP: (1) Military expenditure, 2001 (UNDP); (2) Military expenditure, 1996 (UNDP); (3) Public expenditure on health, 2000 (UNDP); (4) Public expenditure on health, 1995 (UNDP); (5) Public expenditure on education, 1998–2000 (latest figure) (UNDP); (6) Public expenditure on education, 1996 (UNDP); (7) Total tax revenue, 2000 (OECD).

TABLE 6
GOVERNMENT PRIORITIES BY SYSTEM TYPE

Political System Type	Total tax revenue as percentage of GDP 2000	Public expenditure on health as percentage of GDP 2000	Public expenditure on education as percentage of GDP 1998–2000	Military expenditure as percentage of GDP 2001
Fully consolidated democracy				
Mean (st. dev.)	41.0 (6.0)	6.2 (0.8)	5.6 (1.2)	1.4 (0.7)
N	16	18	16	18
Weakly consolidated democracy				
Mean (st. dev.)	38.0 (2.8)	4.9 (0.9)	5.2 (1.1)	2.2 (1.0)
N	6	10	10	10
Minimal liberal democracy				
Mean (st. dev.)	–	4.3 (3.3)	3.7 (0.4)	2.6 (0.1)
N		3	3	3
Electoral democracy				
Mean (st. dev.)	33.4 (-)	3.5 (1.1)	4.0 (0.5)	3.5 (2.7)
N	1	5	3	5
Non-democracy				
Mean (st. dev.)	–	3.6 (1.0)	5.2 (1.1)	4.5 (4.4)
N		3	2	3
Total				
Mean (st. dev.)	39.9 (5.5)	5.2 (1.6)	5.2 (1.2)	2.2 (1.8)
N	23	38	33	38

Sources: As Table 5.

The enormous socio-economic diversity in Europe becomes apparent in these figures. Even adjusted for purchasing power parities, the great discrepancy between Luxembourg, as by far the richest country (US$53,780 per capita), and Moldova (US$2,150 per capita), remains striking. Life expectancy at birth is lowest in Russia, at 66.6 years, by contrast with 79.9 years in Sweden. The differences in levels of literacy are somewhat less pronounced: with the notable exceptions of Albania (85.3 per cent) and Turkey (85.5 per cent), literacy rates are between 95 and 99 per cent in most countries. The overall 'human development index' (HDI) is lowest for Moldova (0.700), followed by Turkey (0.734) and Albania (0.735), with Norway (0.944), Iceland (0.942), and Sweden (0.941) leading the group.

These discrepancies also become apparent if we look at the performance by system type (Table 8).

The longer-established consolidated democracies are clearly also the richest ones with the highest life expectancy and an overall HDI of 0.923, followed by the still 'weakly consolidated' democracies (HDI = 0.854), with all the others considerably below this score. If we take literacy alone, however, the differences are much less pronounced, given the highly developed educational systems in Central and Eastern Europe in the communist era. In the period under consideration, the less-developed countries also seem to have caught up somewhat, with the Baltic countries the best performers in economic terms – with increases in GDP per capita at purchasing power parity of over 90 per cent – starting, admittedly, from a relatively low base.

Social Inequalities and Political Unrest

The World Bank also compiles a measure of what it calls 'political instability and violence', concerning the likelihood of unconstitutional or violent interventions, including terrorism. This can be seen, to some extent, as a negative indicator of 'good governance', showing the continuing existence of potentially anti-democratic forces. The country scores are reported in Table 9.

In this respect, the cases of Bosnia, Serbia and Macedonia clearly stand out as the most turbulent ones, followed by Turkey and Albania. Finland, Sweden and Iceland, by contrast, are the most stable and peaceful. As far as changes over time are concerned, these are, of course, also influenced by individual events, but the situation seems to have become even worse in Albania, Bosnia and Macedonia more recently. (Somewhat surprisingly, France, Germany and the United Kingdom also have experienced minor changes in a negative direction, albeit retaining positive scores overall.)

The scores by system types confirm our expectations, however (see Table 10). The 'fully consolidated' democracies also have the lowest level of political unrest, followed by the more recently democratized ones.

TABLE 7
SOCIO-ECONOMIC PERFORMANCE ON SELECTED INDICATORS

Country	(1)	(2)	(3)	(4)	(5)	(6)	(7)	(8)	(9)	(10)	(11)	(12)
Albania	3,680	2,120	74	73.4	72.8	0.6	85.3	85.0	0.3	0.735	0.698	0.037
Austria	26,730	22,070	21	78.3	77.0	1.3	99.0	99.0	0.0	0.929	0.908	0.021
Belarus	7,620	4,850	57	69.6	68.0	1.6	99.0	99.0	0.0	0.804	0.774	0.030
Belgium	25,520	22,750	12	78.5	77.2	1.3	99.0	99.0	0.0	0.937	0.923	0.014
Bosnia-Herzegovina	5,970	–	–	73.8	–	–	93.0	–	–	0.777	–	–
Bulgaria	6,890	4,010	72	70.9	71.1	-0.2	98.5	98.2	0.3	0.795	0.784	0.011
Croatia	9,170	4,895	87	74.0	72.6	1.4	98.4	97.7	0.7	0.818	0.794	0.024
Cyprus	21,190	14,201	49	78.1	77.8	0.3	97.2	95.9	1.3	0.891	0.864	0.027
Czech Republic	14,720	10,510	40	75.1	73.9	1.2	99.0	99.0	0.0	0.861	0.843	0.018
Denmark	29,000	23,690	22	76.4	75.7	0.7	99.0	99.0	0.0	0.930	0.910	0.020
Estonia	10,170	5,240	94	71.2	68.7	2.5	99.0	99.0	0.0	0.833	0.793	0.040
Finland	24,430	20,150	21	77.8	76.8	1.0	99.0	99.0	0.0	0.930	0.907	0.023
France	23,990	22,030	9	78.7	78.1	0.6	99.0	99.0	0.0	0.925	0.912	0.013
Germany	25,350	21,260	19	78.0	77.2	0.8	99.0	99.0	0.0	0.921	0.908	0.013
Greece	17,440	12,769	37	78.1	78.1	0.0	97.3	96.6	0.7	0.892	0.875	0.017
Hungary	12,340	7,200	71	71.5	70.9	0.6	99.0	99.0	0.0	0.837	0.807	0.030
Iceland	29,990	22,497	33	79.6	79.0	0.6	99.0	99.0	0.0	0.942	0.918	0.024
Ireland	32,410	20,710	56	76.7	76.3	0.4	99.0	99.0	0.0	0.930	0.895	0.035
Italy	24,670	20,290	22	78.6	78.2	0.4	98.5	98.3	0.2	0.916	0.900	0.016
Latvia	7,730	3,940	96	70.5	68.4	2.1	99.0	99.0	0.0	0.811	0.761	0.050
Lithuania	8,470	4,220	101	72.3	69.9	2.4	99.0	99.0	0.0	0.824	0.785	0.039
Luxembourg	53,780	30,863	74	78.1	76.7	1.4	99.0	99.0	0.0	0.930	0.913	0.017

Country	(1)	(2)	(3)	(4)	(5)	(6)	(7)	(8)	(9)	(10)	(11)	(12)
Macedonia	6,110	3,210	90	73.3	73.1	0.2	94.0	94.0	0.0	0.784	–	–
Malta	13,160	13,180	0	78.1	77.2	0.9	92.3	91.1	1.2	0.856	0.835	0.021
Moldova	2,150	1,500	43	68.5	67.5	1.0	99.0	98.3	0.7	0.700	0.704	-0.004
Netherlands	27,190	21,110	29	78.2	77.9	0.3	99.0	99.0	0.0	0.938	0.925	0.013
Norway	29,620	24,450	21	78.7	78.1	0.6	99.0	99.0	0.0	0.944	0.924	0.020
Poland	9,450	6,520	45	73.6	72.5	1.1	99.0	99.0	0.0	0.841	0.810	0.031
Portugal	18,150	14,270	27	75.9	75.3	0.6	92.5	90.8	1.7	0.896	0.876	0.020
Romania	5,830	4,310	35	70.5	69.9	0.6	98.2	97.8	0.4	0.772	0.765	0.009
Russia	7,100	4,370	62	66.6	66.6	0.0	–	–	–	0.779	0.776	0.017
Slovakia	11,960	7,910	51	73.3	73.0	0.3	99.0	99.0	0.0	0.836	0.851	0.030
Slovenia	17,130	11,800	45	75.9	74.4	1.5	99.0	99.0	0.0	0.881	0.901	0.017
Spain	20,150	15,930	26	79.1	78.0	1.1	97.7	97.2	0.5	0.918	0.924	0.017
Sweden	24,180	19,790	22	79.9	78.5	1.4	99.0	99.0	0.0	0.941	0.912	0.020
Switzerland	28,100	25,240	11	79.0	78.6	0.4	99.0	99.0	0.0	0.932	0.712	0.022
Turkey	5,890	6,350	-7	70.1	69.0	1.1	85.5	83.2	2.3	0.734	0.748	0.018
Ukraine	4,350	2,190	99	69.2	68.8	0.4	99.0	99.0	0.0	0.766	0.916	0.014
United Kingdom	24,160	20,730	17	77.9	77.2	0.7	99.0	99.0	0.0	0.930	–	–
Yugoslavia (Serbia and Montenegro)	–	–	–	73.2	–	–	98.0	–	–	–	–	–

Source: United Nations Development Programme (UNDP), *Human Development Report* (New York: United Nations, 1990ff.).

Column Key: (1) GDP per capita at PPP, 2001 (US$); (2) GDP per capita at PPP, 1997 (US$); (3) Increase in GDP, 1997–2001 (per cent); (4) Life expectancy at birth, 2001 (years); (5) Life expectancy at birth, 1997 (years); (6) Change in life expectancy, 1997–2001 (years); (7) Adult Literacy Rate, 2001 (percentage of population); (8) Adult Literacy Rate, 1997 (percentage of population); (9) Change in Adult Literacy Rate, 1997–2000 (percentage of population); (10) Human Development Index, 2001 (0–1 scale); (11) Human Development Index, 1995 (0–1 scale); (12) Change in HDI, 1995–2001.

TABLE 8
SOCIO-ECONOMIC PERFORMANCE BY SYSTEM TYPE

Political System Type	(1)	(2)	(3)	(4)	(5)	(6)	(7)	(8)
Fully consolidated democracy								
Mean	26,280	26.0	78.0	0.9	98.2	0.2	0.923	0.020
(st.dev.)	(8,433)	(17.7)	(1.2)	(0.4)	(2.1)	(0.5)	(0.023)	(0.006)
N	18	18	18	18	18	18	18	18
Weakly consolidated democracy								
Mean	13,814	60.6	74.2	1.1	98.6	0.2	0.854	0.030
(st.dev.)	(5,674)	(28.1)	(3.1)	(0.9)	(0.7)	(0.4)	(0.034)	(0.012)
N	10	10	10	10	10	10	10	10
Minimal liberal democracy								
Mean	7,297	64.8	71.8	0.6	98.4	0.5	0.795	0.015
(st.dev.)	(1,707)	(26.7)	(1.9)	(0.8)	(0.2)	(0.2)	(0.023)	(0.008)
N	3	3	3	3	3	3	3	3
Electoral democracy								
Mean	4,986	52.5	70.9	0.6	93.5	0.7	0.746	0.018
(st.dev.)	(2,019)	(37.5)	(2.9)	(0.5)	(6.5)	(1.0)	(0.035)	(0.017)
N	5	5	6	5	6	5	5	4
Non-democracy								
Mean	5,980	77.9	70.9	1.0	97.0	0.0	0.782	0.024
(st.dev.)	(1,635)	(29.4)	(2.5)	(0.8)	(3.5)	(0.0)	(0.020)	(0.009)
N	3	2	3	2	3	2	3	2
Total								
Mean	17,601	43.9	75.2	0.9	97.5	0.3	0.864	0.066
(st.dev.)	(10,948)	(30.1)	(3.5)	(0.6)	(3.4)	(0.5)	(0.071)	(0.009)
N	38	37	39	37	39	37	38	35

Sources: As Table 7.

Key to columns: (1) GDP per capita at PPP, 2001 (US$); (2) Increase in GDP per capita at PPP, 1997–2001 (per cent); (3) Life expectancy at birth, 2001 (years); (4) Change in life expectancy, 1997–2001 (years); (5) Adult Literacy Rate, 2001 (percentage of population); (6) Change in Adult Literacy Rate, 1997–2000 (percentage of population); (7) Human Development Index, 2001 (0–1 scale); (8) Change in HDI, 1995–2001 (0–1 scale).

TABLE 9
SOCIAL INEQUALITIES AND POLITICAL UNREST

Country	(1)	(2)	(3)	(4)	(5)	(6)	(7)
Albania	−0.47	0.22	−0.69	–	4.2	–	–
Austria	1.29	1.24	0.05	30.5	40.1	33.9	6.2
Belarus	0.19	−0.04	0.23	30.4	2.0	–	–
Belgium	0.97	0.83	0.14	25.0	52.8	41.9	10.9
Bosnia-Herzegovina	−0.83	−0.28	−0.55	–	–	–	–
Bulgaria	0.56	−0.20	0.76	31.9	5.9	–	–
Croatia	0.56	0.38	0.18	29.0	13.1	–	–
Cyprus	0.36	0.50	−0.14	–	25.3	18.4	6.9
Czech Republic	1.02	0.95	0.07	25.4	9.7	–	–
Denmark	1.26	1.14	0.12	24.7	49.3	44.0	5.3
Estonia	0.98	0.74	0.24	37.6	10.4	–	–
Finland	1.63	1.32	0.31	25.6	45.5	41.4	4.1
France	0.73	1.00	−0.27	32.7	47.4	41.8	5.6
Germany	1.06	1.19	−0.13	38.2	42.4	44.3	−1.9
Greece	0.83	0.38	0.45	35.4	34.1	21.6	12.5
Hungary	1.08	0.67	0.41	24.4	12.4	0.5	11.9
Iceland	1.55	1.04	0.51	–	51.3	50.9	0.4
Ireland	1.31	1.10	0.21	35.9	37.6	32.7	4.9
Italy	0.81	0.68	0.13	36.0	41.0	36.7	4.3
Latvia	0.82	0.67	0.15	32.4	10.5	–	–
Lithuania	0.93	0.57	0.36	36.3	10.4	–	–
Luxembourg	1.54	1.23	0.31	30.8	41.2	31.7	9.5
Macedonia	−0.93	−0.18	−0.75	28.2	12.3	–	–
Malta	1.50	0.78	0.72	–	33.9	20.9	13.0
Moldova	−0.12	−0.25	0.13	36.2	3.4	–	–
Netherlands	1.37	1.39	−0.02	32.6	53.5	45.3	8.2
Norway	1.49	1.33	0.16	25.8	50.4	35.8	14.6
Poland	0.71	0.53	0.18	31.6	17.5	10.1	7.4
Portugal	1.43	1.22	0.21	38.5	20.8	11.1	9.7
Romania	0.42	0.54	−0.12	30.3	8.0	1.2	6.8
Russia	−0.40	−0.76	0.36	45.6	4.6	–	–
Slovakia	1.01	0.44	0.57	25.8	–	–	–
Slovenia	1.21	0.96	0.25	28.4	16.7	–	–
Spain	0.82	0.60	0.22	32.5	44.5	32.3	12.2
Sweden	1.43	1.28	0.15	25.0	45.7	44.0	1.7
Switzerland	1.61	1.45	0.16	33.1	38.8	34.3	4.5
Turkey	−0.61	−1.03	0.42	40.0	21.4	9.4	12.0
Ukraine	0.14	−0.25	0.39	29.0	4.0	–	–
United Kingdom	0.81	0.97	−0.16	36.0	46.6	42.2	4.4
Yugoslavia (Serbia and Montenegro)	−0.90	−1.21	0.31	–	16.0	15.7	0.3

Sources: Vanhanen, *Prospects of Democracy*; Vanhanen, *Democratization and Power Resources*; Kaufmann *et al.*, *Governance Matters III*; UNDP, *Human Development Report*.

Key to columns: (1) Political Stability Score 2002 (World Bank) (Scale = +/−2.5); (2) Political Stability Score 1996 (World Bank); (3) Change in Political Stability, 1996–2002; (4) GINI Index 1990s (latest figure) (UNDP); (5) Power Resources, 1998 (Vanhanen: 0–100 scale); (6) Index of Power Resources, 1988 (Vanhanen: 0–100 scale); (7) Change in Index of Power Resources 1988–98.

TABLE 10
SOCIAL INEQUALITY AND POLITICAL UNREST BY SYSTEM TYPE

Political System Type	Political Stability, 2002	Political Stability Change	GINI-Index 1990s (latest figure)	Vanhanen's Index of Power Resources, 1998	Change in IPR, 1988–98
Fully consolidated democracy					
Mean (st. dev.)	1.28 (0.29)	0.16 (0.23)	31.0 (4.8)	42.1 (10.1)	6.66 (4.55)
N	18	18	16	18	17
Weakly consolidated democracy					
Mean (st. dev.)	0.86 (0.21)	0.24 (0.21)	31.7 (5.2)	19.0 (11.7)	8.6 (3.5)
N	10	10	9	9	5
Minimal liberal democracy					
Mean (st. dev.)	0.51 (0.08)	0.27 (0.45)	30.4 (1.5)	9.0 (3.7)	6.8 (–)
N	3	3	3	3	1
Electoral democracy					
Mean (st. dev.)	–0.57 (0.31)	–0.04 (0.54)	37.5 (7.3)	11.5 (7.7)	6.2 (8.3)
N	6	6	4	5	3
Non-democracy					
Mean (st. dev.)	–0.17 (0.58)	0.02 (0.50)	29.7 (1.0)	3.0 (1.4)	–
N	3	3	2	2	
Total					
Mean (st. dev.)	0.76 (0.72)	0.15 (0.33)	31.4 (4.6)	27.6 (17.6)	7.0 (4.4)
N	39	39	33	37	25

Sources: As Table 9.

The 'electoral democracies' and non-democracies both show negative scores, indicating strong and continuing social tensions.

Similar observations can be made for the level of overall economic inequality, as measured by the 'GINI'-index on a scale between 0 (absolute equality) and 100. According to this measure (admittedly often not very reliable though it is), Russia, Turkey, Portugal and Germany show the greatest social inequalities (the last-named possibly because of remaining discrepancies between the Western and Eastern parts), whereas some Central European countries, such as Hungary, Slovakia and the Czech Republic, and the Scandinavian ones, are the most egalitarian. In terms of system types, the 'electoral democracies' again stand out as relatively equal (although there are some missing data and a small number of cases in this category), and the other differences are relatively less pronounced.

Vanhanen's 'Index of Power Resources' (IPR), which is treated by him as the major independent variable affecting the emergence of democracies, can also be used with a certain time lag, as an indication of the socially 'equalizing' effects (or not) of existing democracies. This index is a composite measure of his indicators of occupational diversification (IOD), knowledge distribution (IKD), including levels of literacy and schooling, and the share of family farms (FF) in the agricultural sector, each based on a scale of 0 to 100.[31] The most widely distributed power resources thus exist in the Netherlands, Belgium, Iceland and Norway (in 1998), whereas Belarus, Ukraine and Russia have the lowest scores. The changes in the 1990s, on the whole, also have been in a positive direction, Germany (with the special circumstances of its Eastern part) being the only exception.

In terms of system types, the older established democracies also show the widest distribution of power resources, followed by the more recent democracies. The purely formal 'electoral' democracies and the non-democracies, in accordance with Vanhanen's theory, still have the lowest values. The changes in the 1990s have been strongest, and in a positive direction, in the new democracies. (This must be qualified, however, by pointing out once again the low number of cases in some of these categories.)

Conclusions

The foregoing presentation has attempted to demonstrate how some of our common tools in empirical political science, such as the currently available and widely used indicators of democratization and good governance, enable some limited but nevertheless meaningful and useful analysis of the 'quality' of the political systems of contemporary European states. This in spite of the fact that most of such indices, taken by themselves, have been severely and rightly criticized on both substantive and methodological grounds. It is the contention of this essay that, nevertheless, the information contained in such indicators and indices can be combined to yield more balanced and meaningful accounts when they are integrated into a more comprehensive conceptual framework.

As the presented results show, first of all, there exists a significant distinction between liberal democracies and non-democracies, and the identification of certain sub-types becomes possible on this basis. Secondly, aspects of 'democratic quality' can be distinguished from criteria of 'good governance' in general. The actual performance in these respects points, on the whole, to a better functioning of the longer-standing 'fully consolidated' liberal democracies, but some of the more recently established, still 'weakly consolidated' democracies seem to be catching up in this regard. Some of the reasons for this better performance, as has also been shown, lie in the actual government priorities and policies pursued in some crucial areas such as health, education and other welfare measures that enhance the redistributive and to some extent 'equalizing' effects of such systems. The lower incidence of political instability and violence in the better functioning democracies can also be seen as an indication of a more effective general feedback mechanism bringing into line and balancing out, to a certain extent, the dual demands of 'representativeness' in terms of high levels of political participation and inclusion, on the input side, and of 'accountability' and political responsiveness, including appropriate checks and balances, on the output side of the political system.

It also has been shown that there is no reason for complacency about the continuing quality of existing democracies, in both a functional and a normative sense. In cases such as Italy or Greece, for example, a certain 'regression' may actually have occurred, or, at least, some more distinct 'defects' persist. These, however, can be better detected with more elaborate qualitative case-by-case analyses, such as the 'democratic audit', rather than with the broad overall indicators discussed here. Quantitative and qualitative approaches, therefore, must supplement each other in two ways. One is in going from the broader quantitative assessment to a detailed case analysis in order to check the validity of such findings.[32] The other starts from case studies in order to test the range of identified causal relationships and hypotheses in a broader setting, thus establishing the extent to which they can be generalized (that is, their 'external validity').

More differentiated institutional forms of liberal democracies, such as parliamentarian or presidential,[33] centralized or federal,[34] or majoritarian or consensual ones,[35] and their respective strengths and weaknesses, also could not be discussed here. This, again, has to be done with more finely tuned empirical approaches, but also has to be supplemented with sharper methodological tools going beyond the simple means, correlations or, at best, regressions presented in most of the current studies, given the inevitable 'small N' situation for such analyses. Both the quality of existing democracies in a more demanding sense, and our concepts and tools for dealing with it, can thus still be improved.[36]

NOTES

1. Giuseppe Di Palma, *To Craft Democracies: An Essay on Democratic Transitions* (Berkeley: University of California Press, 1990).
2. See, for example, Axel Hadenius (ed.), *Democracy's Victory and Crisis* (Cambridge: Cambridge University Press, 1997); Susan J. Pharr and Robert D. Putnam, *Disaffected Democracies: What's Troubling the Trilateral Countries?* (Princeton, NJ: Princeton University Press, 2000).
3. See also Leonardo Morlino, 'What is a "Good" Democracy? Theory and Empirical Analysis', paper prepared for the CPS Session on 'The Quality of Democracy in the Twenty-First Century', International Sociological Association World Congress, Brisbane, Australia, 7–13 July 2002.
4. David Beetham and Stuart Weir, 'Democratic Audit in Comparative Perspective', in Hans-Joachim Lauth *et al., Empirische Demokratiemessung* (Opladen: Westdeutscher Verlag, 2000), pp.73–88.
5. International Institute for Democracy and Electoral Assistance (IDEA), 'State of Democracy: Trends from the Pilot Countries', Working Paper, Stockholm, 2001.
6. See also Giovanni Sartori (ed.), *Social Science Concepts: A Systematic Analysis* (Beverly Hills, CA: Sage, 1984).
7. See also Robert A. Dahl, *Democracy and its Critics* (New Haven, CT: Yale University Press, 1989), pp.4ff.
8. See also Juan J. Linz, 'Some Thoughts on the Victory and Future of Democracy', in Dirk Berg-Schlosser (ed.), *Democratization* (Wiesbaden: VS-Verlag, 2004) pp.102–20.
9. David Collier and Steven Levitsky, 'Democracy with Adjectives: Conceptual Innovation in Comparative Research', *World Politics*, Vol.49, No.3 (1997), pp.430–51.
10. See Robert A. Dahl, *Polyarchy: Participation and Opposition* (New Haven, CT: Yale University Press, 1971); Guillermo O'Donnell, Philippe Schmitter and Laurence Whitehead, *Transitions From Authoritarian Rule: Prospects for Democracy* (Baltimore, MD: Johns Hopkins University Press, 1986); Axel Hadenius, *Democracy and Development* (Cambridge: Cambridge University Press, 1992); Georg Sørensen, *Democracy and Democratization* (Boulder, CO: Westview, 1993); Larry J. Diamond, *Developing Democracy: Toward Consolidation* (Baltimore, MD: Johns Hopkins University Press, 1999); Dirk Berg-Schlosser, *Empirische Demokratieforschung: Exemplarische Analysen* (Frankfurt: Campus, 1999), Vol.3, *Studien zur Demokratieforschung.*
11. See, for example, Seymour Martin Lipset, *Political Man: The Social Bases of Politics* (Garden City, NY: Doubleday, 1960); Seymour Martin Lipset, 'The Social Requisites of Democracy Revisited', *American Sociological Review*, Vol.59, No.1 (1994), pp.1–22.
12. See, for example, Talcott Parsons and Edward A. Shils (eds.), *Toward a General Theory of Action* (Cambridge, MA: Harvard University Press, 1952); David Easton, *A Systems Analysis of Political Life* (New York: Wiley, 1965).
13. Dirk Berg-Schlosser and Jeremy Mitchell, 'Introduction', in Dirk Berg-Schlosser and Jeremy Mitchell (eds.), *Conditions of Democracy in Europe, 1919–39: Systematic Case-Studies* (London: Macmillan, 2000), pp.1–40.
14. See, for example, Adam Przeworski, Susan C. Stokes and Bernard Manin, *Democracy, Accountability, and Representation* (Cambridge: Cambridge University Press, 1999).
15. See Benjamin Barber, *Strong Democracy: Participatory Democracy for a New Age* (Berkeley, CA: University of California Press, 1984).
16. See Carole Pateman, *The Sexual Contract* (Cambridge: Polity, 1988).

17. See, for example, Robert Putnam, *Making Democracy Work: Civic Traditions in Modern Italy* (Princeton, NJ: Princeton University Press, 1993).
18. For a fuller discussion of such measures and their respective strengths and weaknesses, see also Alex Inkeles (ed.), *On Measuring Democracy* (New Brunswick, NJ: Transaction Press, 1991); David Beetham, *Defining and Measuring Democracy* (London: Sage, 1994); Lauth *et al., Empirische Demokratiemessung*; Joe Foweraker and Roman Krznaric, 'Measuring Liberal Democratic Performance: An Empirical and Conceptual Critique', *Political Studies*, Vol.48, No.4 (2000), pp.759–87; Dirk Berg-Schlosser, 'Indicators of Democratization and Good Governance as Measures of the Quality of Democracy: A Critical Appraisal', paper prepared for the International Sociological Association Congress, Brisbane, Australia, 7–13 July 2002.
19. Tatu Vanhanen, *The Emergence of Democracy: A Comparative Study of 119 States, 1850–1979* (Helsinki: Societas Scientiarum Fennica, 1984); Tatu Vanhanen, *Prospects of Democracy: A Study of 172 Countries* (London: Routledge, 1997). The data are taken from the data file 'Democratization and Power Resources 1850–2000' (2003), author: Tatu Vanhanen, Department of Political Science and International Relations, University of Tampere; distributor: Finnish Social Science Data Archive.
20. Kenneth Jaggers and Ted R. Gurr, *Polity III: Regime Change and Political Authority, 1800–1994*, 2nd edn (Boulder, CO: ICPSR, 1996); Monty G. Marshall, Keith Jaggers and Ted Robert Gurr, *Polity IV: Political Regime Characteristics and Transitions, 1800–2001* (Maryland, MD: University of Maryland, Integrated Network for Societal Conflict Research, Centre for International Development and Conflict Management, 2001).
21. Freedom House, *Freedom in the World* (New York: Freedom House, 1978 onwards).
22. See Daniel Kaufmann, Aart Kraay and M. Mastruzzi, *Governance Matters III: Governance Indicators for 1996–2002* (Washington, DC: World Bank, 2003).
23. See PIOOM – Interdisciplinary Research Programme on Causes of Human Rights Violations, *World Conflict and Human Rights Map 2001/2002* (Leiden: PIOOM, 2002).
24. For details, see Daniel Kaufmann, Aart Kraay and Pablo Zoido-Lobatón, *Aggregating Governance Indicators*, policy research working paper no.2195 (Washington, DC: World Bank, 1999).
25. See Foweraker and Krznaric, 'Measuring Liberal Democratic Performance'; Gerardo L. Munck and Jay Verkuilen, 'Conceptualizing and Measuring Democracy: Evaluating Alternative Indices', *Comparative Political Studies*, Vol.35, No.1 (2002), pp.5–34.
26. For the use of this term, see also Diamond, *Developing Democracy*.
27. See Kaufman *et al., Governance Matters III*.
28. United Nations Development Programme (UNDP), *Human Development Report* (New York: UNDP, 1990 onwards).
29. The data for the tax share are taken from the *OECD Revenue Statistics* (Paris: OSCE, 2002).
30. See Dirk Berg-Schlosser, 'Typologies of Third World Political Systems', in Anton Bebler and Jim Seroka (eds.), *Contemporary Political Systems: Classification and Typologies* (Boulder, CO: Lynne Rienner, 1990), pp.173–201; Berg-Schlosser, 'Indicators of Democratization'; Przeworski *et al., Democracy and Development: Political Institutions and Material Well-Being in the World, 1950–1990* (Cambridge: Cambridge University Press, 2000).
31. A low value here indicates a low score on these dimensions, and corresponds to a low level of distribution of power resources, or conversely, a high level of inequality.
32. That is, the 'internal validity' in Cook and Campbell's sense: see Thomas D. Cook and David Campbell, *Quasi-Experimentation: Design and Analysis Issues for Field Settings* (Boston, MA: Houghton Mifflin, 1979).
33. See, for example, Juan J. Linz, 'Presidential or Parliamentary Democracy: Does It Make a Difference?', in Juan Linz and Arturo Valenzuela (eds.), *The Failure of Presidential Democracy* (Baltimore, MD: Johns Hopkins University Press, 1994).
34. See, for example, Manfred G. Schmidt, 'Das politische Leistungsprofil der Demokratien', in Michael Greven (ed.), *Demokratie – eine Kultur des Westens?* (Opladen: Leske & Budrich, 1998), pp.181–99.

35. See Arend Lijphart, *Patterns of Democracy: Government Forms and Performance in Thirty-Six Countries* (New Haven, CT: Yale University Press, 1999).
36. Charles C. Ragin, Dirk Berg-Schlosser and Gisèle De Meur, 'Political Methodology: Qualitative Methods in Macropolitical Inquiry', in Robert Goodin and Hans-Dieter Klingemann (eds.), *A New Handbook of Political Science* (Oxford: Oxford University Press, 1996), pp.749–68; Dirk Berg-Schlosser and S. Quenter, 'Macro-Quantitative vs. Macro-Qualitative Methods in Political Science: Advantages and Disadvantages of Comparative Procedures Using the Welfare-State Theory as an Example', *Historical Social Research*, Vol.21, No.1 (1996), pp.3–25.

The Misuse of Referendums in Post-Communist Europe

CLARE McMANUS-CZUBIŃSKA, WILLIAM
L. MILLER, RADOSŁAW MARKOWSKI and
JACEK WASILEWSKI

Introduction

Following the Athens summit in April 2003, when heads of government from 10 applicant countries signed the treaty of accession to the European Union (EU), there has been a series of referendums to ratify the treaty. Majorities in favour of EU accession have been overwhelming. With the exception of a narrow 'yes' vote in Malta, they ranged from 67 per cent to 92 per cent. And the turnout has generally been at least adequate – with the arguable exception of Hungary, where it slipped beneath the psychologically (but no longer legally) important 50 per cent (see Table 1).

But what have these referendums achieved? Legally and constitutionally they have provided a sufficient basis for EU enlargement. But they have told us very little about public support for EU membership. Indeed they raise more questions than they answer. In particular:

Did the voters represent the people as a whole?
Did the voters even represent their own preferences?
If not, why did they vote against their preferences?

These in turn raise further questions about the quality of democracy in post-communist Europe and the role of the accession states within an enlarged European Union. Were referendums an appropriate way to take democratic decisions on what had become, by 2003, an issue of 'deals not ideals' – even if referendums are an appropriate way to take other decisions? Did these particular referendums 'empower the people' in any meaningful way? And even if they were not a valid exercise in popular control, did they at least provide closure to the debate on accession by legitimating accession to the point where it is no longer up for continuous debate and reconsideration? The questions of empowerment and legitimation are related, of course. If these referenda are

TABLE 1
EU ACCESSION REFERENDUMS – ACTUAL RESULTS

Dates		Turnout (%)	YES (%)
None	Cyprus	None	None
16–17 May 2003	Slovakia	52	92
10–11 May	Lithuania	63	90
23 March	Slovenia	60	90
12 April	Hungary	46	84
7–8 June	Poland	59	77
13–14 June	Czech Republic	55	77
20 September	Latvia	73	67
14 September	Estonia	63	67
8 March	Malta	91	54
Average		62	78

Notes: Cyprus did not hold a referendum. Table ranked in descending order of
percentage 'yes' in EU referendum. In Slovenia there was a double referendum on EU and NATO membership.

Source: <http://europa.eu.int/comm/enlargement/negotiations/
accession_process.htm> (accessed Dec. 2003).

not seen as a valid exercise in popular control they will not provide much
long-term legitimacy. And in that case the accession states may prove to be
'bad members of the club' if, indeed, they choose to remain members at all.

Did the voters misrepresent the people as a whole? There is always a
possibility that voters misrepresent the public as a whole since non-voters
may have different views from voters. That was perhaps important in Latvia,
where a fifth of the public were excluded (as 'non-citizens') from voting, and
the evidence shows that the excluded non-citizens had very different views
from the voters.[1] Elsewhere it probably mattered less. Our own calculations
for Poland suggest that the voters were only about five per cent more inclined
to a 'yes' vote than the public as a whole. So the misrepresentation of the
public by the voters was not perhaps of great importance there.

Did voters misrepresent themselves? They did. Voters did not and could not
express their own true feelings about accession. A referendum imposes far more
constraints on the electorate than a parliamentary election. Typically elections
offer voters a wide range of choice among different parties. And if there is widespread public disquiet at the limited range of available parties, then it is always
possible for a new party to offer an additional alternative. But the EU referendums offered only two options, 'yes' or 'no', and it was impossible for any
political entrepreneur to widen the choice by adding even a third option, let
alone a fourth or a fifth. It was a forced choice between unwelcome alternatives.

Consequently voters voted without enthusiasm, for something they did not
want. The referendums grossly overstate the degree of popular enthusiasm for

EU membership throughout the accession states. In reality voters chose not to block elite moves towards a greater European Union, but they acquiesced with reluctance.

Results of the 2003 Eurobarometer poll – which was held in the midst of the 'referendum season' – came reasonably close to the actual levels of 'yes' votes in most accession states (82 per cent). But simultaneously, only 58 per cent of respondents describe their country's membership of the EU as 'a good thing'. Although fewer said it would be 'a bad thing', a considerable number had neutral or mixed views about membership (see Table 2).

Across ten items of concern, an average of 38 per cent express fears about the consequences of EU membership. Only 50 per cent have a clear view that membership will bring 'more advantages than disadvantages' to their country. Still less – only 39 per cent – have a clear view that membership will bring 'more advantages than disadvantages' to themselves personally. Again, many

TABLE 2
HOPES AND FEARS (PER CENT)

		EU membership will bring ...		
	'Yes' Vote	EU membership is 'a good thing'	Average expressing fears (across ten items)	More advantages than disadvantages for country	More personal advantages than disadvantages
Cyprus	91	72	43	69	51
Slovenia	89	57	38	47	38
Slovakia	87	59	40	46	36
Hungary	86	63	42	56	40
Lithuania	86	65	32	62	52
Poland	83	61	33	53	40
Czech Republic	76	46	47	35	30
Latvia	64	37	42	38	31
Malta	64	51	41	49	47
Estonia	56	31	47	33	26
Average	82	58	38	50	39

Notes: 'Yes' figures are expressed as a percentage of those answering 'yes' plus 'no', others excluded. Table ranked in descending order of percentage 'yes' in Eurobarometer poll. Large numbers of ethnic Russians in Baltic States were excluded from participation in the referendums despite long-term residence or even birth. Eurobarometer surveys adults (over 15 years), not citizens. Those perceived – by the general public – to be most disadvantaged by EU membership were: farmers (22 per cent), inhabitants of rural areas (22 per cent), elderly people (22 per cent), and those who do not speak foreign languages (34 per cent).

Source: Eurobarometer EB59 – CC-EB 2003.2 (July 2003, fieldwork May 2003), accessible via <http://www.europa.eu.int/comm/public_opinion>, pp.69, 72, 90, 93, 102, 104, 114.

have mixed rather than clearly pessimistic views. So it would be wrong to claim that the referendums produce the *wrong answer* to the question 'yes' or 'no', but that is clearly the *wrong question*. So, the referendums misleadingly imply far more positive support, or even enthusiasm, than actually exists. In reality, support for EU accession is widespread but weak, reluctant and conditional. It is combined with almost as much pessimism as optimism. It could be described perhaps as 'a mile wide but an inch deep'[2] – something that is extremely difficult if not altogether impossible to measure by the crude procedure of a 'yes/no' referendum.

Although the Eurobarometer survey does not aim to reveal the criteria used by referendum voters to decide between 'yes' and 'no', it does provide some evidence on the nature of their hopes and fears. Significantly, it shows that more than twice as many express economic fears (57 per cent) as cultural fears, such as concern about their language (25 per cent), identity or culture (21 per cent). Only fears of an increase in crime and drug-trafficking (53 per cent) rival economic fears.

To investigate in greater depth whether voters 'misrepresented themselves' and, more importantly, whether these referendums were an appropriate way to take decisions, we will focus on Poland, where we had an opportunity to insert a wide range of accession-oriented questions into the 2001 PNES (Polish National Election Survey).[3] These allow us to investigate Polish voters' enthusiasm (or the lack of it) for accession in much greater detail than Eurobarometer polls permit. In particular we can examine the *criteria* that voters use to make their referendum choice. Eurobarometer data hint that economic fears are far greater than cultural fears. But fears are not quite the same as criteria for decision. We shall argue that it is criteria for decision that largely determine whether referendums are an appropriate or inappropriate device for decision in particular circumstances, and our own PNES data allow us to address that key question of criteria explicitly.

Before we embark on our analysis of PNES data, however, we should consider the degree to which Poland is typical of the accession states – and of the accession peoples. Poland ranks exactly halfway down the list of accession states in terms of the actual 'yes' vote – or 'yes' preferences if we were to include Cyprus. Poland is also reasonably typical of accession countries on more general attitudes towards the EU: 62 per cent of Poles trust the EU compared with 63 per cent overall – and Poland comes almost exactly halfway down the list of accession countries in terms of trusting the EU.

But Poland is not just another accession state. Over half the entire population joining the EU in 2004 lives in Poland. So inevitably, Polish attitudes are even more typical of attitudes among the accession peoples than among the accession states. Cross-country variations are interesting but cross-country averages are misleading.

A Civilizational Choice?

As the referendum result was announced Polish President Kwaśniewski expressed the 'civilizational choice' view in the now-familiar slogan, 'We are coming back to Europe'[4] – which had come to imply much more about Western democratic values than about geography. More brutally, Latvian President Vaira Vike-Freiberga said the vote 'wiped out for ever the divisions on the map of Europe that the odious Molotov-Ribbentrop pact of 1939 placed there'.[5] Such claims present the referendum choice as a simple choice that could be made by the public, with understanding and enthusiasm, on the basis of gut instinct.

But by 2003 the EU could no longer be equated with Western democracy, and the 2003 referendums could not therefore be about a simple 'civilizational choice' as they might have been in 1989 or even 1993. The unity of Western democracy had been called into question on both sides of the Atlantic by those who saw not one but two Western democratic civilizations – a militant neo-conservative American and a soft 'old' European, operating in economic and ideological competition, with increasingly divergent values on fundamental concepts of international order.

Could Poland join both? Or would joining with 'old Europe' in the EU inevitably mean turning against the United States? If there are to be two Western civilizations in the twenty-first century (as there were, according to Huntington, in the nineteenth[6]), then it is not quite obvious where Poland fits. The *Economist* noted that 'Poland's strong pro-Americanism tempers its European instincts', quoting one Polish official as saying that a choice between Europe and America was similar to a choice between a father and mother: 'we love them both'.[7] But it might be worse than that: like Britain, Poland might prove to be 'in but not of' the EU – reluctant, hyper-critical, unreliable and troublesome, a 'Trojan donkey' for the United States.[8] Our 2001 PNES survey shows that 72 per cent of Poles trusted the US, and 76 per cent the American-dominated NATO, compared with only 54 per cent who trusted the EU.[9] Judged by that benchmark, Iraq seems to have at once exposed the strong historic Polish–American link more clearly and, at the same time, tested and considerably eroded its strength. But 2003 Eurobarometer data still show that, although Polish trust in the EU is typical of that throughout the accession states, Polish trust in NATO is exceptionally high.[10] And a poll for *Polityka*, taken just before the referendum, shows that 54 per cent of Poles still cite the US as Poland's 'closest ally' against only 46 per cent who cite the EU.[11] Yet the very fact that this is a meaningful question is far more significant than the numerical findings: Poles simply cannot equate the EU with 'Western civilization'.

At the referendum Polish diplomats were reported as 'knowing that our place is in Europe' and that 'Poland is not Canada'.[12] But three million

Polish émigrés lived in the US; the US administration lavished praise on Poland for being the core of a 'new Europe' opposed to the 'old Europe' of France and Germany, even if others contest this view;[13] Poland 'snubbed' the EU by equipping its air force with US jets;[14] and the US 'outflanked' old Europe by 'inviting Poland to the Iraq victors' table', assigning Poland to command a sector of occupied Iraq.[15] Moreover, an obsolescent focus on Catholic–Protestant divisions tends to obscure the rising significance of secular–religious divisions. And on religiosity, relatively religious Poland and the US have more in common with each other than with what is now largely secular, if still nominally Christian, 'old' Europe.

An Unequal Treaty

There is a second, and perhaps more important, reason why the referendum choice was unlikely to be a simple 'civilizational choice' by 2003: hard bargaining and long-drawn-out negotiations had exposed the fact that EU accession was more about 'deals than ideals'. It was about taxes and subsidies, about ensuring that the agricultural subsidies paid in the new Europe would never reach the levels that farmers in the old Europe had enjoyed, at least in the past. And accession was also about the burden of EU 'conditionality', which, even when it aimed to cut corruption and strengthen democracy or 'good government', also underlined the inferior status of the new Europe by imposing conditions that some states in the old Europe could not meet. Old Europe set the conditions and set the timetable.

Eastern Europe's hope for a 'return to Europe' remained a distant and remote possibility during more than 40 years of communist rule, but the Yalta agreement to divide Europe was always regarded by East Europeans as artificial and ultimately transient. When communism collapsed there were high expectations of a speedy end to this artificial division. But 'Europe' had changed. West European visions of Europe had not only deepened but also narrowed as the economic European Community (EC) moved towards reinventing itself as the political and even cultural EU.

So, the Iron Curtain was replaced by a barrier that was almost as impenetrable, the *acquis communautaire*, a body of laws, rules and regulations to which prospective applicants must conform if they wish to be accepted as member states. Instead of being 'welcomed home', Eastern Europe faced 13 arduous and acrimonious years of being forced to conform to EU-imposed demands. In the early 1990s naive and unskilled negotiators succumbed to EU pressure. And during the final stages, EU pressure to conform or risk forfeiting a place in the first wave of eastward enlargement was immense. The EU made clear that there would be no exceptions. There was no appreciation, for example, of the fact that Poland's size, in terms of population and land, meant that agricultural and industrial restructuring was especially onerous there. Initial claims by the Polish government that it had secured the best deal out of all the applicant states on the agricultural chapter of the treaty of accession proved mistaken. It emerged that the Polish government's version of what it had signed up to was completely different from that of the EU – and of course it was the latter that counted. Whatever accession was, it was not an 'equal treaty'. There was a whiff of colonialism in the air.

Even on non-economic affairs, pressure from the EU was recognized and resented. In recent talks on the EU's new Constitution for example, EU diplomats have been highly critical of Poland's 'egoistic' stance – leading the Polish foreign minister to respond that 'portraying Poland as an egoistic country, which does not understand what the EU is about, is a form of pressure', adding bravely that 'no such pressure will succeed'.[16]

All these years of arduous and acrimonious negotiations left a deep wound in the psyche of East European publics. Shocked by the EU's tough negotiating stance and frustrated at the perceived unfairness of the Europe Agreements,[17] many became disillusioned with the project of European union. Support for Poland's membership of the EU fell from the dizzy heights of over 80 per cent in the early 1990s to barely over 50 per cent before recovering later – in extent though not in enthusiasm.

Originally, the new post-communist elites throughout Eastern Europe intended to hold referendums that would underline the historical and cultural symbolism – as well as the economic importance – of joining the EU. The people would trade their newly won and much-treasured sovereignty for recognition as full members of a restored Europe. But that opportunity slowly faded with the years.

By announcing its intention in July 2000 to hold a referendum in the near future on EU membership, the Polish government was merely trying to force the EU into announcing a date for the end to the interminable and debilitating accession negotiations in which they had invested so much for so long.[18] As disenchantment with the EU grew among the citizens of Central and Eastern Europe, the wisdom of such an intention was questioned. But despite the collapse of popular enthusiasm for accession, the Polish elite still wished to go ahead with the referendum, if only because confidence in their own government had fallen to an all-time low in the wake of economic crises and successive corruption scandals at home.

Yet the decision to hold a referendum could hardly be described as an exercise in popular control. The Polish government had written in a number of 'escape routes' if the referendum went wrong. First, a clause was belatedly written into the Polish Constitution which would allow a referendum to be declared constitutionally invalid if the turnout fell below 50 per cent – and in such an event, the Polish Parliament could take Poland into the EU irrespective of the referendum vote. Second, if the referendum produced a majority of 'no' votes on a valid turnout it is likely that Poland would have followed the Irish example by having another referendum a few months later when the people could be threatened with ostracization if they dared to vote 'no' again.

Poles identify fairly strongly with Europe,[19] and pro-EU campaigners in Poland tried to obscure the distinction between 'Europe' and the EU.[20] Conversely anti-EU campaigners pictured the EU as a structure, an organization, indeed an empire, using slogans such as 'Yesterday Moscow, Tomorrow Brussels'[21] to suggest that Poland's independence was threatened by the EU.

That was over-dramatic. In fact, far more Poles see Moscow (38 per cent) rather than Brussels (only 8 per cent) as the 'greater threat to Poland's sovereignty and independence'. NATO provides a better point of comparison than Moscow. Only 8 per cent of Poles see the EU as the primary threat to their 'sovereignty and independence', that is four times as many as see NATO as the primary threat. Similarly, they rate NATO much higher than the EU in positive terms. On balance 62 per cent see the EU as 'good for Poland'. But that judgement derives very much from balancing advantages and disadvantages. And it compares unfavourably with the 87 per cent who see NATO as 'good for Poland'. A large majority of Poles (76 per cent) see the EU as a guarantor of 'freedom in Central Europe'. But again, that compares unfavourably with the considerably greater number, 91 per cent, who see NATO as defending freedom in Central Europe.

And whether or not they see the EU as the primary threat to their independence, many Poles do indeed see the EU *as more a threat than a protection.* Poles are evenly divided on whether the EU 'protects' (46 per cent) or 'threatens' (45 per cent) Polish 'independence and culture' – whereas an overwhelming majority of 82 per cent see NATO as 'protecting' rather than 'restricting' their independence. Poles are overwhelmingly suspicious (76 per cent) that the EU will put the interests of 'old Europe' above the interests of the countries in the 'new Europe'. By contrast, only a minority (31 per cent) suspect that NATO will 'not take risks to defend Poland'.

So, even if we accept that the one organization is more economic and the other more military in orientation (and in reality that is far too simplistic), this combination of answers suggests that Poles have a strongly Atlanticist but only moderately pro-EU perspective on Poland's national interest. The warmth of Polish attitudes to NATO highlights their cold suspicion of the EU.

The conditions for EU accession include closing the eastern frontier, opening the western frontier, allowing foreigners to buy Polish land, and joining the euro – the latter a condition that does not apply to existing members. But the złoty lacks the symbolic power of the British pound and only 25 per cent would prefer to keep it as the only currency in Poland.

In principle, a majority (51 per cent in favour, 32 per cent against) support the opening of the western frontier together with the closure of the eastern one, even if they have reservations in practice. However, land touches a particularly raw nerve: three-quarters of Poles reject the right of incomers from the EU to buy Polish land. Indeed 45 per cent are 'strongly' opposed to EU citizens buying Polish land (though somewhat less opposed in the western 'regained territories' than further east – the issue plays rather differently as a symbolic issue on the one hand, and as an economic issue on the other).[22] Poles are markedly more enthusiastic about taking jobs in the EU than about letting EU citizens compete for scarce jobs in Poland (see Table 3).

The EU accession treaty fails to resolve these fears. Instead, it merely phases in both the advantages and disadvantages of membership. EU subsidies to Polish farmers will gradually increase over a nine-year period from just 25 per cent of the subsidy given to West European farmers – but the size of the subsidy will be cut as the rates of subsidy converge.[23] Temporary restrictions on the purchase of Polish land will be balanced by temporary restrictions on Polish workers' access to jobs in the West. And so on. But in the end, Poles will have to accept foreigners' rights to take Polish jobs and buy Polish land. And they will never ever enjoy agricultural subsidies on the scale that western farmers have done in the past.

There is a broad consensus that accession will benefit foreign firms while damaging Polish agriculture and state industries: 84 per cent think foreign firms will benefit, while 68 per cent think state industries will be damaged and almost as many (60 per cent) think Polish agriculture will be damaged. Whatever the compensating benefits, accession is viewed as a threat to Polish agriculture and state industries.

TABLE 3
JOBS, LAND AND THE EU (PER CENT)

Do you agree or disagree with each of the following, and how strongly? If we join the European Union ...	Poles should have a right to take jobs in other EU countries	Foreigners from the EU should have a right to take jobs in Poland	Foreigners from the EU should have a right to own land in Poland
Strongly agree	74	56	9
Agree	24	34	14
Disagree	1	7	30
Strongly disagree	0	2	45
Neither/mixed/depends (do not read out)	1	1	2

Note: Percentages of those with a view, excluding 'Don't knows' (DKs).

Source: Polish National Election Survey (PNES) 2001.

And Poles are almost evenly divided on whether accession will benefit rather than damage private Polish firms or their own family living standards – although more inclined towards pessimism. Amongst those with an opinion, there are slightly more who are pessimistic (48 per cent) than optimistic (46 per cent) about private Polish firms; and also slightly more who are pessimistic (45 per cent) than optimistic (41 per cent) about their own family living standards. But (as we discuss in detail later) an unusually and remarkably large number simply do not have any clear view on whether or not accession will benefit or damage their family living standards.

A Forced Choice: When 'Yes' Means 'Maybe Sometime, Not Now'

The brutal simplicity of a 'yes/no' choice contrasts dramatically with the fog of ignorance in which that choice had to be made. We might well ask whether a referendum in such circumstances could ever have much validity. If there is any case for including a 'none of the above/against all' option on an election ballot (a subject examined by Hutcheson later in this collection), there is surely an equally strong case for including a corresponding 'insufficient information for decision' option along with 'yes' and 'no' on a referendum ballot. No referendum can adequately express the complexity of perspectives on accession – in Poland or anywhere else – but a simple 'yes/no' choice provides a particularly misleading indicator.

Given only a slightly wider choice, an absolute majority (54 per cent) say they would prefer to join the EU 'at some more favourable time in the future' rather than join immediately (25 per cent) or stay out indefinitely (12 per cent). Indeed, three months after the referendum, a survey by Taylor Nelson Sofres– Osrodka Badan Opinii Publicznej (TNS OBOP) found that 50 per cent of Poles were still convinced that Poland was not yet ready for membership, compared with only nine per cent who felt that Poland was fully prepared.[24]

Yet the unspoken implication of the unequal treaty negotiations and the subsequent referendums was that the only options were immediate entry, on the one hand, or a very real possibility of indefinite exclusion, on the other. The example of the UK was enough to show that failure to grasp the opportunity of entry when offered could lead to long-term exclusion even for a state as strong economically, diplomatically and militarily as the UK. And none of the accession states were in that league. So a 'yes/no' referendum not only failed to offer an option that truly expressed the public's perspective on the EU, it also imposed a forced choice under conditions of implied threat.

The referendum produced a large majority for entry because the largest section of voters – those who would 'prefer to join later' – split two-to-one in favour of accepting rather than rejecting accession when forced to choose. Consequently 68 per cent of our respondents said they would vote 'yes' rather than 'no' – if they voted at all. Among the 56 per cent who said they certainly would vote, those who would vote 'yes' rose to 73 per cent. Although our survey took place at the end of 2001, these figures are remarkably close to the actual outcome of a 59 per cent turnout and a 77 per cent 'yes' vote, which tends to confirm Szczerbiak's view that Polish opinion on EU accession had been 'extremely stable since mid-1999' and 'most Poles had actually made their minds up about it a long time ago', so that there was 'little new' that could have any impact in the referendum campaign itself.[25] But their minds were not made up in the mould of the referendum choice: they were forced into that mould. Indeed, only a minority of 'yes' voters actually wanted to 'join now' and the views of the majority of even the 'yes' voters could be aptly characterized as 'sometime maybe, not now'.

Criteria for Decision: Deals or Ideals?

Perhaps a simple 'yes/no' referendum could represent a broad political or cultural choice well enough, but not a choice based on all the doubts, details, hesitation and uncertainties of economic hopes and fears. A referendum is a far better tool for expressing *ideals* than for exercising judgement on technical *deals*.

Many good democrats, including at least three British prime ministers – Attlee, Thatcher and Major – have derided referendums as 'the device of demagogues and dictators'.[26] That may be over-critical, but even populist democrats would have to concede that referendums are a bad tool for technical decision-making as distinct from a tool for deciding questions of principle.[27] So if the question of accession were an issue of broad principle, which the public understood fully and cared about passionately, then a referendum might be appropriate. But if it were merely a technical issue, shrouded in technicalities and uncertainties, on which the public were ill-informed, confused, doubtful and unenthusiastic, then there is no democratic case for a referendum.

There are two ways of assessing this critical question of the relative importance of 'deals versus ideals', or economic versus political and cultural considerations – and thus the appropriateness of a 'yes/no' referendum. One is to ask the people explicitly about the criteria that are important to them. The other is to use statistical analysis to correlate potential criteria against referendum votes. Happily, both approaches lead to the same conclusion.

Asking the People: 'Economic' versus 'Political and Cultural' Criteria

Roughly four-fifths of Poles told us they would base their referendum decision on 'economic' rather than 'political and cultural' criteria of any kind. More surprisingly, that was true both of those who intended to vote 'yes' (22 per cent of whom stressed 'political and cultural criteria') and of those who intended to vote 'no' (20 per cent). Surprisingly also, it does not seem that those who wanted to postpone a decision on entry to a more favourable time in the future were encouraged to do so merely by an economic calculus. Only 16 per cent of those who wanted either to join immediately or to stay out indefinitely said that their decision was based on 'political and cultural' criteria. By contrast, 25 per cent of those who wanted to postpone the decision stressed 'political and cultural' criteria. It seems that this 25 per cent at least were waiting for a more politically and culturally secure, respected and self-confident Poland that could negotiate from strength, rather than for some economic window of opportunity.

In terms of social groups, 'cultural' criteria are stressed more by women (25 per cent) than men (18 per cent); and more by those who were either 'devout' or 'non-believers' (27 per cent) than by ordinary believers (20 per cent), who form the great majority of Poles. 'Cultural' criteria are stressed by those who sympathize with either the Catholic Liga Rodzin Polskich (LPR) (32 per cent) or the aggressively modernizing Platforma Obywatelska (PO) (25 per cent), more than by those who sympathize with Samoobrona (12 per cent). Conversely, 'economic' criteria are stressed especially by 'transition losers' (84 per cent) and by Samoobrona sympathizers (88 per cent). Although these variations are not large, they show that some social and political groups are a little more self-consciously sensitive to cultural criteria than others – although none of them put anywhere near as much stress on cultural as on economic criteria.

It is plausible, but not surprising, that those who are hardest-pressed economically should be unusually sensitive to economic criteria and relatively insensitive therefore to cultural criteria. More importantly, our figures suggest something much less obvious: that cultural criteria constitute a dimension of impact, not a direction. Cultural criteria not only influence the conservative Catholic minority, they also influence the relatively secular minority; and cultural criteria are as likely to influence some Poles in favour of accession as influence others against it. It is not the case that economic criteria point in one direction and cultural criteria in another. Poles are divided over culture as well as over economic matters. They are divided over whether accession will have a positive or negative cultural impact, as well as divided over whether it will have a positive or negative economic impact. They disagree over what cultural changes they *want*, as well as over what cultural changes they *expect*.

The Statistical Approach: Weighing the Impact of Economic versus Cultural Criteria

The alternative approach is to correlate various indicators of cultural and economic attitudes with referendum votes. This has the advantage that we can compare many different aspects of cultural and economic attitudes.

So not only can we resolve the big question of whether cultural criteria predominate over economic hopes and fears, but we can also determine which aspect of culture and which element of economic hopes and fears have most influence.

Polish decisions on EU accession might have reflected the 'civilizational choice' stressed by the president, between a communist past and a European or Atlanticist future; or other cultural choices, notably the choice between a religious or secular culture, or between a nationalist or multiculturalist and cosmopolitan culture; or simply reflected economic hopes and fears, whether personal or societal.

Cultural criteria – the 'civilizational' choice. Opposition to accession correlates with perspectives on the first transition – the transition from communism. And general nostalgia for the pre-1989 regime is more influential than mere 'transition loss'. That is the ultimate retrospective on the 'civilizational choice'. Opposition to accession is relatively high (at 42 per cent) among 'transition losers' whose own family living standards have declined sharply since 1989, but even greater (at 50 per cent) among those who express a more general nostalgia for the pre-1989 regime (see Table 4).

Conversely, support for accession correlates quite strongly with support for democracy – both as a principle of governance and as an operating system in Poland. Attitudes towards the practice of democracy – 'the way it works in Poland' – make a difference of 27 per cent to support for accession. And attitudes to the principle – 'democracy is better than any other form of government' – made a slightly greater difference of 30 per cent. Either way, the most enthusiastic democrats are also the most enthusiastic supporters of accession (see Table 5).

TABLE 4

EU VOTE – BY ATTITUDES TO THE DEMOCRATIC TRANSITION (PER CENT OF YES VOTE)

	Among those who think ...		
	current regime is ...	economy works ...	family living standards are ...
Much better than before 1989	83	88	80
Slightly better now	71	77	78
Neither better, nor worse	66	72	68
Slightly worse now	61	65	69
Much worse now	50	53	58

Note: Percentages of those with a view, excluding DKs.

Source: PNES 2001.

TABLE 5
EU VOTE – BY ATTITUDE TO DEMOCRACY (PER CENT OF YES + NO
VOTES)

	YES-vote in a referendum
Among those whose attitude to the way democracy works in Poland is, on the whole, that they are . . .	
Very satisfied	83
Fairly satisfied	79
Not very satisfied	60
Not at all satisfied	56
Among those whose attitude to the statement: 'Democracy may have problems but it's better than any other form of government' is that they . . .	
Agree strongly	78
Agree	68
Disagree	53
Disagree strongly	48

Note: Percentages of those with a view, excluding DKs.

Source: PNES 2001.

Cultural criteria – religious versus secular. Polish identification with the Catholic Church rivals identification with Poland itself – and far exceeds such social or political identifications as class or party. Cardinal Glemp, head of the Polish Church, had called for the accession treaty to recognize the 'separateness' and indeed 'sovereignty'[28] of Poland on moral issues such as abortion – which it failed to do. The LPR and, more bitterly, the Catholic nationalist Radio Maryja both campaigned against accession.[29] But, in the end, a very Polish Pope intervened to bless accession with a very Polish slogan: 'From the Union of Lublin to the European Union';[30] and Cardinal Glemp himself described accession as 'a question of human solidarity'[31] across Europe. So the Church sent out mixed messages on accession, clearly pro-accession at the top but perhaps on balance anti-accession at the grassroots.

In 2001, opposition to accession was particularly high among the religiously 'devout': only 56 per cent of the self-described 'devout' compared with 77 per cent of 'atheists' intended to vote 'yes'.

While the Pope's dramatic late intervention allegedly had an impact,[32] it could not fully reverse that tendency. A comparison of our 2001 PNES survey with 2003 referendum exit polls is illuminating. In 2001, 85 per cent of PO voters but only 50 per cent of LPR voters told us they would vote 'yes' in the referendum; referendum exit polls in 2003 showed 92 per cent of those PO voters but only 64 per cent of LPR voters cast a 'yes' vote.[33]

So the gap narrowed from 35 to 28 per cent. But a similar comparison suggests that the gap between PO and Samoobrona voters' support for a 'yes' vote widened from 22 to 42 per cent. So the Pope's intervention (which would have influenced the relatively devout LPR voters much more than the much less religious Samoobrona voters) almost certainly prevented a further slide of devout (or LPR) opinion against EU accession. Indeed his intervention probably increased EU support by a small amount, though not by much. The devout – and especially LPR sympathizers – still remained relatively sceptical compared with other Poles and especially compared with the aggressively modernizing PO voters.

Cultural criteria – nationalism versus multiculturalism. Support for EU accession correlates moderately with trusting Polish political institutions such as the president, MPs, the courts or the Central Bank – though less with trusting other Polish institutions. In every case bar one, however, where there is a statistically significant correlation at all, trust correlates with support for accession, and distrust with opposition – reflecting the elite's broad commitment to accession. The single exception is trust in the Church – which correlated (albeit in 2001, and then only weakly) with opposition to accession!

With one exception – again involving the Church – support for accession does not correlate significantly with identities unless they include a specific reference to 'Europe'. Those who feel 'equally European and Polish', for example, are 21 per cent more likely to support accession than those who feel exclusively Polish. The single exception is religious identification: those with a very strong sense of religious identity were, in 2001 at least, 19 per cent more likely to oppose accession than those with a very weak or no religious identity (see Table 6).

There are much stronger correlations, however, between opposition to accession and distrusting Western countries or organizations, in particular NATO itself along with NATO countries such as the United States, Britain or Germany. Counter-intuitively, however, trusting Poland's eastern neighbours, Russia and Ukraine, does not increase opposition to EU accession. Indeed, there is a low but statistically significant correlation between trusting Russia or Ukraine and supporting accession – almost certainly this indicates a weak 'internationalist' or 'cosmopolitan' impact on support for accession rather than anything specifically linked to the former Soviet Union.

EU hopes and fears. So far we have asked: 'what kind of people support or oppose accession?' Now we refocus on a different set of questions: 'what is it about the EU that is so attractive or repulsive?'; and, in particular, 'is it the cultural or economic aspects of the EU that are so attractive or repulsive?' Most of all, opposition to accession correlates with simple distrust for the EU ($r = 0.60$) and even more with the general feeling that the EU is simply 'bad

TABLE 6
CORRELATIONS BETWEEN OPPOSITION TO ACCESSION AND
DOMESTIC OR INTERNATIONAL DISTRUST

	Correlation with: prefer to join 'never'	Correlation with: NO vote in referendum
IDENTIFICATIONS		
Identification – Polish v. European	.16**	.16**
Identification with religion	.11**	.10**
DISTRUST – DOMESTIC		
Distrust – President	.16**	.18**
Distrust – MPs	.13**	.13**
Distrust – courts	.13**	.08*
Distrust – Central Bank	.09**	.12**
DISTRUST – INTERNATIONAL		
Distrust – NATO	.28**	.31**
Distrust – Britain	.25**	.21**
Distrust – USA	.24**	.21**
Distrust – Germany	.23**	.22**
Distrust – Ukraine	.08*	.10**
Distrust – Russia	.07*	.10**

Note: Correlations calculated, excluding DKs and those with views coded as 'nether/mixed/depends'. ** = statistically significant at $p < .01$, * = statistically significant at $p < .05$.

Source: PNES 2001.

for Poland' ($r = 0.79$). But these correlations are so tautologous as to be substantively trivial despite their statistical significance. There are other, more meaningful, and scarcely much weaker correlations that tell us what it is about the EU that is particularly attractive or repulsive for voters.

Some specific concerns about the cultural consequences correlate with opposition to accession, especially concerns about incomers bringing in a different culture and, to a slightly lesser extent, concerns about the introduction of the euro – a potentially symbolic as well as economic issue – and the closure of the eastern border – potentially a cultural as well as an economic 'turn to the West' (see Table 7).

Perceptions that the EU bureaucracy is corrupt and wasteful, that it will remain biased towards the interests of 'old Europe', or especially that it might threaten Polish freedom and independence correlate even more strongly with opposition to accession (see Table 8).

But opposition to accession correlates most strongly of all with hopes and fears about its economic impact – especially its impact on family living standards or Polish agriculture (see Table 9).

However, there is great uncertainty about the likely economic impact of accession, especially on the family. Few are confident that accession will

TABLE 7
CORRELATIONS BETWEEN OPPOSITION TO ACCESSION AND PERCEPTIONS OF
THE CULTURAL CONSEQUENCES OF ACCESSION

	Correlation with: prefer to join 'never'	Correlation with: NO vote in referendum
Worse place if incomers bring different culture	.40**	.36**
Keep złoty	.34**	.32**
Border changes bad	.31**	.36**
Poland does NOT have a lot to learn from other countries	.21**	.21**
We should NOT co-operate at the cost of our independence	.19**	.17**

Notes: ** = statistically significant at p < .01. Correlations calculated, excluding DKs and those with views coded as 'nether/mixed/depends'. An unusually large number (33 per cent) spontaneously replied that incomers with a different culture would make the locality neither better nor worse. If these respondents were included in the analysis, by treating 'neither better nor worse' as intermediate between 'better' and 'worse' the correlations between 'never join' and 'vote no' are reduced from 0.40 to 0.33 and from 0.36 to 0.29 respectively.

Source: PNES 2001.

bring neither benefit nor damage, but many simply have no idea which of the two it will be. Only about three per cent feel that accession will have no great impact on agriculture, state or private enterprise, or foreign firms; but some 20 per cent simply cannot guess whether that impact will be positive or negative. And they are particularly uncertain about the impact on their own family: ten per cent think that it will have no impact but 33 per cent simply

TABLE 8
CORRELATIONS BETWEEN OPPOSITION TO ACCESSION AND PERCEPTIONS OF
THE CHARACTER OF THE EU

	Correlation with: prefer to join 'never'	Correlation with: NO vote in referendum
EU threatens independence	.42**	.49**
EU threatens freedom	.41**	.49**
EU officials corrupt and wasteful	.30**	.39**
EU would put old Europe first	.32**	.33**

Notes: ** = statistically significant at p < .01. Correlations calculated excluding DKs and those with views coded as 'nether/mixed/depends'.

Source: PNES 2001.

TABLE 9
CORRELATIONS BETWEEN OPPOSITION TO ACCESSION AND PERCEPTIONS OF
THE ECONOMIC CONSEQUENCES OF ACCESSION

	Correlation with: prefer to join 'never'	Correlation with: NO vote in referendum
Damage family living standard	.52** (.44)	.60** (.48)
Damage agriculture	.44** (.41)	.51** (.49)
Damage private Polish firms	.38**	.37**
Damage state firms	.36**	.37**
Damage foreign-owned firms	.06*	.07*

Notes: ** = statistically significant at p < .01, * = statistically significant at p < .05. Correlations calculated excluding DKs and those with views coded as 'nether/mixed/
depends'. Figures in brackets show the correlations if 'neither' and 'DK' answers are
treated as intermediate between expected 'benefit' and 'damage'.

Source: PNES 2001.

do not know. So only a little over half have a clear idea about whether they
themselves will be accession winners or accession losers.

Typically we might expect up to 15 per cent 'don't knows' on attitude and
perception questions: that merely tells us something about the public – that it
includes a proportion of diffident and uncertain people. But a figure of 20 per
cent hints at something special about the question, about the subject matter,
rather than about the people. And a figure of 33 per cent alerts us to a very
real phenomenon of uncertainty on that specific question.

Yet by any calculation opposition to accession correlates more strongly
with hopes and fears about the impact of accession on family incomes and
Polish agriculture than with anything else. Among those who have a clear
view about the likely impact on their family incomes, that is the key criterion.
But so many are uncertain about the impact on their family that, across the
public as a whole, perceptions of the impact on Polish agriculture are at
least equally important.

Weighing the Influences

We have found a number of fairly strong correlations with support for accession. But many of these may be effectively duplicates, no more than different
aspects of a single phenomenon. We use multiple regression to reveal and
assess the independent impact of different factors underlying support for
accession. Our model for the analysis comprises five blocks of variables
selected from those already discussed:

Social Background. Age (in years); gender; education (11-point scale
from 'none' to 'university'); church attendance (8-point scale from 'never' to

'several times per week'); urban or rural location (6-point scale from 'village' to 'city over 500,000'); region (Russian partition, Austrian, Prussian, and 'regained territories'); self-assessed family income (4-point scale from 'not really enough to live on' to 'enough for a good standard of living'); and self-assessed trend in family living standard since 1989 (5-point scale from 'much better' to 'much worse').

Civilizational Culture. Satisfaction with the way democracy is working in Poland (4-point scale from 'very satisfied' to 'not at all satisfied'); attitude towards the statement that 'democracy is the best form of government' (4-point scale from 'agree strongly' to 'disagree strongly'); preference for pre-1989 regime (5-point scale from 'pre-1989 regime much better' to 'much worse than present').

Religious Culture. Devout scale (4-point scale from 'atheist' to 'devout'); trust Church (4-point scale from 'trust a lot' to 'distrust a lot'); and three 'church and state' scales, indicating pleasure or displeasure with the public display of crosses, religious instruction in schools, and Church pronouncements on parliamentary legislation.

Nationalist Culture. Attitude to incomers with different cultures (3-point scale from 'making the locality better' to 'making it worse'); self-identification (5-point scale from 'exclusively Polish' to 'more European than Polish'); attitude to the statement that 'Poland has a lot to learn from other countries' (4-point scale from 'agree strongly' to 'disagree strongly').

Economic Hopes and Fears. Five scales indicating whether the respondent thinks accession will benefit or damage Polish agriculture, state and private enterprises, foreign businesses and the respondent's family (2-point and 3-point scales, depending upon whether 'don't knows' are included or excluded).

In constructing this list, we have chosen a similar number of indicators to represent and span the different facets of each of the potential criteria for accession choice.

Our basic model assumes that social background affects cultural values and economic hopes or fears; and then both economic background and values, hopes and fears combine to influence support for accession. However, we expect that most of the influence of social background would operate through values rather than independently of values. For example, church attendance might instil a religious culture – and then culture rather than mere attendance might influence attitudes to accession. Similarly, income or education might affect support for accession through their influence upon economic hopes and fears rather than directly.

The exception might be where some aspect of social background has no associated value. Thus region – essentially proximity to the 'old Europe' of the old EU – might be expected to have a direct rather than an indirect influence on support for accession, reflecting geography and geographically defined economic interests rather than values.

But the analysis itself will reveal whether these influences are direct or indirect. In fact, the regression analysis shows that only a few of these potential influences actually exert a statistically significant, direct and independent influence. Only three of the 24 have an influence strong enough to produce beta coefficients that exceed 0.10 – notably concerns about family living standards and Polish agriculture, both of which have large and independent influences.

Across the public as a whole, uncertainty about the impact of accession on family living standards moderates its influence (beta = 0.24 in Table 10, Column 1). Among those with a view about the economic consequences of

TABLE 10
MULTIPLE REGRESSIONS PREDICTING OPPOSITION TO ACCESSION

Predictors:	Dependent variable: Vote NO (rather than YES)		
	beta	beta	beta
Social Background			
region (east)	+8	ns	ns
age (young)	ns	+8	ns
Civilizational Culture			
dissatisfied with way democracy works	+9	ns	ns
Religious Culture			
trust in church	+7	+7	ns
Nationalist Culture			
incomers would make locality worse	+11	+8	+14
Economic Hopes and Fears			
damage family living standard	+24	+45	no view
damage Polish agriculture	+30	+21	+39
damage Polish private enterprises	+8	ns	+17
$R^2 \rightarrow$	35	41	26
	all respondents	excluding those unsure about economic impact on family	those unsure about economic impact on family

Notes: Using stepwise regression with pairwise deletion. All beta coefficients shown are standardized and significant at one per cent level. Regressions used the full set of 24 social, political, cultural and economic predictors listed in the text – but no other predictors than those in the table proved statistically significant at the one per cent level. 'ns' = not significant.

Source: PNES 2001.

accession, the perceived impact on family living standards is the more predominant influence (beta = 0.45 in Column 2). Conversely, if we focus on the very large number (43 per cent) who are uncertain about the impact of accession on their families – and therefore cannot use that as a criterion for decision – then the predominant influence is concern about Polish agriculture, about which there is far less uncertainty (Column 3).

Beyond these economic concerns about family living standards and Polish agriculture, the only sizeable cultural influence is cosmopolitanism: those who fear that incomers with different cultures will make their area worse are somewhat more opposed to accession. But the impact of this cultural concern (beta = 0.14 in Column 3) is much less than that of economic concerns.

Conclusion: The Misuse of Referendums and the Quality of Democracy in Post-Communist Europe

The regression analysis not only reinforces but also greatly sharpens the impression given by our earlier bivariate analyses. The choice was not, in essence, a civilizational choice. Culture played only a minor role – and even then it was nationalist or cosmopolitan culture rather than civilizational or strictly religious factor that mattered. Referendum choices were dictated mainly by economic hopes and fears, and primarily by very *personal* hopes and fears that focused on family rather than country. Only uncertainty about the impact of accession on the family limited the power of these very private emotions.

Of course, expectations about the impact of accession on family living standards are themselves influenced by many other factors – which therefore exercise an indirect – but usually *only* indirect – influence upon referendum choice. A regression on social background variables indicates that the greatest social influence on optimism or pessimism about the impact of accession on the family is that favourite of amateur weather forecasters: persistence forecasting. Those who feel they have already done well out of the first transition (from communism) are optimistic about the impact of the second transition (towards accession); and those who have already done badly out of the first transition fear the second transition will only make things worse for them. More generally, a regression on all our social, political, cultural and economic predictors indicates that pessimism about the impact of accession on family living standards is closely tied to pessimism about its impact on Polish agriculture and industry. General economic pessimism (or optimism) about accession clearly has a strong influence upon personal, family-oriented pessimism (or optimism) and thus a significant indirect influence on referendum voting. But in the end what matters most is personal concern about the impact of accession on family living standards.

We have focused our analysis on Poland, but our argument is not primarily about Poland. And we have focused our analysis on the decision about whether Poland – and the other accession states – should or should not join the EU in 2004, but our argument is not primarily about accession. Our argument is primarily about the question posed by Clement Attlee, about the democratic credentials of referendums.

Certainly, referendums can be used to 'let the people decide'. But they can also be used to 'co-opt the people', to legitimize a decision taken by the elite, to make the people accomplices in a decision they do not themselves make – and would prefer to avoid. So referendums can be as much a technique of elite governance as they are a technique of popular control.

Referendums may be a good device for articulating the 'settled will of the people'.[34] But referendums can only be a device of popular control if a broad issue of principle is at stake, if the people clearly understand the issue, if they have strong, settled, enduring views about it, and if the options on the referendum ballot correspond to those views. The evidence from our detailed analysis of Polish opinion, as well as from the Eurobarometer's wider but less detailed survey of opinion across all the accession states, suggests that these conditions were not met by the EU referendums of 2003.

Referendums in 1989 or the early 1990s on the 'civilizational choice' of continuing with communism or abandoning it might have met those conditions. That was a broad question of principle on which people had strong and settled views. And indeed the first post-communist elections were often interpreted as referendums on the transition from communism. If there had been the prospect of accession at that time it seems likely that accession would also have been a broad question of principle, appropriate to a popular referendum, at that time.

But by 2003, accession was no longer a question of principle. It was a question of hard-headed expert negotiation, of 'deals not ideals', and of deals about economic details whose consequences were, for the public, shrouded in uncertainty. When we asked the public explicitly, four out of five told us their referendum decision would depend on economic guesswork, neither on culture nor on politics. Similarly Eurobarometer found that the fears and misgivings of the public across the whole range of accession states centred on economic rather than cultural or political concerns. Our statistical analysis corroborates the public's introspective self-assessment: that their referendum votes really were determined by economic rather than cultural considerations – and above all by their expectations of the costs and benefits to themselves and their families. For them it was not even, except indirectly, an issue of the costs or benefits to their country. So it was not an issue of principle but of calculation, indeed of personal calculation. Unfortunately it was a calculation that could not be based on knowledge since almost half the public felt they simply did not know whether they would win or lose.

So how do the 2003 referendums measure against our four conditions for popular control?

1. *Was a broad issue of principle at stake?* – No, it was about 'deals' not 'ideals'.
2. *Did the people clearly understand the issue?* – No, almost half said that they did not have information on the key element of their calculations, the economic costs and benefits to their families.
3. *Did the people have strong, settled, enduring views about it?* – No, a decision based on calculation rather than principle could not express a 'settled, enduring will'; and a decision based on calculation could not even represent a strongly held, albeit transient, judgement when people self-consciously lacked the key information on costs and benefits to their families.
4. *Did the options on the ballot correspond to the views of major sections of the public?* – No: a YES/NO referendum excluded the choice of the majority, which was to join at some other time when the deal might be better.

So, the democratic character of these referendums was weak. From a democratic perspective this was a misuse of the referendum device. In 2003, the accession referendums did not allow voters to express their own views. In self-consciously recognized ignorance, and under the duress of an implied 'now or never' threat, these referendums imposed a forced choice between two uncertain and unpopular alternatives. They manufactured an overwhelmingly large 'yes' vote – but without any popular commitment or public responsibility. The result was all breadth and no depth.

It is doubtful whether such referendums can have an enduring impact. These referendums were neither a good device for popular control nor for elite governance. Aware of the doubts and uncertainties that underpinned the large but unenthusiastic 'yes' votes, the public are not likely to feel personally committed to the referendum decision, nor overawed by the numbers that voted 'yes'. Therefore, continuing EU membership will have to be continuously legitimized by what it delivers. The proposed Constitution for this 'ever-closer union' now includes an 'exit clause', and even continuing participation can be grudging and obstructive. Accession is not an 'irreversible' decision. Both physical and psychological 'exit' remain possibilities and these referendums have not closed the debate on EU membership.

NOTES

1. A Latvian Facts Survey in May 2003 showed that 57 per cent of Latvian citizens, and only 36 per cent of non-citizens in Latvia, supported EU accession; non-Latvians constitute two-fifths

of Latvia's population and half of them are excluded from citizenship or participation in the referendum: see *Latvian Facts Survey*, May 2003, p.8, accessible via <http://www. eip.gov.lv>.

2. For comparison with public support for the 'first transition', see James L. Gibson, 'A Mile Wide But an Inch Deep'(?): The Structure of Democratic Commitments in the Former USSR', *American Journal of Political Science*, Vol.40, No.2 (1996), pp.396–420.

3. This essay is based on an analysis of the Polish National Election Survey, Sept. 2001 – a random sample representative of the adult population of Poland (aged 18 and above). It was funded by a grant from the Polish National Science Foundation (Komitet Badan Naukowych) to the Institute of Political Studies of the Polish Academy of Sciences, with additional funding from the UK ESRC under grant R000223685 to Glasgow University. Fieldwork, by CBOS, started on 29 October 2001 and ended on 11 November; 1,794 interviews were completed (the refusal rate was 22 per cent). The data set has been weighted by gender, age, educational attainment, place of residence and economic activity.

4. Paweł Wroński, 'Tak Jesteśmy w Unii', *Gazeta Wyborcza*, 9 June 2003, p.1; see also Colleen Barry, 'Poland Celebrates Vote to Rejoin European Nations', *Herald* (Glasgow), 9 June 2003, p.8.

5. *Guardian*, 22 Sept. 2003, p.13.

6. While 'twentieth-century America has defined itself as a part of and, indeed, the leader of a broad entity, the West, that includes Europe', according to Huntington, 'nineteenth-century America defined itself as *different from and opposed to* Europe' (our emphasis): Samuel P. Huntington, *The Clash of Civilizations and the Remaking of World Order* (London: Touchstone Books, 1998), p.46.

7. *Economist*, 30 Aug.–5 Sept. 2003, pp.19–20 (p.20).

8. Recalling de Gaulle's description of Britain as 'America's Trojan Horse', the French and German media devised the more abusive term 'Trojan Donkey' for Poland: see Martin Walker, 'The European Problem', *National Review Online*, 10 June 2003, p.2, accessible via <http://www.nationalreview.com/comment/comment-walker061003.asp>; Nick Thorpe, 'Why Poland Loves America', *BBC News Online*, 30 May 2003, pp.2–3, accessible via <http://www.bbc.co.uk>; and TVP's interview with President Bush, 29 May 2003, p.1, accessible via <http://www.whitehouse.gov/g8/interview5.html>. For the Polish media's response to the term 'kon' trojański, see Krzysztof Darewicz, 'Przydatna Umiejętność Manewrowania. Rozmowa ze Zigniewem Brzezińskim', *Rzeszpospolita*, 30 April–1 May 2003, p.A6.

9. Although not quite comparable with each other, two questions in the Pew Center's 2002 *Global Attitudes Project* reinforce this point: 79 per cent of Poles had a 'favourable' opinion of the US, but only 48 per cent felt the EU had a 'good influence' on 'the way things are going in Poland'; according to these Pew data, Poles were notably more pro-American and less pro-EU than the public in 'old Europe': Pew Center, *Global Attitudes Project: What the World Thinks in 2002*, Tables T48 and T37, accessible via <http://www.people-press.org>.

10. See Eurobarometer EB59 – CC-EB 2003.2 (published July 2003 – fieldwork May 2003), accessible via <http://www.europa.eu.int/comm/public_opinion>, Annex B-98, B-99, B-83.

11. See 'Pytanie Tygodnia: Kto Jest Bliższym Sojusznikiem Polski?', *Polityka*, 7 June 2003, p.22.

12. Stephen Castle, 'Bush Visit and EU Poll Test Divided Loyalties of Poles', *Independent*, 30 May 2003, p.13.

13. Timothy Garton Ash, for example, opposed this almost normative division of Europe into 'old' and 'new': see Timothy Garton Ash, 'Europa i Ameryka Są na Siebie Skazane', *Gazeta Wyborcza*, 20 June 2003, accessible via <http://www1.gazeta.pl/ue/1,36136,1538890. html#dale > .

14. Ian Taylor, 'Poland Snubs EU by Buying US Jets', *Guardian*, 19 April 2003, p.14.

15. Alison Chiesa, 'Bush Outflanked Old Europe by Inviting Poland to the Victors' Table', *Herald*, 12 April 2003, p.1; see also Jacek Żakowski, 'Nasz Ciężki Kawałek Iraku', *Polityka*, 17 May 2003, pp.28–32.

16. Foreign Minister Włodzimierz Cimoszewicz, quoted in Ian Black, 'Irritation Grows as Stubborn Poland Joins the EU's Awkward Squad', *Guardian Weekly*, 13 Nov. 2003, accessible via <http://www.guardian.co.uk/guardianweekly>.

17. Clare McManus, 'Poland and the Europe Agreements: The EU as a Regional Actor', in John Peterson and Helena Sjursen (eds.), *A Common Foreign Policy for Europe? Competing Visions of the CFSP* (London and New York: Routledge, 1998).

18. Oana Lungescu, 'Poland Presses for EU Action', *BBC World News*, 18 July 2003, accessible via <http://news.bbc.co.uk/1/hi/world/europe/839162.stm>.

19. The importance of possessing a European identity while simultaneously retaining a regional and Polish identity has been discussed extensively in the Polish media by leading academics such as Professor Janusz Reykowski: see Wojciech Szacki in conversation with Janusz Reykowski, 'Europejczyk Wielopoziomowy', *Gazeta Wyborcza*, 19 Aug 2003, p.12; see also Piotr Sztompka, 'My, Europejczycy', *Gazeta Wyborcza*, 19 Aug. 2003, accessible via <wysiwyg://dol.232/http://www2.gazeta.pl.../htm/1626/a1626776.htm&tablica = DOCUMENT>; Clare McManus-Czubińska *et al.*, 'Understanding Dual Identities in Poland', *Political Studies*, Vol.51, No.1 (2003), pp.121–43.

20. Aleks Szczerbiak, *Referendum Briefing No.5: The Polish EU Accession Referendum* (2003), p.1, accessible at <http//www.sussex.ac.uk/Units/SEI/oern/index.html>.

21. Ibid., p.6.

22. Concerns over the right of foreigners to buy Polish land after EU accession have been consistently debated in the Polish media: see Sylwia Szparkowska and Andrzej Stankiewicz, 'Nie Wykupujś Polskiej Ziemi', *Rzeczpospolita*, 22 April 2003, pp.A1 and A3.

23. However, EU funding will also be available to promote regional cooperation and to fight unemployment; for details of the amounts for which Poland may apply during its first years of EU membership (2004–06), see Jakub Jasiński, 'Dla Regionów i Bezrobotnych', *Rzeczpospolita*, 1 Sept. 2003, accessible via <wysiwyg://23/http://www.rzeczpospolita.pl/dodatki/plun_030901/plun_a_2.html >.

24. See 'Lepiej za Parę Lat', *Rzeczpospolita*, 2 Sept. 2003, accessible via <wysiwyg://162/ http://www.rzeczpospolita...j/kraj_a_2.html?k = on;t = 2003082820030903>.

25. Szczerbiak, *Referendum Briefing*, p.7.

26. See, for example, Prime Minister John Major, *Commons Hansard Debates*, 29 June 1992, col.585; Attlee's phrase is regularly quoted in the British parliament by anyone opposed to a referendum.

27. For a brief summary of the case for and against the use of referendums, see David Butler and Austin Ranney, 'Theory', in David Butler and Austin Ranney (eds.), *Referendums Around the World: The Growing Use of Direct Democracy* (Washington, DC: American Enterprise Institute, 1994), pp.11–23.

28. Ian Traynor, 'Abortion Issue Threatens Polish Admission to EU', *Guardian*, 30 Jan. 2003, p.17.

29. Mikołaj Lizut, 'Masoni Podrzucili Giertycha', *Gazeta Wyborcza*, 23 July 2003, accessible via <http://www1.gazeta.pl/ue/1,36136,1590426.html>; see also 'Giertych o UE z Zagranicznymi Dziennikarzami', *Gazeta Wyborcza*, 3 June 2003, accessible via <http://www1.gazeta.pl/ue/1,42343,1511639.html>.

30. Szczerbiak, *Referendum Briefing*, p.7.

31. Stephen Castle, 'Poland Backs EU Membership with a Resounding "Yes"', *Independent*, 9 June 2003, p.8.

32. Marcin Kowalski, 'W Unii Dzięki Papieżowi – Mowi Abp Henryk Muszyński', *Gazeta Wyborcza*, 10 June 2003, accessible via <http://www1.gazeta.pl/ue/1,36136,1522826.html>.

33. Szczerbiak, *Referendum Briefing*, p.10.

34. For a generation that phrase, 'settled will of the people', characterized the moves towards devolution in the UK which culminated in the referendums of 1997: see, for example, its use in the speech of Secretary of State for Scotland John Reid, *Devolution – a Partnership of Parliaments*, 19 July 1999, accessible via <http://www.scottishsecretary.gov.uk>.

Dimensions of Disengagement in Post-Communist Russia

STEPHEN WHITE and IAN McALLISTER

Introduction

Formally, Russia's post-communist institutions provide every opportunity for its citizens to choose the government they want and to influence its actions. There are secret and competitive elections, held at regular intervals. The new Constitution, adopted by popular vote in 1993, makes a formal commitment to political diversity and multiparty politics. There is a separation of powers, and an independent judiciary. The classic liberal freedoms are all secured: freedom of speech, movement and assembly, freedom of conscience, and equality before the law. In the event of any disagreement, international norms take precedence over the laws of the state itself. There are freedoms that go beyond the practice of many liberal democracies, including the requirement that official bodies make available any information they hold on private individuals unless national security considerations are involved. And there are freedoms that have a particular resonance in post-communist conditions: freedom of entrepreneurship, and the right of private as well as other forms of ownership. The new Constitution even begins, in words that are hardly accidental, 'We the multinational people . . .'.

Russians themselves have taken a less positive view. Asked to consider the changes that have taken place since 1991, a large proportion of ordinary Russians think it has become much easier to practise a religion, to join any organization they wish, to speak their mind, and (by a rather smaller margin) to travel and live wherever they wish. But the same people, compared with the late Soviet period, think they are no less likely to be arrested improperly, and they are less likely to think government will treat them 'honestly and fairly'. Remarkably, nearly twice as many think it is more difficult than it was in the late Soviet period for ordinary people to influence the government that rules in their name. Communist rule, it emerges, was 'close to the people', 'legal', even 'honest and open'. Post-communist rule, by contrast, is most closely associated with criminality and corruption, but also with being 'remote' and 'irresolute', and hardly less bureaucratic than the communist system it has replaced.[1] Within the academic literature, some Russian scholars have suggested that elections have undergone an 'authoritarian adaptation', and that so far from eliminating the alienation of ordinary people from government they have 'only deepened it'.[2] More generally, the USSR as a concept remains as popular as it was in the spring of 1991, when it secured the support of more than three-quarters of the electorate in a national referendum.

This contribution examines these contrasting judgements. In particular, it explores the paradox by which ordinary Russians have acquired all the mechanisms that in other countries are thought to give ordinary citizens an effective means of holding their government to account – independent courts, a free press, political parties and competitive elections – but believe themselves to have less influence than in the years before *perestroika*, when the political system began to undergo a limited democratization. The discussion is based on a representative national survey that was fielded in the spring of 2001 (full details are provided in the appendix); comparisons are drawn between these results and those that emerged from a similar survey by the present authors and associates in 1993, and between the results that emerge from Russian surveys and those conducted with a common questionnaire in Belarus and Ukraine in the spring of 2000. We consider, first of all, orientations towards the political system within this broadly comparative context, and the distribution of those orientations by age, gender and other variables, with particular reference to trust and various measures of political efficacy. We move on to consider rival explanations for the differences that we observe in levels of engagement or disengagement, particularly resource and social learning theories. In our final section we explore the implications of these findings for the development of patterns of engagement or disengagement in Russian politics over coming decades.

Orientations Towards the Political System

Among the most fundamental attributes of a pluralist political order is trust in civic institutions, and indeed in other citizens. In one of the most influential of scholarly writings on regime and society, Almond and Verba in the early 1960s pointed to the close association between the establishment and consolidation of liberal democracy, and popular attitudes that were supportive of a political system of this kind.[3] There has been little consensus, over the intervening years, about causality: did the attitudes account for the institutions, or were they shaped by them? But either way, it was clear that pluralist politics were stronger where popular attitudes were supportive, and that supportive attitudes helped to sustain a corresponding set of political institutions. Within this complex of attitudes, trust was one of the most important: trust, for instance, can 'indicate the extent of diffuse political support', and a high level of trust in some institutions can 'compensate for low or declining confidence in others, or cushion and blunt the effect of their temporarily deficient credibility'.[4]

One of the clearest conclusions of earlier studies of political values in post-communist Russia is that ordinary citizens have low levels of trust in their civic institutions, and particularly their political institutions. This is not an exclusively Russian phenomenon (across the post-communist nations, as Rose and Mishler have observed, 'even skepticism is in short supply'[5]); nor was it unknown during the years of Soviet rule. It is, however, one of the defining features of the contemporary Russian system. Russians, according to an accumulating series of investigations, are actually quite ready to trust their fellow citizens – it was through social networks of this kind that they survived the communist period, and through such networks that they continue to make good the shortcomings of the consumer market.[6] But there are much lower levels of trust in civic institutions of all kinds: from the churches to organs of government, including structures such as trade unions and political parties that nominally represent the interests of newly enfranchised citizens. Indeed, there is less trust in the new and independent trade unions than in their Soviet-period equivalents.[7] Levels of trust, moreover, have generally been declining, even for the churches and armed forces, which have traditionally enjoyed the greatest public confidence.[8]

Russians took broadly the same view in our own survey, which was fielded in the spring of 2001. As before, there was most confidence in the Church and the armed forces, which have articulated the interests of the whole nation for hundreds of years. There were comparable levels of confidence in the mass media, particularly state television and radio (which is also, overwhelmingly, a state service). The press had a slightly higher rating, especially at intermediate levels of confidence. The institutions of government themselves, however, enjoyed little support, with low levels of confidence and particularly high levels of mistrust. Just 16 per cent had some confidence in their elected parliament, for instance, and only 11 per cent expressed some confidence in political parties, with 79 per cent taking the opposite view (the only institutions that have ever been found to enjoy less support than political parties were the investment funds set up after privatization, many of which were organized swindles that defrauded ordinary citizens of their vouchers).[9] It was notable, moreover, that even institutions with relatively high levels of support inspired far from unqualified confidence: the churches, in particular, were distrusted almost as much as they were trusted.

Some degree of distrust of political institutions is, of course, a universal; but the comparative evidence leaves little doubt that Russians are more distrustful of their civic institutions than their counterparts in Ukraine and Belarus, and much more distrustful than in other European countries (see Table 1). Certainly, there are some common elements. Russians, for instance,

TABLE 1
TRUST IN CIVIC INSTITUTIONS: RUSSIA IN COMPARATIVE PERSPECTIVE
(PERCENTAGES)

	Russia	Ukraine	Belarus	EU 15
Army	49	49	50	70
Church	48	35	56	44
President	22	30	41	48
Trade unions	21	19	25	39
Courts	18	20	28	51
Police	18	16	20	67
Private enterprises	16	20	27	33
Parliament	12	10	23	51
Political parties	9	7	12	18

Sources: Authors' surveys (see Appendix), combining the percentage scores for 'full' and 'considerable confidence'. Data for the EU15 are derived from *Eurobarometer 56*, fieldwork Nov. 2001, accessed at <http://europa.eu.int/comm/public_opinion/archives/eb/eb56/eb56_en.htm>. The figures for 'President' in the EU case refer to 'national government' and for 'private enterprises' to 'big companies'.

are reasonably typical in their attitude to organized religion, with high levels of distrust as well as confidence. But with very few exceptions, Russians have less confidence in their civic institutions than their counterparts in the other Slavic republics, and far less confidence than citizens in the EU member states: by a substantial margin in the case of business and the institutions of government, and by a spectacular margin in the case of law enforcement. Political parties are, everywhere, the least trusted of all civic institutions; but here again, Russians are much less supportive than their counterparts in the member countries of the European Union.

We asked several other questions that related to political efficacy, or the extent to which individual citizens believe they can exercise real influence over the process of government (see Table 2). What opportunity, for instance, did ordinary Russians have to make use of the rights with which they had nominally been endowed under the post-communist Constitution? The overwhelming majority (88 per cent) agreed largely or entirely that it was difficult for them to do so. At least in part, this was because politicians had little interest in the views of the citizens they represented: politicians 'don't care what ordinary people think', and Duma deputies in particular 'soon [lost] contact with their electors'. We asked a more general question – familiar in cross-national investigations – about the extent to which 'people like you can have a direct influence on the actions of central government'. Overwhelmingly, our respondents took the view that ordinary people could have 'not the slightest' influence upon such actions (60 per cent), or very little (a further 24 per cent); only 12 per cent took a more positive view. Again, it is

TABLE 2
MEASURES OF POLITICAL RESPONSIVENESS, 2001 (PERCENTAGES)

	Russia		Belarus		Ukraine	
	Agree	*Disagree*	*Agree*	*Disagree*	*Agree*	*Disagree*
Equality of treatment						
'Government treats people equally and fairly'	8	85	12	82	4	93
'Difficult for ordinary people to secure their legal rights'	88	9	77	18	88	11
'Human rights respected'	18	76	28	67	9	89
Efficacy						
'Politicians don't care what ordinary people think'	86	10	n.a.	n.a.	n.a.	n.a.
'Duma deputies lose contact with electors'	88	7	n.a.	n.a.	n.a.	n.a.
'People like me can influence the central government'	12	84	23	74	16	81

Source: As Table 1 (the figures are for Russia in 2001, Belarus and Ukraine in 2000). Estimates
exclude 'Don't knows' and therefore do not sum to 100.

not only in Russia that ordinary citizens believe they have little influence on
government decisions; but they are more likely to take this view in Russia than
in the other Slavic republics, let alone the established Western democracies
(Russians, other studies have found, are much less likely than either their
British or their Ukrainian counterparts to believe that elections play a part
in 'holding government accountable for their past actions', and they are less
likely to believe that elections allow ordinary citizens to 'choose among
particular policies' or to 'comment on the state of their country').[10]

Competitive elections, ten years after the end of communist rule, are certainly welcome in principle. More than a third of our respondents 'entirely
approved' of them and another quarter did so to some extent, although a
substantial minority (21 per cent) took a different view. When elections
took place, a clear majority of our respondents (66 per cent) thought they
should definitely take part, and another 14 per cent were inclined to do so provided it did not involve undue inconvenience. Was voting, however, likely to
make any difference to public policy? And was it of particular significance
within the repertoire of political action that is available to ordinary citizens?
Opinion was quite evenly divided on the extent to which elections could
'change the future course of events', but a small plurality were pessimistic

(42 per cent agreed they could change the course of events and 49 per cent disagreed). Ukrainians and Belarusians, by contrast, leaned in the opposite direction (see Table 3). Russians were also less likely than their counterparts in the other two Slavic republics to believe they should vote; and they were less likely than Ukrainians, and particularly Belarusians, to believe that the election mechanism in particular gave them a means of influencing national policy.

Russians, similarly, were less likely than their counterparts to believe elections offered ordinary people an opportunity to influence the way in which the country was governed. Only five per cent agreed strongly that they offered an opportunity of this kind and another 24 per cent agreed to some extent, but 62 per cent took the opposite view (Ukrainians were less sceptical, and still more so our Belarusian respondents). Elections, moreover, counted for relatively little among the mechanisms that were available to ordinary people to influence national decisions on matters they thought important. About a third (32 per cent) thought that voting in local and national elections was the most effective way in which they could seek to exercise political influence; a few mentioned demonstrations (seven per cent), or letters to government bodies or the newspapers (two per cent each). The largest proportion of all, however (43 per cent), thought there was simply no effective way in which they could seek to influence decisions on matters of national policy. Not surprisingly, there was substantial support for the proposition that a 'strong, powerful leader [could] achieve more than any laws': fully 60 per cent agreed in varying degrees, compared with 19 per cent who took the opposite view. In Ukraine, 44 per cent shared this faith in a strong leader but 45 per cent disagreed; and in Belarus opinion was still more strongly opposed to a strong leader, with 22 per cent in favour but 63 per cent against.

TABLE 3
MEASURES OF SUPPORT FOR ELECTIONS, 2001 (PERCENTAGES)

	Russia		Belarus		Ukraine	
	Agree	*Disagree*	*Agree*	*Disagree*	*Agree*	*Disagree*
'People should vote in national elections'	66	26	74	20	76	20
'Elections allow me to influence national policy'	29	62	51	40	40	54
'Elections can change the course of events'	42	49	64	29	53	41

Source: As Table 1 (the figures are for Russia in 2001, Belarus and Ukraine in 2000). Estimates exclude 'Don't knows' and therefore do not sum to 100.

Civic Engagement and Social Capital

As well as orientations towards the political system, we explored forms of participation – unconventional as well as conventional. Western democracies typically rest upon a dense network of interpersonal associations, or a 'civil society'. Communist rule made it more difficult if not impossible for ordinary citizens to associate on a voluntary basis: as it was sometimes put, 'everything that was not banned was compulsory'. Mass organizations such as the trade unions and youth associations had a very high proportion of the relevant group enrolled within their ranks; the ruling parties were more selective in their membership, but typically enrolled at least ten per cent of the adult population and up to a third of all college graduates. A decade later, trade union membership has remained relatively high, at between a quarter and a third of the adult population. Membership of all other forms of civic association, however, is very low indeed, and membership of a political party is lower than all other forms (see Table 4). Again, there is a geographical gradient: in almost every case levels of membership are lower in Russia than in either of the other two republics, and higher in Belarus than almost anywhere else.

Levels of membership of these various associations, moreover, are themselves very low in comparative terms. As Howard has shown, drawing on the World Values Survey, 'with the partial exception of labour unions, participation in voluntary organizations is much lower in post-communist countries than in the older democracies and the post-authoritarian countries'. In older democracies, such as West Germany, the United States and Japan, a representative adult is a member of 2.4 organizations; in a post-authoritarian country such as Argentina or South Africa, membership levels average 1.8; while in the post-communist countries, membership levels averaged 0.9. The post-communist countries had particularly low levels of membership of organizations that were more political in character, such as political parties and environmental groups; but there were also low membership levels of religious organizations, sports or recreational societies, educational or cultural

TABLE 4
MEASURES OF CIVIC ENGAGEMENT, 2001 (PERCENTAGES)

	Sports club	Musical society	Political party	Neighbourhood body	Charity	Trade union
Russia	8	2	1	2	1	19
Belarus	10	4	2	3	2	38
Ukraine	6	3	1	2	3	24

Source: As Table 1 (Russia 2001, Belarus and Ukraine 2000). Estimates exclude 'Don't knows' and therefore do not sum to 100.

societies, professional associations and charities. Levels of membership, moreover, were tending to decline further in the late 1990s.[11]

It will not surprise most students of comparative politics to find that these measures are associated with one another. In each of the three countries with which we are concerned, the more that ordinary citizens believe they can influence national policy, the more likely they are to have attempted to do so (by petition, letter, demonstration or voting). And in turn, the more likely they are to have engaged in various forms of conventional or unconventional political action, the more likely they are to believe their actions can have some influence on government. In Russia, for instance, seven per cent of those who thought they had a 'significant' influence on government policy abstained from voting in the December 1999 Duma elections, but 26 per cent of those who thought they had 'no influence'. Those who thought they had a 'significant' influence were two or three times more likely than other respondents to consult their elected representative, three or four times more likely to take part in a strike or demonstration, and five or six times more likely to sign a petition or send a letter to the newspapers than those who thought they had 'no influence'. Similarly, it is no surprise that levels of electoral turnout are higher where there are higher levels of individual political efficacy. In the last parliamentary and presidential elections in Russia, for instance, turnout was 61.7 and 68.6 per cent respectively; in Ukraine it was slightly higher at 69.3 and 70.2 per cent; but in Belarus, where there were the highest levels of belief that (rightly or wrongly) elections offered an effective means of political influence, turnout was highest of all, at 83.9 per cent in the 2001 presidential contest.

What underpins civic engagement across the population? Studies by Putnam and others have suggested that social trust develops slowly, over time, and is predicated on prolonged periods of political stability and effective governance. This suggests that civic engagement may not have strong roots in Russian society and the societies of the two former Soviet republics; in fact, as the results in Table 5 suggest, there is a moderate relationship between civic engagement and the six basic socio-economic measures. The most consistently important influence – and indeed the most important in each of the equations – is participation in the labour force, with higher levels of participation leading to strong civic engagement. Clearly, the type of regular social contact that accompanies labour force participation also encourages involvement in social groups. It is important to note that the effect of labour force participation is net of other aspects of social attainment, notably education and income.

Among the other effects, gender is important only in Belarus, where males seem to be more engaged, and age consistently operates to make the young more engaged than the old. Indeed, in the case of Belarus, age is the second

TABLE 5
SOCIOECONOMIC CORRELATES OF CIVIC
ENGAGEMENT, 2001 (REGRESSION ESTIMATES)

	Number of civic memberships		
	Russia	Belarus	Ukraine
Gender (male)	ns	.10**	ns
Age (years)	−.11**	−.19**	ns
Urban resident	.06**	.07*	ns
Tertiary education	ns	.08**	.08**
Labour force participation	.18**	.21**	.24**
Family income	ns	−.08*	.13**
Adjusted R-squared	ns	ns	ns

Notes: ** = statistically significant at $p < .01$, * = statistically significant at $p < .05$. 'ns' = not significant. Regression equations showing standardized regression coefficients predicting civic engagement, which is measured as the number of civic institutions in Table 4 that the respondent reported being a member of. All regression coefficients below 0.1 are identified here as 'not significant.

Source: As Table 1.

most important variable in the equation, after labour force participation. Living in a city promotes engagement in Russia and Belarus, but not in Ukraine; and possessing tertiary education is important for engagement in the two ex-Soviet republics, but not in Russia itself. The only significant differences in effects emerge with income: while it is not statistically significant in Russia, more income promotes engagement in Ukraine, but reduces it in Belarus. This may reflect the differing roles of income derived from the formal economy – as opposed to the informal economy – in the three countries. But despite this, there is a clear consistency in the types of effects and, by and large, in their magnitude in shaping civic engagement across the three countries.

Explaining Patterns of Engagement and Disengagement

The measures of support for the political system identified in the previous section provide three important measures – confidence, responsiveness and propensity to vote – of the extent to which voters feel engaged with various aspects of the political system in Russia, Ukraine and Belarus. We focus in this section on the sources of these attitudes across the electorate, limiting ourselves to the Russian case. It is a commonplace in the comparative literature that some social groups will be more influential in the political process than others, despite the existence of procedures in most democratic societies that place all citizens in a position of formal equality. Empirical theories of political participation explain these inequalities in terms of differential access to socio-economic resources, such as education, occupation and income. Access to these resources helps to determine the lifestyle, social networks and motivations of individuals, in various ways; it shapes different levels of political participation, and ultimately determines the ability of ordinary citizens to influence government policy. The practical consequence is that some citizens possess more political influence than others, simply by virtue of their socio-economic position.[12]

In contrast to resource theories, social learning theories of political participation emphasize the political socialization that individuals experience within the society, and the beliefs and feelings about politics that they accumulate in childhood and pre-adulthood. Studies by Easton and Dennis[13] and others have argued that this pre-adult socialization has important consequences for adult political values and may offset negative political experiences in later life. From the perspective of the political system, the diffuse regime support that flows from this socialization acts as 'a reservoir upon which the system typically draws in times of crises, such as depressions, wars, and internecine conflicts, when perceived benefits may recede to their lowest ebb'.[14] Sniderman has refined this approach by examining the role of personality and motivational factors in shaping political beliefs and, more specifically, democratic commitment. His theory rests on two main propositions. First, since support for the democratic ideal involves a complex array of beliefs and values, its most common source within a society will be the political culture. Second, the extent to which individuals acquire this commitment from the political culture will depend, at least in part, on their personality, and those with high self-esteem will be 'more likely to have internalized the modal values of the political culture'.[15]

The resources that individuals can bring to political participation are derived from their socio-economic status as reflected in urban residence, educational level, employment and income, all of which are relatively amenable to measurement.[16] By contrast, measuring social learning is more problematic. As operationalized by Sniderman, it is one of two intervening variables linking personality and democratic commitment. As Sniderman puts it, 'democratic values for a variety of reasons are not easy to learn, and whatever affects an individual's capacity for social learning also affects his chances of learning those values'.[17] To accommodate the major components of this model, we measure social learning by three variables: by the period in which the person entered the active electorate (after the collapse of communism, or during the years of Gorbachevian *perestroika*); by whether or not they were a member of the Communist Party of the Soviet Union; and by whether or not they believed that there was more democracy in the communist than in the current period.

TABLE 6

RESOURCES, LEARNING AND POLITICAL EVALUATIONS, 2001 (REGRESSION
ESTIMATES)

	Confidence		Responsiveness		
	Institutions	Media	Equality	Efficacy	Elections
Resources					
Urban	−.10**	−.10**	−.05*	ns	ns
Tertiary education	ns	−.05*	ns	.07**	ns
Employed	−.09**	−.09**	−.04*	ns	−.07**
Family income	−.04*	−.04*	ns	.06*	−.07**
Learning					
CPSU member, self	ns	−.01	ns	.05*	.08**
CPSU member, family	ns	.00	ns	ns	.06**
Democracy generation	−.12**	−.06*	.11**	ns	ns
Glasnost generation	−.10**	ns	ns	ns	ns
Soviet democracy better	−.09**	ns	−.15**	ns	−.09**
Adjusted R − sq	.12	.03	.04	.01	.02

Notes: ** = statistically significant at p < .01, * = statistically significant at p < .05. 'ns' = not significant. All regression coefficients below 0.1 are identified here as 'not significant'. Regression equations showing standardized regression coefficients predicting confidence in institutions, responsiveness, and support for democratic elections. The dependent variables are defined as follows. 'Confidence in institutions' is made up of the nine items in Table 1 combined into a single scale. 'Confidence in the media' combines three items relating to trust in newspapers, television and radio into a single scale. 'Equality' combines the three items listed under that subheading in Table 2 into a single scale, and 'efficacy' combines the three items listed under that subheading in Table 2 into a single scale. 'Elections' combines the three items in Table 3 into a single scale.

Source: As Table 1.

Both resources and learning have a significant impact on disengagement, though the overall fit of the models suggests that we know relatively little about responsiveness in the form of efficacy or about support for elections. The most substantial effect comes from the measure of social learning; for example, entering the active electorate during the period of democratization in the late 1980s tends to reduce confidence in political institutions, but increases a belief in equality of treatment. Perhaps surprisingly, former CPSU membership has little impact other than increasing a sense of efficacy and promoting the propensity to electoral participation. As we might have expected, a hankering for the democracy of the Soviet era reduces support for all of the measures, notably the belief that the current system provides equality of treatment. In contrast to the established democracies, the resources that voters bring to the political system almost always lead to disengagement, most notably employment and income. The only exception concerns efficacy, where tertiary-educated, higher-income citizens are more likely to believe that they have the skills to ensure that they receive fair treatment from government.

The Consequences of Disengagement

Disengagement is important not only in its mainsprings within the electorate – through resources or learning – but in its political implications. A disengaged electorate may be one that is more compliant in its political behaviour, by abstaining from voting or withdrawing from other conventional forms of political participation. Equally, however, a disengaged electorate might be one in which other, less conventional forms of political participation become an important channel for expressing grievances to government. Studies of political participation have drawn a major distinction between conventional and unconventional forms of participation, but within each of the two categories there is a variety of different methods.[18] Among conventional or democratic modes of participation, the most common is the act of voting. Unconventional methods are much more diverse. For example, during the Brezhnev era, Bahry and Silver identified four types of political participation: unconventional political activism, involving such activities as the distribution of *samizdat*; compliant activism, mainly concerning party-initiated work; social activism, involving residential and neighbourhood groups; and contacting public officials.[19] DiFranceisco and Gitelman identify three forms of political participation which distinguish between symbolic participation, such as voting, and contacts with public officials.[20]

The survey asked two questions concerning recalled vote in the December 1999 Duma elections and in the March 2000 presidential elections. Table 8 shows that the survey recorded 25 per cent of the respondents as non-voters in 1999, with a further 13 per cent not recalling either whether they voted or for whom they voted. In 2000 these numbers were reduced, with 16 per cent abstaining and just five per cent unable to recall their voting behaviour. Combining the results of the two questions shows that 13 per cent of the electorate were consistently abstentionist between the two elections, and 58 per cent were consistently voters; the remaining 29 per cent fell between these two categories. Less conventional methods of participation were measured in the survey by four questions asking the respondents whether they had engaged in various activities ranging from signing a petition to participating in a strike. Table 7 shows that relatively few had engaged in any of the four activities; just eight per cent had engaged in one or more over the previous two years.

Political participation in post-communist Russia, then, conforms very closely to what has been found in Western societies, with citizens dividing on the use of conventional rather than unconventional forms of participation. Studies in the liberal democracies have found that rather than moving between different forms of participation to match their resources and needs, citizens

TABLE 7
FORMS OF PARTICIPATION AND DISENGAGEMENT (PERCENTAGES)

	Conventional				
	1999	2000	Both elections	Unconventional	
Voter	62	79	58	Signed petition	4
Don't recall	13	5	29	Written to newspaper	2
Non-voter	25	16	13	Contacted MP	4
Total	100	100	100	Participated in strike	2
				(At least one)	8

Notes: The questions were: 'If you voted in the elections to the Duma in December 1999/presidential elections in March 2000, which party did you vote for?'; 'In the course of the past two years, have you signed a petition?; written to a newspaper about a political or personal problem?; consulted an elected individual (MP) about a political or personal problem?; or taken part in a strike?'

Source: As Table 1.

tend to specialize in a particular mode and employ it to the exclusion of others. This appears to be borne out in Russia, and the two dimensions are only modestly correlated $(r = -.06)$. Conventional political activity does, however, appear to be a prerequisite to the use of unconventional modes of participation.[21] As Muller argues, those who engage in conventional activity do not necessarily progress to the use of unconventional forms, but all of those who have engaged in unconventional methods have, at some stage, also used conventional forms.[22] In Russia, as in other societies, we would therefore expect to find a correlation between various individual characteristics and the use of one particular method of participation.

How far do political evaluations go towards explaining disengagement, while also taking into account the individual resources that a voter has at his or her disposal, and the political learning they will have experienced as they enter the active electorate? The regression results in Table 8 suggest that political evaluations have an important role, more so in predicting abstention than in shaping protest. Abstention has strong roots in social and political learning, but in the opposite direction to what we might predict. Those with positive experiences and commitments stemming from the Soviet era are less likely to abstain in elections, compared with those with more recent experiences in the post-1990 era. For example, there is a major effect for those coming of political age since 1990, and the strength of the effect is on a par with all the other measures of learning combined. However, the most important predictor of disengagement is, as we might expect, expressing a lack of support for elections. In contrast to the conventional measure of

TABLE 8
RESOURCES, LEARNING, POLITICAL EVALUATIONS
AND DISENGAGEMENT (REGRESSION ESTIMATES)

	Standardized Coefficients	
	Abstention	Protest
Resources		
Urban	ns	$-.04^*$
Tertiary education	ns	$.06^{**}$
Employed	$-.10^{**}$	ns
Family income	ns	ns
Learning		
CPSU member, self	$-.04^*$	$.05^*$
CPSU member, family	$-.07^{**}$	$.09^{**}$
Democracy generation	$.22^{**}$	ns
Glasnost generation	$.06^{**}$	ns
Soviet democracy better	$-.07^{**}$	$.13^{**}$
Political Evaluations		
Confidence in institutions	ns	ns
Confidence in media	ns	$-.05^*$
Equality of treatment	$.09^{**}$	ns
Efficacy	ns	$.10^{**}$
Support for elections	$-.37^{**}$	ns
Adjusted R-squared	$.20$	$.04$

Notes: ** = statistically significant at $p < .01$, * = statistically significant at $p < .05$. 'ns' = not significant. All regression coefficients below 0.1 are identified here as 'not significant'. Regression equations showing standardized regression coefficients predicting abstention and protest. Dependent variables are defined in Table 7. Abstention is scored 1 = non-voter, 0.5 = don't recall, 0 = voter. Protest is scored one for each of the unconventional activities in Table 7 that the respondent reported participating in. The exact questions are shown in Table 7.

Source: As Table 1.

participation, the likelihood of engaging in less conventional forms has few correlates among the three sets of variables in Table 8. Those engaging in such activities are more likely to have a tertiary education – an important skill, say, in contacting a public representative, to have been members of the CPSU, and to believe that Soviet democracy was better than the current variety. They are also more likely to have a sense of political efficacy.

Conclusion

Our findings, we suggest, have important implications for the development of political participation in post-communist Russia. In the resource model, levels of participation depend on the socio-economic status of the electorate, so that a society with a significant under-privileged group will be more likely to experience lower levels of conventional participation; as standards of living either improve or deteriorate, levels of participation co-vary. The social learning model, by contrast, identifies participation as being a consequence of absorbing values from the political culture. Absorbing these values is, in turn, a lengthy process, and change occurs over many generations. In turn, learning and resources influence political evaluations, which help to shape disengagement, particularly with regard to voting. All of this suggests that patterns of political participation in Russia will be shaped for some years to come by the norms established during the communist era.

APPENDIX

Nationally representative surveys were conducted in each of the three countries using a common questionnaire and a well-established local agency. In Russia our surveys were conducted respectively by the All-Russian Centre for the Study of Public Opinion (VTsIOM) and by Russian Research. Fieldwork took place between 19 and 29 January 2000 and between 17 June and 3 July 2001. In the former case, the universe was the resident population of the Russian Federation aged 16 and over, and 2,003 interviews were conducted on a face-to-face basis in respondents' homes (our results are based on the 1,940 interviews that took place with those aged 18 and over). A four-stage stratified sample was constructed in accordance with the agency's normal practices. Interviews took place in 107 primary sampling units in 38 of the 89 subjects of the Federation; 193 interviewers were employed, and 16 per cent of the interviews themselves were monitored by agency supervisors. In the latter case the universe consisted of Russian Federation residents aged 18 and over, excluding soldiers, convicts and those of no fixed address. Interviews took place in 195 primary sampling units in 42 different subjects of the Federation; 197 interviewers were employed, yielding a total N of 2,000.

Our survey in Belarus was conducted by Novak under the direction of Andrei Vardomatsky. Fieldwork took place between 13 and 27 April 2000. There were 62 sampling points, and 90 interviewers conducted face-to-face interviews in respondents' homes. The total number of interviews was 1,090, using the agency's normal three-stage stratified sampling model to secure representation of the resident population aged 18 and over. All seven of the country's regions were included.

In Ukraine our survey was conducted by the Kyiv International Institute of Sociology under the direction of Vladimir Paniotto and Valeriya Karuk.

The questionnaire was piloted between 28 and 31 January and fieldwork took place between 18 February and 3 March 2000. A four-stage stratified sample was constructed, and 110 primary sampling units were employed. A total of 125 interviewers took part, who conducted 1,600 interviews on a face-to-face basis in respondents' homes, of which ten per cent were subject to a check by supervisors, yielding a valid total of 1,590.

NOTES

1. Stephen White, 'Ten Years On, What Do the Russians Think?', *Journal of Communist Studies and Transition Politics*, Vol.18, No.1 (2002), pp.35–50 (pp.40, 39).
2. See respectively Mikhail N. Afanas'ev, *Klientelizm i rossiiskaya gosudarstvennost'*, 2nd edn. (Moscow: MONF, 2000), p.17; and A.V. Zinov'ev and I. S. Polyashova, *Izbiratel'naya sistema Rossii (teoriya, praktika i perspektivy)* (St Petersburg: Yuridicheskii tsentr Press, 2003), p.8.
3. Gabriel A. Almond and Sidney Verba, *The Civic Culture: Political Attitudes and Democracy in Five Nations* (Princeton, NJ: Princeton University Press, 1963).
4. Fritz Plasser, Peter A. Ulram and Harald Waldrauch, *Democratic Consolidation in East–Central Europe* (London: Macmillan, and New York: St Martin's, 1998), p.111.
5. William Mishler and Richard Rose, 'What are the Origins of Political Trust?', *Comparative Political Studies*, Vol.34, No.1 (Feb. 2001), pp.30–62 (p.41).
6. William L. Miller, Stephen White and Paul M. Heywood, *Values and Political Change in Postcommunist Europe* (London: Macmillan, and New York: St Martin's, 1998), p.100.
7. Ibid., p.102; and (for trade unions) Richard Rose and Christian Haerpfer, *New Russia Barometer III: The Results* (Glasgow: Centre for the Study of Public Policy, 1994), p.32.
8. For VTsIOM time-series data, see Stephen White, *Russia's New Politics* (Cambridge: Cambridge University Press, 2000), p.270.
9. Cited in ibid.
10. Jon H. Pammett, 'Elections and Democracy in Russia', *Communist and Post-Communist Studies*, Vol.32, No.1 (March 1999), pp.45–60 (pp.53, 55).
11. Marc Morje Howard, *The Weakness of Civil Society in Post-Communist Europe* (Cambridge: Cambridge University Press, 2003), pp.11, 58–60, 67.
12. See, for instance, Lester W. Milbrath and M.L. Goel, *Political Participation: How and Why Do People Get Involved in Politics?*, 2nd edn. (Chicago: Rand McNally, 1977); and Paul M. Sniderman, *A Question of Loyalty* (Berkeley: University of California Press, 1981). Perhaps the most influential works in this tradition are Almond and Verba, *The Civic Culture*; and Sidney Verba, Norman H. Nie and Jae-On Kim, *Participation and Political Equality: A Seven-Nation Comparison* (Cambridge: Cambridge University Press, 1978).
13. David Easton and Jack Dennis, 'The Child's Acquisition of Regime Norms: Political Efficacy', *American Political Science Review*, Vol.61, No.1 (1967), pp.25–38; see also, by the same authors, *Children in the Political System* (New York: McGraw Hill, 1969).
14. Easton and Dennis, 'The Child's Acquisition', p.63.
15. Sniderman, 'Personality and Democratic Politics', p.254.
16. Lester W. Milbrath, *Political Participation* (Chicago: Rand McNally, 1965); and Sidney Verba and Normal H. Nie, *Participation in America* (Chicago: University of Chicago Press, 1972), p.125ff.
17. Sniderman, 'Personality and Democratic Politics', p.207.
18. Verba, Nie and Kim, *Participation and Political Equality*; Samuel Barnes and Max Kaase (eds.), *Political Action: Mass Participation in Five Western Democracies* (Beverly Hills, CA: Sage, 1979).
19. Donna Bahry and Brian D. Silver, 'Soviet Citizen Participation on the Eve of Democratization', *American Political Science Review*, Vol.84, No.3 (1990), pp.821–47.

20. Wayne DiFranceisco and Zvi Gitelman, 'Soviet Political Culture and "Covert Participation" in Policy Implementation', *American Political Science Review*, Vol.78, No.3 (1984), pp.603–21.
21. Clive Bean, 'Participation and Political Protest: A Causal Model with Australian Evidence', *Political Behaviour*, Vol.13 (1991), pp.253–83.
22. Edward N. Muller, *Aggressive Political Participation* (Princeton, NJ: Princeton University Press, 1979), pp.230–31.

Disengaged or Disenchanted? The Vote 'Against All' in Post-Communist Russia

DEREK S. HUTCHESON

Introduction

Many scholars – including some in this collection – have highlighted a world-wide decline in political engagement. Fragmenting social networks, together with the diminishing membership and importance of political parties and the reduced role of civic society, have been used as evidence of fundamental changes taking place in the nature of political participation.[1] In particular, falling voter turnouts in elections worldwide have attracted increasing scholarly attention.[2] Recently, these investigations have turned to the transition states of post-communist Europe.[3]

The previous contribution looked at the patterns of engagement, disengagement and political protest in the Russian Federation and its two largest Slavic neighbours. The present analysis seeks to develop this line of examination further, on the basis of voting behaviour in Russia over the past decade. Falling electoral turnouts in Western Europe have in some cases been attributed not only to voter disengagement but also disenchantment. Rather than make a forced choice amongst unsuitable candidates, it has been argued, some register their protest by failing to vote at all. Russian voters, however, have two electoral instruments through which they can register a protest: either they can abstain from voting altogether, or else they can actually vote *against all* candidates. Hitherto, there has been remarkably little academic examination of the latter phenomenon, and only a handful of articles outside the Russian press have examined it in any detail.[4] Are non-voters disengaged or disenchanted? Are the 'positive negatives' (those who consciously vote against the list of candidates) fundamentally different from the 'negative negatives' (who simply fail to vote)?

Methods of Protest in Russian Elections

As noted above, it is open to Russian voters disenchanted with the political process to emulate the actions of their Western counterparts and simply to abstain from voting. At least in terms of rational choice theory, for the disenchanted voter this would be the logical outcome of a cost–benefit analysis. Such voters would evaluate the consequences of casting a vote and assess the utility obtained from their single vote to be so insignificant as to be outweighed by the costs of voting. They would register their discontent by withdrawing from political participation altogether, in effect refusing through abstention to legitimize the electoral process.[5]

However, as in some other former Soviet states, the Russian electorate can also express its disenchantment using a provision retained from the Soviet voting system: voting 'against all' candidates (or parties).[6] Fundamentally, this differs from simple abstention. The voter incurs the same costs of voting as other voters (the problems of getting to the polling station and the opportunity cost in terms of time and effort), and also legitimizes the electoral process through participation. However, rather than contributing to the voting totals for any of the candidates, he or she is able to register a protest by consciously casting a vote *against all* contenders – a 'positive' negative vote, in effect, as opposed to a simple abstention.

The provision to vote 'against all' was retained in 1993 when the fundamentals of the post-Soviet electoral system were established. At this time the decision was aimed primarily at increasing turnout figures above the legal minimum, the reasoning being that voters would be less likely to abstain from voting altogether if given the chance to participate but vote against all candidates. However, until 1997 the legal position of the 'against all' vote was ambiguous, in many cases carrying only indicative status.

For the founding State Duma election in 1993, the contests in the single-member districts were to be considered invalid 'if the number of votes in the column "against all" [were] higher than for the candidate with the largest number of votes'.[7] By contrast, in 1995 the victor in a single-member district seat was considered to be 'the candidate who receive[d] the largest number of votes from participating voters'.[8] In other words, regardless of the number of votes cast 'against all', the first placed *candidate* was to be elected. In fact, there were some cases in which this was salient: in three constituencies the elected members actually polled fewer votes than the 'against all' option.[9] The same applied until the second round of the 1996 presidential election: if no candidate won more than half the vote in the first round, 'the two *candidates* who achieved the greatest share of the vote' were to contest the second round, making no mention of what would happen were the 'against all' option to receive more votes than one or both of these protagonists. Only in the second round did the 'against all' option carry legal significance, the winner's status being confirmed only if he or she had more votes than were cast 'against all'.[10]

Since 1997, however, the status of this option has been more firmly enshrined in electoral legislation, effectively giving it parity with the voting totals for real candidates. The 1997 version of the framework election law, 'On Fundamental Guarantees of Electoral Rights', declared explicitly that an election would be declared invalid if 'the number of votes cast for the candidate receiving the greatest number of votes relative to other candidates was less than the number of votes . . . cast against all candidates'[11] – provisions mirrored in the single-member district part of the 1999 State Duma election[12] and the 2000 presidential election, in which a first place for 'against all' in the first round would have rendered the election invalid. (Seemingly, however, as long as one candidate had received more votes than 'against all', the second-placed *candidate* could still have contested the second round, even if he or she had received fewer votes than 'against all'.)[13] Much the same formulations have been retained in the latest versions of these laws, rendering 'against all' a fundamental part of the Russian electoral system at all levels.[14]

Thus the status and significance of the provision to vote 'against all' has changed over the past decade. In the early to mid-1990s it performed the role of a 'safety valve', allowing institutionalized protest voting, but only under certain circumstances influencing election results materially. Since 1997, however, it has effectively become a legal entity in its own right, with the potential to render elections invalid.

Theoretical effects of the vote 'against all' have been examined elsewhere,[15] and it is not necessary to recount them all here. None the less, it is worth noting that the possible consequences of voting 'against all' may not conform with the aims of voters who, by definition, do not wish to vote to see any of the other candidates on the list elected. The State Duma electoral law does not take explicit account of votes cast 'against all' in the party list half of the election, but does require that at least 50 per cent of participating voters be represented in the parliament. An overall majority cast 'against all' (unlikely, but theoretically possible) would therefore leave all 225 seats – or half the State Duma – unfilled. More realistically, though, a substantial but not overwhelming share of the vote cast 'against all' may actually *increase* the number of seats allocated to the leading parties, rather than reduce it. If people were to vote 'against all' in preference to abstaining, this would have the effect of increasing the turnout and consequently the level of the five per cent barrier.[16] Hypothetically, small parties that might otherwise have obtained just over five per cent of the vote could consequently find themselves fractionally short of this total, thereby splitting the 225 seats allocated proportionally among fewer parties. (Of course, had the 'against all' votes been cast for parties that would not in any case have passed the five per cent barrier, then it would make no difference.)

In the single-member district part of the State Duma contests, the real effects of the vote 'against all' have been more significant. Since the option was formalized in the electoral law, elections in specific constituencies have been declared invalid when 'against all' has garnered more votes than any single candidate. In 1999, this happened in eight seats, leaving them unfilled until by-elections were held in March 2000. Similar occurrences have been noted in various regional elections; for example, in the December 1999 elections to the Ul'yanovsk legislative assembly, 'against all' polled more votes than the first-placed candidate in six districts out of 25, all of which were in the city of Ul'yanovsk itself.[17] Once again, the effects of this were paradoxical: the assembly was still quorate, but the 19 members elected were mainly from the rural parts of the province, and were broadly loyal to the incumbent governor. By protesting, presumably in part against the regional administration, 'against all' voters actually created a smaller assembly that was more loyal to it.

To summarize, therefore, the provision to vote 'against all' allows voters to register a 'positive' negative vote, rather than simply disengaging by default through non-participation, and in sufficient numbers this can have real effects on election results. It prevents any of the candidates against whom the 'against all' voters have voted from being elected, but it can also be counterproductive. In a legislative election, voters are left unrepresented in the parliament or assembly until a by-election can be held, arguably giving them *less* influence over the decision-making process. Moreover, in certain circumstances a vote 'against all' can actually increase, rather than curb, the influence enjoyed by key actors in the political process. Thus the effects of a vote 'against all' are by no means straightforward.

The second method of protest – abstention – can be an equally effective weapon, if once again potentially counter-productive. Federal and regional elections have minimum turnout figures – 50 per cent for presidential elections, 25 per cent for State Duma elections and 20 per cent for other elections – and a failure to reach these minimum levels has the effect of rendering the election invalid. For example, in the case of Ul'yanovsk cited above, it took three rounds of by-elections before the turnout was sufficiently high to elect the remaining six deputies to the regional parliament. Whether this was down to disinterest or disenchantment, the effect was that the legislative assembly continued to operate while the districts in question remained unrepresented.

Examining Protest in Russian Voting Behaviour[18]

Evidence of voter alienation in Russia through falling turnout figures at the federal level is somewhat tenuous. As Table 1 shows, turnout in presidential elections fell marginally between 1991 and 1996, but in general it has been fairly consistent since the first election in June 1991. In State Duma elections, meanwhile, turnout actually rose marginally between 1993 and 1995 before falling by a smaller amount in 1999. While this still means that nearly two in five voters failed to vote, it is important to note that this is not a problem

TABLE 1
VOTER TURNOUT, FEDERAL AND REGIONAL ELECTIONS, 1991–2003, BY TYPE OF CONSTITUENT SUBJECT

Type of region	1991 Pres	1993 SMD	1993 PL	1995 SMD	1996 Pres (1)	1996 Pres (2)	1999 PL	2000 Pres	Gub 1 (1)	Gub 1 (2)	Gub 2 (1)	Gub 2 (2)
Republic [21]	70.3	51.1	50.8	64.8	69.5	70.3	65.8	73.6	67.0	57.9	61.1	61.6
Territories [6]	76.8	56.0	55.5	64.6	69.3	66.7	59.6	66.3	50.7	61.1	55.6	49.5
Provinces [49]	66.2	52.7	51.9	66.0	70.3	68.4	61.5	68.7	53.1	42.7	53.0	44.7
Fed. Cities [2]	69.1	47.5	46.9	62.3	65.8	67.9	59.6	66.9	58.7	44.2	56.9	–
Autonomous regions [11]				65.0	68.5	66.9	65.0	69.0	55.9	61.0	64.5	51.9
Total/Mean	74.7	54.8	54.3	64.7	69.8	68.9	61.9	68.7	56.7	47.7	55.9	47.2

Sources: As note 18, plus Michael McFaul and Nikolai Petrov, *Politicheskii al'manakh Rossii 1997* (Moscow: Carnegie, 1998), pp. 379–81 and 390–96 for 1991 and 1993 results.

Key: 'Pres' = Presidential election; 'SMD' = Single-member district (State Duma election); 'PL' = Party list (State Duma election); 'Gub X (Y)': X refers to the election number (i.e., the first and second post-Soviet gubernatorial elections); Y refers to the round. Similarly, the numbers in brackets for the 1996 presidential election refer to the two rounds. For single-member district State Duma results, and gubernatorial elections, mean figures are given, since individual election results are region-specific. For party list and presidential results, the total across the Russian Federation is given. The turnout figures for gubernatorial elections include all elections; if those held concurrently with federal elections (i.e., State Duma or presidential) are excluded, the first round turnouts were 54.8 per cent and 52.7 per cent respectively.

that affects Russia exclusively; turnout in the parliamentary and presidential elections in 1999–2000 was higher than the analogous elections in the United States and Britain in the two years following, for example.

As in many other countries, turnout levels in Russia are greater for higher-level elections. The mean turnout figures for the two waves of gubernatorial elections since 1995 show that voters are less likely to vote in regional elections than in federal ones. Excluding the gubernatorial elections that took place concurrently with State Duma or presidential elections, turnout in the first rounds of gubernatorial elections was actually slightly lower than the figures given here, averaging just under 55 per cent in the first (1995–99) wave, and less than 53 per cent in the second (1997–2003). In those provinces and autonomous regions where second rounds took place, on average fewer than half the electorate voted. Indeed, in some cases, the figure has been closer to a quarter: in the second round of the St Petersburg gubernatorial contest in October 2003, for example, only 28.3 per cent of the electorate actually voted, and in Tyumen' in January 1997, even fewer – 25.3 per cent – did so.

In sub-regional elections, generally turnouts have been lower still. Vladivostok – where there were more than 18 invalid elections and by-elections to the city Duma due to insufficient turnout – is the arch-example of a wider trend of low engagement in local politics. Partly as a result of this, in the latest version of the law 'On Municipal Elections' the requirement of a minimum turnout figure for the validation of local elections has been removed.[19]

The overall picture is that, although there has been some variation in turnout from election to election, participation figures have remained relatively stable and have not declined dramatically. However, it is important to bear in mind an important caveat regarding the use of turnout figures as an indicator of political engagement: in rural areas, where the majority of voters tend to be elderly, one of the legacies of the Soviet period has been that the culture of compulsory voting has remained ingrained, and local administrations strongly encourage high voter turnout in order to legitimize their rule. In many cases they use 'administrative resources' to achieve this (such as organizing transport to take people to the polling station, reminding voters that their village is dependent on the good will of higher-level administrations for its basic resources, and recreating the Soviet-era 'carnival' atmosphere on polling day).[20] Thus the highest voter turnouts may occur, not where people are most politically engaged and educated, but, paradoxically, where the least critical voters reside.

Votes 'against all' – the alternative method of opting out of the mainstream voting process – do, however, show a clear upward trend. Table 2 shows the figures in different types of election since 1991, once again

TABLE 2
VOTES 'AGAINST ALL', BY TYPE OF REGION, 1995–2003

Type of region	1991 Pres	1993 SMD	1993 PL	1995 SMD	1995 PL	1996 Pres (1)	1996 Pres (2)	1999 SMD	1999 PL	2000 Pres	Gub 1 (1)	Gub 1 (2)	Gub 2 (1)	Gub 2 (2)
Republic [21]	2.3	11.2	4.4	6.7	2.5	1.4	3.6	7.4	2.2	1.2	4.3	4.5	4.7	4.2
Territories [6]	1.9	15.0	3.9	9.2	3.0	1.7	5.4	11.6	3.6	1.8	4.3	3.4	5.1	4.8
Provinces [49]	1.8	18.3	3.4	9.8	2.9	1.7	5.4	11.5	3.4	1.6	5.4	7.4	7.4	6.8
Fed. Cities [2]	1.7	17.6	5.8	12.5	2.9	1.3	4.4	14.8	4.1	4.2	1.9	5.8	4.7	–
Autonomous regions [11]				12.0	4.8	2.1	5.0	9.0	3.9	1.5	7.8	7.3	7.4	13.1
Total/Mean	1.9	14.8	3.9	9.9	2.8	1.4	4.8	11.5	3.3	1.9	5.3	6.6	6.7	6.6

Sources/Notes: As Table 1.

compared by type of constituent subject. It can be seen that there has been a rise in the number of voters choosing to cast a 'positive' negative vote, rather than simply abstaining – in particular, in the two main federal cities of Moscow and St Petersburg. The percentage of the electorate voting 'against all' has generally been higher in elections that use district-based majoritarian systems – such as the single-member district State Duma seats and gubernatorial elections – than in a single, nationwide constituency (for example, the party list section of the State Duma elections, and the presidential elections). Indeed, in gubernatorial elections, some districts within regions have voted in substantial numbers against all; in one district of Tyumen' in the 1996–97 contest, 44.7 per cent of the electorate voted thus.

As noted above, and confirmed by Table 2, at the federal level the 'against all' option has had the highest impact in State Duma elections, particularly in the single-member district sections. In 1999, the voters of eight constituencies temporarily remained unrepresented when the votes cast against all candidates exceeded the total for any one individual. Moreover, as the comparative data in Table 3 show, between 1995 and 1999 there was a noticeable increase in both the share of the vote for and the impact of the 'against all' option. An average of 9.9 per cent of voters in each constituency cast such protest votes in the 225 single-member district contests in 1995, and 11.5 per cent in 1999.[21] When analysed on a constituency-by-constituency basis, the 'against all' share of the vote increased by a mean of 1.23 times between 1995 and 1999.

The relative extent to which the 'against all' option has been used by voters is perhaps best illustrated by Table 4. If 'against all' is treated as though it were a real candidate, it came in first place – beating all candidates – in three constituencies in 1995, and eight in 1999 (although, as noted earlier, this

TABLE 3
COMPARISON OF KEY INDICATORS, 1995 AND 1999 STATE DUMA ELECTIONS

Indicator	1995	1999	Difference
Total party list 'against all' vote	2.8%	3.3%	+0.5%
Mean single-member district 'against all' vote	9.9%	11.5%	+1.6%
Mean number of candidates	11.7	9.9	−1.8
Mean number of candidates ahead of 'against all'	3.2	2.5	−0.7
Number of constituencies where 'against all' came first	3	8	+5
Mean difference between SMD and PL 'against all' vote in each constituency	7.0%	8.1%	+1.1
Total number of candidates	2,627	2,226	−401
Candidates ahead of 'against all'	708	557	−151
Percentage of candidates ahead of 'against all'	27.0%	25.0%	−2.0%

Sources: As note 18.

TABLE 4
EFFECTIVE PLACING OF 'AGAINST ALL' AMONG CANDIDATES, 1995 AND 1999
SMD STATE DUMA ELECTIONS

Effective placing	1995 N=	1995 Per cent	1995 Cumulative	1999 N=	1999 Per cent	1999 Cumulative
1	3	1.3	1.3	8	3.6	3.6
2	26	11.6	12.9	43	19.2	22.8
3	54	24.0	36.9	77	34.4	57.1
4	66	29.3	66.2	53	23.7	80.8
5	31	13.8	80.0	22	9.8	90.6
6	26	11.6	91.6	16	7.1	97.8
7	14	6.2	97.8	3	1.3	99.1
8	4	1.8	99.6	1	0.4	99.6
9	0	0.0	99.6	1	0.4	100.0
10	0	0.0	99.6	0	0.0	100.0
11	1	0.4	100.0	0	0.0	100.0
Total	225	100.0		224	100.0	

Sources: Calculated from *Vybory deputatov Gosudarstvennoi Dumy. 1995. Elektoral'naya statis-
tika* (Moscow: CEC/Ves' Mir, 1996), pp.157–98; *Vybory deputatov Gosudarstvennoi
Dumy Federal'nogo Sobraniya Rossiiskoi Federatsii. 1999. Elektoral'naya statistika*
(Moscow: CEC/Ves' Mir, 2000), pp.182–208.

did not deny the leading candidates their seats in 1995, owing to the electoral
legislation in use at the time). In 1995 the 'against all' vote came amongst
the top four candidates in virtually two-thirds (149 of 225) of constituencies.
In 1999 it achieved this feat in four-fifths of seats. Of course, there were
varying numbers of candidates in the constituencies – but in the vast majority
of cases (86 per cent in 1995, and 88 per cent in 1999), the 'against all' option
beat at least half the real candidates. In highly competitive constituencies,
often it came ahead of a dozen or more contenders. As Table 3 shows,
approximately three-quarters of all candidates contesting the 1995 and 1999
elections obtained fewer votes individually than were cast against them and
their counterparts.

It will be noted from Tables 2 and 3 that the 'against all' option was used
considerably more in the single-member districts than in the party list part of
the State Duma elections. Only in three constituencies out of 225 in 1995, and
one out of 224 in 1999, did fewer people vote 'against all' in the single-
member district part of the election than in the party list. While the number
of 'positive negative' voters in the party list vote was not insignificant in
absolute terms – 1.9 million voters in 1995, and 2.2 million four years
later – on average more than three times as many voters voted 'against all'
in the single-member districts. This means that several million voters cast
their ballots *for* a party but *against* a single-member district candidate. To
what can this be attributed?

There are a number of possible explanations. In the first instance, the number of candidates in the party list part of the election was significantly higher than in the constituencies. The proportional sections were contested by 43 parties in 1995 and 26 in 1999, compared with averages of 11.7 and 9.9 candidates respectively per single-member district constituency. It could be assumed that voters were more likely to find a party that reflected their own views from such a large selection than from the more restricted choice of candidates at constituency level. None the less, neither in 1995 nor in 1999 was there a significant correlation between the number of candidates and the share of the 'against all' vote in the single-member districts, which would suggest that the breadth of choice had little influence on the voters' decision to vote negatively.

An alternative explanation may lie in the different electoral systems used for the two parts of the election. Whereas the party list section is based on proportional representation within a single, all-Russia district (albeit with a regional element in terms of seat distribution), single-member districts are constituency-based. The 'winner takes all' system in this half of the election means that voters' disenchantment can be more effectively expressed by voting against all candidates than by wasting their franchise on a candidate with little chance of success. If sufficiently large numbers of voters do this, it can result in the annulment of the election. By contrast, the proportional system used to allocate seats from the party lists encourages people to vote more positively. As noted above, an 'against all' vote of similar magnitude to that in the single-member districts would not necessarily result in any fewer party list deputies being elected, and it could even lead to a greater advantage for the leading parties. In this case, the rational voter's interest lies in choosing an alternative party, since victory for one party does not automatically mean the exclusion of all the others.

Another factor worth considering is that elections in Russia are generally based on personality rather than party.[22] Of course, many parties in Russia are set up around their leaders, who provide a personal focus to their organizations' activities. However, in the list section of the State Duma elections, voters are constrained by design to choose between parties rather than individuals. In constituency-based contests, the focus is very much on the candidates rather than on their affiliations, and thus the 'against all' voters are able to focus their disenchantment more specifically on individuals.

Comparison with other types of election can perhaps give an indication of which of these explanations is the more useful. As in the single-member district contests, in presidential elections only the winner gains the prize of office, and the focus is on the candidates rather than parties. Yet Table 2 shows that the 'against all' vote in presidential elections has generally been below two per cent (except in the second round in 1996). Gubernatorial elections, meanwhile, could be construed in structure as 'mini-presidential'. The figures in Table 2 indicate, however, that the average 'against all' vote is much higher. This suggests that district magnitude may play a role in the decision to vote 'against all'. In elections with small districts and majoritarian systems, it is easier to achieve a concentration of 'against all' votes. In contests with larger district magnitude (such as the presidential and list elections) or proportional systems, this vote is more thinly spread and a plurality for the 'against all' option is less likely. Thus voters appear more inclined to vote positively for a candidate or party.

Patterns of 'Against All' Voting

How consistent is the vote 'against all'? Are certain regions more inclined to vote 'against all' than others?[23] To establish this, we can turn to the results of all federal elections since 1995, together with the first two gubernatorial elections in each region. In the first instance, we can examine the correlations between the 'against all' shares of the vote in different elections, in order to establish whether or not there are recognizable patterns of protest voting.

The strong and generally positive relationships seen in Table 5 suggest that certain regions are likely to have consistently high figures from one election to the next. Interestingly, the correlations of the 'against all' votes in the 1996 and 2000 presidential elections with the results from the preceding State Duma elections were stronger for the party-list than for the single-member districts. Moreover, in both cases the correlations of party list and presidential results were actually slightly greater than those between the two halves of the Duma elections themselves, possibly corroborating the earlier hypothesis that district magnitude is significant in explaining the 'against all' vote. However, the consistent patterns of regional protest voting do not appear to extend to the sub-federal level.

This being the case, we can begin to construct a regional index examining which regions' voters are consistently more likely to vote 'against all'. There are several ways of doing this. First, it must be decided whether to include or exclude gubernatorial and other sub-federal elections. While inclusion would give the fullest picture, the above correlation analysis has suggested that 'against all' voting behaviour differs between the federal and sub-federal levels. To yield information about consistency of voting behaviour, it is probably better to concentrate solely on federal elections – namely, those to the State Duma and the Russian presidency.[24]

Second, the decision must be made whether to utilize absolute 'against all' values, or relative ones. In the first case, the arithmetical mean of the 'against all' vote across all seven sets of voting data would be calculated. In the latter, the relative order of 'against all' results would be used. The former would take into account actual voting behaviour, but the regional mean could be artificially raised or lowered by one election or constituency in which there was an anomalously high vote 'against all'. In order to guard against such

TABLE 5
BIVARIATE PEARSON CORRELATIONS BETWEEN 'AGAINST ALL' FIGURES, 1995–2003

Election	1995 SMD	1995 PL	1996 Pres (1)	1996 Pres (2)	1999 SMD	1999 PL	2000 Pres	Gub 1 (1)	Gub 1 (2)	Gub 2 (1)	Gub 2 (2)
1995 SMD	1	–	–	–	–	–	–	–	–	–	–
1995 PL	.562**	1	–	–	–	–	–	–	–	–	–
1996 Pres (1)	.408**	.772**	1	–	–	–	–	–	–	–	–
1996 Pres (2)	.517**	.572**	.734**	1	–	–	–	–	–	–	–
1999 SMD	.444**	.165	.274**	.466**	1	–	–	–	–	–	–
1999 PL	.632**	.653**	.586**	.649**	.591**	1	–	–	–	–	–
2000 Pres	.416**	.296**	.343**	.404**	.538**	.629**	1	–	–	–	–
Gub 1 (1)	.393**	.464**	.441**	.440**	.271*	.398**	.220*	1	–	–	–
Gub 1 (2)	.099	.273	.392*	.294	.195	.113	.097	.528**	1	–	–
Gub 2 (1)	.130	.103	.119	-.016	.174	.216	-.007	.166	.024	1	–
Gub 2 (2)	.041	.399	.303	-.256	.012	.275	-.044	.248	-.074	.623**	1

Notes: Shows Pearson r, where $-1 < r < +1$.

** = statistically significant at $p < .01$, * = statistically significant at $p < .05$

TABLE 6
INDEX OF REGIONAL 'AGAINST ALL' VOTING, 1995–2000 FEDERAL ELECTIONS

'Against all' rank	Region type	Region name	Mean rank
1	(P)	Kamchatka	11.93
2	(AP)	Jewish AP	14.64
3	(P)	Murmansk	14.71
4=	(T)	Krasnoyarsk	14.79
4=	(AT)	Taimyr AT	14.79
6	(T)	Khabarovsk	15.86
7	(P)	Arkhangelsk	16.00
8	(T)	Primor'e	16.86
9	(P)	Sakhalin	17.07
10	(AT)	Chukotka AT	18.29
11	(AT)	Nenets AT	19.00
12	(P)	Omsk	20.36
13	(R)	Kareliya	20.43
14	(P)	Moscow Province	20.57
15	(P)	Vologda	25.36
16	(AT)	Koryak AT	25.64
17	(AT)	Evenki AT	26.21
18	(P)	Perm'	26.50
19	(R)	Komi	27.64
20	(P)	Leningrad	27.79
21	(C)	Moscow City	28.43
22	(P)	Yaroslavl'	28.57
23	(P)	Tula	29.07
24	(AT)	Yamalo-Nenetskii AT	29.14
25	(P)	Vladimir	30.36
27=	(P)	Ivanovo	30.50
27=	(P)	Novosibirsk	30.50
27=	(P)	Sverdlovsk	30.50
29	(P)	Nizhny Novgorod	31.36
30	(P)	Amur	32.36
31	(C)	St Petersburg	32.43
32	(P)	Tver'	33.86
33	(P)	Magadan	34.64
34	(P)	Irkutsk	35.07
35	(P)	Kirov	36.07
36	(P)	Kostroma	38.07
37	(R)	Marii El	38.29
38	(P)	Kaliningrad	38.50
39	(AT)	Khanty-Mansy AT	38.57
40=	(R)	Sakha (Yakutiya)	40.93
40=	(AT)	Komi-Permyat AT	40.93
42	(P)	Kurgan	41.07
43	(P)	Ryazan'	41.64
44	(P)	Novgorod	41.93
45	(R)	Udmurtiya	42.43
46	(P)	Lipetsk	42.64
47	(P)	Voronezh	44.00
48	(P)	Chita	44.43
49	(P)	Saratov	44.71

(*Continued*)

TABLE 6 *CONTINUED*

'Against all' rank	Region type	Region name	Mean rank
50	(P)	Tomsk	44.86
51	(P)	Tyumen'	45.50
52	(P)	Kaluga	46.50
53	(P)	Chelyabinsk	46.79
54	(P)	Orel	50.07
55	(P)	Smolensk	51.36
56	(P)	Samara	52.43
57	(R)	Buryatiya	52.71
58	(P)	Kemerovo	53.64
59=	(R)	Altai Republic	54.14
59=	(R)	Khakasiya	54.14
61	(R)	Tatarstan	54.64
62	(P)	Pskov	55.21
63	(P)	Ul'yanovsk	55.29
64	(P)	Belgorod	56.29
65	(P)	Penza	56.86
66	(P)	Tambov	57.79
67	(P)	Rostov	59.07
68	(P)	Volgograd	62.00
69	(P)	Orenburg	64.43
70	(T)	Stavropol'	65.50
71	(P)	Astrakhan	67.29
72	(T)	Altai Krai	67.64
73	(P)	Kursk	68.14
74	(P)	Bryansk	68.21
75	(T)	Krasnodar	68.57
76	(R)	Bashkortostan	69.07
77	(R)	Ingushetiya	72.71
78	(R)	Tyva	74.86
79	(R)	Chuvashiya	76.57
80	(R)	Mordoviya	77.29
81	(AT)	Ust'-Orda AT	77.36
82	(R)	Adyegaya	78.07
83	(R)	Kalmykiya	79.07
84	(AT)	Aga-Buryat AT	80.21
85	(R)	Northern Osetiya	81.14
86	(R)	Karachaevo-Cherkessiya	82.93
87	(R)	Dagestan	85.14
88	(R)	Kabardino-Balkariya	85.36

Source: See note 25.

Key: (R) = National republic; (T) = Territory [*Krai*]; (O) = Province [*Oblast'*]; (C) = Federal city; (AP) = Autonomous province [*Avtonomnaya oblast'*]; (AT) = Autonomous territory [*Avtonomnyi okrug*].

one-off fluctuations, the results given in Table 6 are based on an index calcu- lated using mean rankings, rather than absolute voting figures.[25] This does not guard against the effects of one-off anomalies, but the use of uniform intervals between each case slightly offsets their impact.[26]

Some interesting patterns are discernible from Table 6. Geographically, a very strong north–south geographical split can be observed. Regions in the northern half of Russia, it seems, are much more likely to vote 'against all' than those in the south. Of the 44 regions in the upper half of the list, only six (in descending order, the Jewish autonomous province, Primor'e, Sakhalin, Tula, Kaliningrad and Ryazan') are entirely south of the 56th parallel, which runs through Moscow province just to the north of the capital city. By contrast, no region that lies entirely north of the parallel appears in the bottom half of the list (although the main parts of four regions which are bisected by it – Urdmurtiya, Tomsk, Tyumen' and Pskov – do lie to the north).

This pattern is confirmed by Map 1, which divides the Russian regions into octiles (eight groups of 11 regions). All but one of the top 11 regions are in the northern and eastern peripheries of the Russian Federation. The following 11 are mostly contiguous with them, forming a large tranche of European Russia north of Moscow. The next two octiles largely fill in the gaps in the northern half of Russia and Siberia. The fifth and sixth octiles form a mid-southern belt in European Russia, extending continuously from Pskov in the west to Tatarstan in the east, and covering most of the remaining southern regions beyond the Urals. The regions in the seventh octile are largely contiguous with each other and cover the southern and south-western peripheries. Every region in the final octile – comprising the 11 regions in which there

MAP 1
RUSSIAN REGIONS BY OCTILE ACCORDING TO PROPENSITY TO VOTE
'AGAINST ALL' CANDIDATES

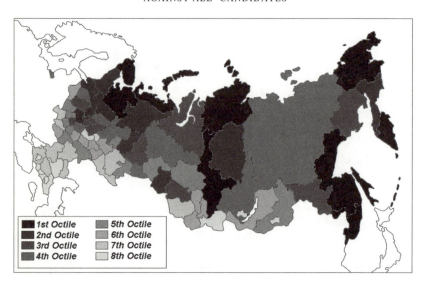

is the least propensity to vote 'against all' – is either a national republic or an autonomous district in which non-Russian ethnic groups are prevalent. Six of them are in the northern Caucasus.

When analysed by type of region, it is found that most of the national republics (16 out of 20) are in the bottom half of the list. By contrast, eight of the ten autonomous territories, which also feature stronger representations of non-Russian ethnic groups, are in the top half of the list. The propensity of the territories (*kraya*) to utilize the 'against all' option is mixed, whilst the two major cities, Moscow and St Petersburg, show fairly high 'against all' voting figures. The provinces, which form the majority of the Russian regions, are distributed throughout, with a slight majority in the upper half of the distribution.

To summarize, therefore, there are noticeable regional variations in the tendency of voters to vote 'against all'. Voters in southern areas are less likely to express their disenchantment with the political system and its actors than are their counterparts in northern Russia – in particular, in the northern and eastern peripheries of the country. What accounts for these variations? In the final section we turn to a wider discussion of the bases of electoral disengagement, contrasting the behaviour of those who abstain from voting with those 'positive negative' voters who cast their votes against all candidates.

The Bases of Protest Voting Among the Russian Electorate

Having examined the patterns of 'against all' voting, we turn now to some of the possible explanations of it. In addition to examining the bases of 'against all' voting *per se*, we can also contrast the 'positive negative' voters with their counterparts – those who abstain from the political process altogether.

The comparisons in Table 7 give some indication of the contrasts between 'positive voters' (those who cast their ballots in 1999 for one of the parties in the party list section of the election), 'negative' voters (who voted against all) and non-voters (who abstained altogether). The 'against all' subsection in the survey is relatively small, and thus care should be taken in extrapolating the results. None the less, Table 7 shows that voters who protest in some way – either through abstention or through voting 'against all' – tend to be younger than their 'positive voting' counterparts. 'Positive' voters are also more likely to be married, and a higher proportion of them are former members of the Communist Party of the Soviet Union. This suggests that those who are at present less engaged in the political system have been less engaged in the long term as well, and have lower 'social capital' than their more engaged counterparts.[27] The proportion of non-voters who have been unemployed in the past 12 months is almost twice as high as among those

TABLE 7
DEMOGRAPHIC CHARACTERISTICS, STATE DUMA ELECTION, 1999

Indicator	'Positive' voters	'Against all' voters	Non-voters	Whole electorate
N =	1129	57	743	1940
Male	46.5	51.0	44.1	45.6
Female	53.5	49.0	55.9	54.4
Mean age (years)	48.4	43.9	38.7	44.5
Pensioners	34.4	31.5	17.8	27.8
Miscellaneous				
Completed higher education	12.6	7.9	12.0	12.2
Married	61.4	52.3	48.9	56.2
Former CPSU member	14.8	1.3	5.8	10.9
Non-religious	55.9	55.5	59.3	57.2
Unemployed in last 12 months	7.8	7.9	13.8	10.0
Income				
Quartile 1	14.6	14.4	12.8	13.9
Quartile 2	31.6	29.4	29.1	30.5
Quartile 3	31.2	33.8	29.7	30.7
Quartile 4	22.7	22.4	28.4	24.9
Size of voters' village/town (inhabitants)				
Village-9,999	32.1	34.1	30.5	31.6
10,000–49,999	10.4	1.6	10.5	10.1
50,000–249,999	17.7	22.1	18.7	18.3
250,000–499,999	10.6	8.9	12.4	11.2
500,000–999,999	9.0	11.3	11.5	10.0
1,000,000 and over	20.2	22.0	16.4	18.8

Note: 'Non-religious' = never attend a religious service.

Source: New Russia Barometer VIII, conducted by VTsIOM on behalf of the Centre for the Study of Public Policy, University of Strathclyde, fieldwork 13–29 January 2000, N = 1,940. Except where indicated, the figures refer to the percentage of each category's voters, treated as discrete entities.

who voted (either for a candidate or against all of them). Similarly, the proportion of pensioners amongst the non-voting section of the electorate is significantly smaller than for positive or negative voters. In other words, it seems that those who abstain are more likely to be younger and disaffected voters who have become disengaged from the political system and abstain by default, whereas those who vote 'against all' differ from them and are actually closer in profile to positive voters.

As noted above, turnout fell marginally between the 1995 and 1999 State Duma elections. Survey data collected in the immediate aftermath of these elections indicate that one of the reasons for this was growing disenchantment with the political process. Aside from practical difficulties of getting to the polling station on election day, the most common reasons cited for non-participation were a lack of trust in politicians, a lack of political efficacy, a lack of interest in politics *per se*, and exasperation with 'fights at the top'. Between 1995 and 1999 there were marked increases in each of these indicators of political efficacy.[28] Moreover, while a slim majority (52.2 per cent) of those who participated in the Duma election in 1999 thought that the result would 'definitely' or 'somewhat' change things, the overwhelming majority of non-voters (71.5 per cent) were of the opinion that it would have little or no effect.

What, though, explains the upsurge in 'against all' voting throughout the 1990s, and in particular in the State Duma elections? Unfortunately, the survey data available did not ask why people who voted 'against all' had done so. None the less, through the use of various data it is possible to build up a pattern of what sort of regions and people are likely to vote 'against all'. It would be unwise to infer causal relationships, but there are a number of factors that do appear to be related to the 'against all' vote.

The bivariate correlations shown in Table 8 yield some fascinating information. There are a number of statistically significant correlations of varying strengths between the 'against all' vote and other factors. It might be expected that constituencies in which there was a higher turnout would also be those in which there would be a greater propensity to vote 'against all' (on the basis that, since fewer protest voters were abstaining, a greater number of them would be tempted to go to the polls but vote 'against all'). In fact, though, it can be seen that there is a negative correlation between the turnout in each constituency in the 1995 State Duma election and the proportion of votes cast against all candidates. In other words, proportionately fewer votes were cast 'against all' in constituencies where turnout was highest, a finding counter-intuitive to our hypothesis. However, this is perhaps explained by the negative correlations between turnout and both the levels of higher education and the proportion of urban dwellers in each constituency; and a positive correlation between turnout and the proportion of elderly voters in a constituency. This confirms the observation made above that it is difficult to assess levels of civic disengagement in Russia through turnout figures alone, since the voting culture is strongest in regions where the population is predominantly rural, elderly and politically compliant – and therefore least likely to vote 'against all'. By contrast, urban dwellers have less compunction about voting in protest.

On the other hand, significant positive correlations between the 'against all' vote and the proportion of ethnic Russians in constituencies is of great interest. It suggests that those seats in which non-Russians are to be found in greater number are less likely to vote 'against all' than their more Slavic-dominated counterparts. This confirms the finding from the regional index of 'against all' voting, in which the majority of the ethnic-based national

TABLE 8
BIVARIATE CORRELATIONS, 1995 AND 1999 STATE DUMA ELECTIONS

	Turnout 1995	SMD against all vote 1995	PL against all vote 1995	SMD against all vote 1999	PL against all vote 1999	Ethnic Russians	Higher education	Urban population	Elderly (>60 years)
Turnout 1995	1	–	–	–	–	–	–	–	–
SMD against all vote 1995	−.288**	1	–	–	–	–	–	–	–
PL against all vote 1995	−.302**	.492**	1	–	–	–	–	–	–
SMD % against all 1999	−.308**	.445**	.240**	1	–	–	–	–	–
PL against all vote 1999	−.361**	.515**	.606**	.575**	1	–	–	–	–
Ethnic Russians	−.093	.362**	.066	.418**	.490**	1	–	–	–
Higher education	−.338**	.324**	.152*	.416**	.453**	0.234**	1	–	–
Urban population	−.588**	.409**	.232**	.509**	.577**	0.371**	.716**	1	–
Elderly (>60 years) (excluding federal cities)	.347**	−.174*	−.519**	−.007	−.167*	0.401**	−.226**	−.210**	1
Ethnic Russians (excluding federal cities)	−.077	.345**	.065	.408**	.475**	1	–	–	–
Higher education (excluding federal cities)	−.417**	.195**	.236**	.345**	.488**	0.187**	1	–	–

Sources: As tables 1–4 for electoral data; Michael McFaul *et al.*, *Primer on Russia's 1999 Duma Elections* (Moscow: Carnegie, 1999), pp.132–7, for non-election parameters – expressed in the data set as the percentage of the population falling into the category shown (i.e., percentage of Russians, percentage of urban dwellers, etc.).

Notes: The figures for Moscow city and St Petersburg are averages for the whole city, rather than for each specific seat. To preserve accuracy, these were excluded from the analysis in the bottom three lines to retain a true seat-by-seat comparison. Table 8 gives Pearson *r*, where $-1 < r < +1$. ** = statistically significant at $p < .01$, * = statistically significant at $p < .05$.

republics were to be found in the bottom half of the list. It is also consistent with the findings of an earlier analysis by Akhremenko and Meleshkina (admittedly using regional-level data, rather than the constituency-level figures utilized for the present investigation).[29] Some of these ethnic regions (such as Tatarstan, Bashkortostan and various republics in the North Caucasus) are well known for the level of control apparently exerted over the electorate by their ruling elites, and traditionally have recorded high numbers of votes for the 'party of power'. Thus it can be observed that in the regions and republics with more *upravlyaemyi* ('managed') electorates, voters are more reluctant to vote 'against all'.

It will be recalled, however, that there were a few 'ethnic outliers' – particularly some of the autonomous territories – which were to be found near the top of the list. Akhremenko and Meleshkina explain this by observing that republics and autonomous areas where the 'titular' ethnic group forms a relatively small proportion of the population tend to vote in more substantial numbers 'against all' than those in which non-Russians are in the majority.

Among the strongest relationships in the table are those between the 'against all' vote and the proportion of urban voters. This suggests once again that the rural electorate is more politically compliant than its urban counterpart, and it is confirmed by the high proportions of votes 'against all' seen in the two largest cities in Russia, Moscow and St Petersburg. The relationship between the 'against all' vote and the proportion of elderly voters has generally been relatively weak, although the significant negative correlations in three of the four election results examined here indicates that 'against all' voters are indeed slightly more likely to be young than elderly.

When combined with the other data in the table, we can begin to build up a picture of the profile of protest voters. People who vote against all candidates are more likely to be highly educated urban dwellers than poorly educated rural ones; to be slightly younger than their 'positive voting' equivalents; and to be ethnic Russians. Whilst non-voters appear to lack the social capital and political engagement of those who go to the polls, the 'against all' vote is by contrast greatest amongst voters who are better able to scrutinize the political situation, possessing not only a wider range of information resources (rural media coverage tends to be relatively narrow by comparison with towns and cities), but also higher levels of education with which to analyse this information. The slightly more critical attitudes of the 'positive negative' voters are confirmed in their attitudes towards democracy itself. Substantial numbers in both categories thought in 2000 that a key facet of democracy was the 'freedom to criticize the government'. However, the percentage of 'against all' voters who thought that it was 'essential' or at least 'important' (83.4 per cent) was somewhat higher than among non-voters (71.4 per cent).[30]

Conclusion

The foregoing analysis has examined the growing tendency among the Russian electorate to vote 'against all', and has, where appropriate, contrasted the behaviour of 'against all' voters with those who abstain from voting altogether. It was seen in the first section that the 'against all' option has become more significant as a legal concept over the past decade, and can now, in certain circumstances, invalidate elections. However, sometimes the consequences of an 'against all' vote can be more far-reaching than a voter may foresee. The second section used election data to examine the phenomenon in greater detail. It was seen that voters tend to vote 'against all' in greater number when a large proportion of such protest votes can make a difference – namely, in plurality or majoritarian contests with relatively small district magnitude. Thereafter, an attempt to map the patterns of 'against all' voting showed a significant north–south split in voting behaviour. The final section attempted to explain the variations in abstention and 'against all' voting by examining factors that may be related to the two phenomena, and discovered some significant relationships between 'against all' voting, ethnic origin, urban dwelling and education levels.

In general, non-voters appear to be disengaged. By contrast, the 'against all' voter may be politically disaffected. As was seen above, 'against all' voters are more likely to be found in areas with good information resources and high levels of education. Rather than simply dropping out of the political system altogether as non-voters do, the 'against all' voter instead chooses to incur the costs of voting in order to register a conscious protest *against* all candidates. Thus it may be misleading to talk of 'civic disengagement' *per se* when discussing the vote 'against all' in the Russian Federation. Rather, it seems that the phenomenon can be seen as an example of 'positive' negative voting, allowing the disaffected and disenchanted to register their protest while remaining engaged with the political system in a broader sense.

NOTES

1. Robert D. Putnam, *Bowling Alone: The Collapse and Revival of American Community* (New York and London: Simon & Schuster, 2000); Peter Mair and Ingrid van Biezen, 'Party Membership in Twenty European Democracies, 1980–2000', *Party Politics*, Vol.7, No.1 (2001), pp.5–22; Pippa Norris, *Democratic Phoenix: Reinventing Political Activism* (Cambridge: Cambridge University Press, 2002).
2. Ruy A. Teixeira, *Why Americans Don't Vote: Turnout Decline in the United States* (New York and London: Greenwood, 1987); Alan Siaroff and John W. Merer, 'Parliamentary Election Turnout in Europe since 1990', *Political Studies*, Vol.50, No.5 (2002), pp.916–27; Martin P. Wattenburg, *Where Have All the Voters Gone?* (Cambridge, MA and London: Harvard University Press, 2002); Colin Rallings, Michael Thrasher and G. Borisyuk, 'Seasonal Factors, Voter Fatigue and the Costs of Voting', *Electoral Studies*, Vol.22, No.1 (2003), pp.65–79.

3. Stephen White and Ian McAllister, *Political Participation in Postcommunist Russia: Voting, Activism and the Potential for Mass Protest* (Glasgow: Centre for the Study of Public Policy, 1994); Stephen White and Ian McAllister, 'To Vote or Not to Vote: Election Turnout in Post-Communist Russia', in Matthew Wyman, Stephen White and Sarah Oates (eds.), *Elections and Voters in Post-Communist Russia* (Cheltenham: Edward Elgar, 1998), pp.15–39; Robert E. Bohrer II, Alexander C. Pacek and Benjamin Radcliff, 'Electoral Participation, Ideology, and Party Politics in Post-Communist Europe', *Journal of Politics*, Vol.62, No.4 (2000), pp.1161–72; Tatiana Kostadinova, 'Voter Turnout Dynamics in Post-Communist Europe', *European Journal of Political Research*, Vol.42, No.6 (2003), pp.741–59.

4. A.S. Akhremenko, 'Golosovanie "protiv vsekh" na rossiiskom regional'nom fone', *Vestnik Moskovskogo Universiteta*, Series 12, No.5 (2001), pp.97–111; A.S. Akhremenko and E.Yu. Meleshkina, 'Golosovanie "protiv vsekh" kak forma politicheskogo protesta: problemy izucheniya', *Politicheskaya nauka*, No.1 (2002), pp.21–43; K.V. D'yakova, 'Protiv vsekh byvayut ne tol'ko mukhomory', *Zhurnal o vyborakh*, No.1 (2002), pp.37–9; Hans Oversloot, Joop van Holsteyn and Ger P. van der Berg, 'Against All: Exploring the Vote "Against All" in the Russian Federation's Electoral System', *Journal of Communist Studies and Transition Politics*, Vol.18, No.4 (2002), pp.31–50.

5. For further examination of theoretical background to this discussion, see Anthony Downs, *An Economic Theory of Democracy* (New York: Harper & Row, 1957); and Mancur Olson, *The Logic of Collective Action* (New York: Schocken, 1965).

6. In the USSR, voters were deemed to have voted in favour of the (usually single) candidate on the ballot paper if they simply left it unmarked. They could, however, choose to vote against the candidate by crossing his or her name out. This provision was rarely used, since it involved going into the polling booth, which drew attention to their non-conformity. In the present Russian voting system, 'against all candidates' is listed at the bottom of the ballot paper alongside 'real' candidates. Voters put a mark against their favoured candidate, or in the box for 'against all'.

7. Polozhenie, 'O vyborakh deputatov Gosudarstvennoi Dumy v 1993 godu', Presidential Decree No.1557 (1 Oct. 1993), §39, in *Rossiiskaya Gazeta*, 8 Oct. 1993, pp.3–5. Elections to the State Duma are split into two halves: 225 deputies are elected from single-member districts through a 'first past the post' system similar to that used in Britain, and the remaining 225 are elected from federal party lists.

8. Federal'nyi zakon, 'O vyborakh deputatov Gosudarstvennoi Dumy Federal'nogo Sobraniya Rossiiskoi Federatsii', Law No.90-F3 (21 June 1995), §61, in *Rossiiskaya Gazeta*, 28 June 1995, pp.3–7.

9. The deputies in question were V.F. Grigor'ev and V.A. Vorogushin (constituencies 99 and 100, Leningrad province); and I.S. Anichkin (constituency 125, Novosibirsk province).

10. Federal'nyi zakon, 'O vyborakh Prezidenta Rossiiskoi Federatsii', No.76-F3 (17 May 1995), Section 1924, §§55–56, in *Sobranie Zakonodatel'stva Rossiiskoi Federatsii*, 1995, No.21.

11. Federal'nyi zakon, 'Ob osnovnykh garantiyakh izbiratel'nykh prav i prava na uchastie v referendume grazhdan Rossiiskoi Federatsii', No.124-F3 (19 Sept. 1997), amendments on 30 March 1999 (No.55-F3), published in *Rossiiskaya Gazeta*, 6 April 1999. Full revised text contained in *Federal'nyi zakon' 'Ob osnovnykh garantiyakh izbiratel'nykh prav i prava na uchastie v referendume grazhdan Rossiiskoi Federatsii'* (Moscow: Yurisprudentsiya, 1999); the article referred to here is §58.2.

12. Federal'nyi zakon, 'O vyborakh deputatov Gosudarstvennoi Dumy Federal'nogo Sobraniya Rossiiskoi Federatsii', Law No.121-F3 (24 June 1999), in *Rossiiskaya Gazeta*, 1 July 1999, pp.9–16 (Part 1); ibid., 3 July 1999, pp.9–16 (Part 2), §79.2.

13. Federal'nyi zakon, 'O vyborakh Prezidenta Rossiiskoi Federatsii', No.228-F3 (31 Dec. 1999), in *Rossiiskaya Gazeta*, 5 Jan. 2000, §§72.4 and 73.4.

14. Federal'nyi zakon, 'Ob osnovnykh garantiyakh izbiratel'nykh prav i prava na uchastie v referendume grazhdan Rossiiskoi Federatsii', Law No.67-F3 (12 June 2002), §70.2, in *Rossiiskaya Gazeta*, 15 June 2002, pp.7–14.

15. Oversloot *et al.*, 'Against All', pp.31–50.

16. Parties are required, in the first instance, to obtain more than five per cent of the vote in the party list section of State Duma elections before winning representation in the parliament.

17. *Vybory v organy gosudarstvennoi vlasti sub"ektov Rossiiskoi Federatsii. 1997–2000* (Moscow: CEC/Ves' Mir, 2001), Vol.2, pp.635–41; and contemporary observation by the author.

18. For the analysis in this and the following section, a data set of election results was compiled from official electoral commission statistics. For federal elections, the following sources were used: *Byulleten' Tsentral'noi Izbiratel'noi Komissii Rossiiskoi Federatsii*, No.1, 12 (1994); *Vybory deputatov Gosudarstvennoi Dumy. 1995. Elektoral'naya statistika* (Moscow: CEC/Ves' Mir, 1996), pp.103–44 and 157–98; *Vybory Prezidenta Rossiiskoi Federatsii. 1996. Elektoral'naya statistika* (Moscow: CEC/Ves' Mir, 1996), pp.47–9 and 151–69; *Vybory deputatov Gosudarstvennoi Dumy Federal'nogo Sobraniya Rossiiskoi Federatsii. 1999. Elektoral'naya statistika* (Moscow: CEC/Ves' Mir, 2000), pp.138–71 and 182–208; *Vybory Prezidenta Rossiiskoi Federatsii. 2000. Elektoral'naya statistika* (Moscow: CEC/ Ves' Mir, 2000), pp.184–6 and 203–8. For regional and local elections, data were taken from *Vybory glav izpolnitel'noi vlasti sub"ektov Rossiiskoi Federatsii. 1995–97. Elektoral'- naya statistika* (Moscow: CEC/Ves' Mir, 1997); *Vybory v organy gosudarstvennoi vlasti sub"ektov Rossiiskoi Federatsii. 1997–2000*, 2 vols (Moscow: CEC/Ves' Mir, 2001); A.Kh. Khasanov, V.N. Kamen'kova and R.M. Vakhitova (eds.), *Po veleniyu serdtsa: Vybory Prezidenta Respubliki Tatarstan 25 marta 2001 goda: Dokumenty. Materialy. Itogi* (Kazan': Matbugat yuorty, 2002); Central Electoral Commission website <http:// www.cikrf.ru>; website of the Electoral Commission of the Republic of Buryatiya <http://electoral. buryatia.ru>; website of the Electoral Commission of the Republic of Komi <http://www.rkomi.ru/izbirkom/glava_2001/itog.html>. For a significant number of post-2000 gubernatorial elections, the details available on the Central Electoral Commis- sion or subject electoral commission websites are incomplete. For the purposes of the present analysis, gubernatorial elections have been included only if complete information is available on them from an official source; for this reason, only 63 of the 89 regions are used for analysis of the second wave of gubernatorial elections (1997–2003).

19. *Nezavisimaya Gazeta*, 10 June 2003, p.4. In the latest election to the Vladivostok city Duma, in June 2003, average turnout was just 17 per cent, but on this occasion the election was declared valid.

20. For example, in Tatarstan – which traditionally has one of the highest turnout figures in the Russian Federation – the turnout for the 2000 presidential election was officially recorded as being above 95 per cent in more than half the rural districts, but was below 85 per cent in all but one of 19 urban districts: 'Svedeniya ob itogakh vyborov Prezidenta Rossiiskoi Federatsii 26 Marta 2000 goda', given to the author by the Central Electoral Commission of the Republic of Tatarstan, 25 May 2000.

21. Figures recalculated from the results published by the Central Electoral Commission (see note 18). In 1999 only 224 seats were contested, since no election took place in Chechnya.

22. Derek S. Hutcheson, *Political Parties in the Russian Regions* (London and New York: RoutledgeCurzon, 2003), Ch.6.

23. The Russian Federation is divided into 89 regions – or 'constituent 'subjects' – with varying levels of autonomy.

24. The elections used were the 1995 and 1999 State Duma elections (single-member district and party list treated discretely); the 1996 presidential election (first and second rounds treated discretely); and the 2000 presidential election.

25. To calculate the index, the 'against all' vote totals for each region in each of the major federal elections from 1995 to 2000 were placed in descending order. (Mean values from all the con- stituencies within each region were used for the single-member district State Duma elections.) The mean rank for all federal elections (seven categories from four elections) was calculated. The regions with the lowest mean figures were those that had ranked highest overall for 'against all' votes. Where figures were available for Chechnya, they were included for ranking purposes for the individual elections, but the republic was excluded from the final cal- culation, since the data were incomplete. The mean figures were then placed in descending order to give an index of 'against all' voting across the Russian regions, shown in Table 6.

26. When the rankings produced by the two methods (mean vote and mean ranking) are com- pared, the variation in placing is in most cases not substantial. Six regions would move

more than ten places up the table using mean vote share rather than mean ranking; five would move more than ten places down; and the remaining 77 regions would shift by fewer than ten places.

27. For further discussion of 'social capital' see Putnam, *Bowling Alone*.
28. National Representative Survey conducted for the University of Glasgow by VTsIOM (All-Russian Centre for the Investigation of Public Opinion), fieldwork 20–26 Dec. 1995, N = 1,568, question 16; and NRB VIII survey, question d.9.
29. Akhremenko, 'Golosovanie "protiv vsekh"', pp.104–5; Akhremenko and Meleshkina, 'Golosovanie "protiv vsekh" kak forma politicheskogo protesta', pp.21–43.
30. New Russia Barometer VIII, conducted by VTsIOM on behalf of the Centre for the Study of Public Policy, University of Strathclyde, fieldwork 13–29 Jan. 2000, N = 1,940.

The Quality of Democracy in Belarus and Ukraine

ELENA A. KOROSTELEVA

Introduction

The objectives of this essay are to examine the quality of democracy[1] in Belarus and Ukraine comparatively, and to define what kind of polities are at present developing in these countries.

Before embarking upon this discussion, however, a delineation of some preceding analytical grounds is necessary. First, when discussing new regimes we shall not mean transitions, but consolidated entities, no matter how 'informal' or 'illusory'[2] they appear to be. That is, entities that have acquired some level of 'normalcy'[3] characterized by a degree of stability and predictability for further development.

Second, despite the fact that the term 'democracy' has been in use for more than 2,000 years, there remains much confusion about the meaning and the forms democracy may take, and by virtue of this, less democratic regimes.[4] Contemporary debates in political science find defining *modern* regimes difficult owing to their diversification and proliferation. Not only have older regimes now evolved to display features that sometimes challenge our conventional expectations of democracy, but also the rise of new regimes associated with more complex and mixed environments necessitates the conceptual clarification of what modern democracy should really connote. Our discussion will, therefore, be premised on the conviction that, first, there can be as many forms of democracy – from liberal to delegative and demagogical – as there are different states, so long as the citizenry are formally granted an opportunity to elect and control government under a constitutional law.[5]

Third, this leads us to postulate that a liberal democracy (the conventional Western theory of democracy) may not necessarily be the only or the best way to form a sustainable government. Furthermore, there may be other forms of regime that could theoretically compete with democracy in their provision of governance for stable states accommodating cultural diversity of their citizenry and structural foundations for forming a partnership.

This brings us to the final thesis of our preamble. Not only it is important to refine our understanding of democracy *per se*, but what matters too is the yielding of adequate instruments with which we can measure democratic progress and achieve a better theory of democracy in its various incarnations. This article will follow the course set by Guillermo O'Donnell, who reiterates the significance of the *agency* (citizenry, in Aristotle's term), along with elections and freedoms, viewing 'every individual as a legal person, a carrier of subjective rights that makes choices and is assigned responsibility for them'.[6] It will be demonstrated that our procedural definition of democracy as 'the only game in town'[7] which includes 'free and fair institutionalized elections' and some surrounding 'freedoms or guarantees' that are necessary for holding such elections, may not be sufficient for understanding the workings of democracy or indeed for explaining why liberal democracy is not occurring in many new regimes around the world. What is needed instead is a fresh focus on citizens' 'enlightened understanding'[8] of democracy and its institutional forms, and re-evaluation of the role of 'agency' acting within the legal framework of a newly consolidated polity.

Revisiting the Role of 'Agency' in Defining Democracy

Existing definitions of democracy seemingly fail to address adequately the proliferation and diversification of new regimes. In an attempt to anchor their expanding quantity and differing quality, scholars reduced their efforts to deploying various minimalist, parsimonious approaches to identify, forecast and compare the development of new regimes with established democracies. The most influential definitions of democracy essentially identify the practice of elections as the focal point of democracy-building that allows citizens, through universal franchise, to exercise their right to vote and choose a government of their own preference.

Schumpeter's oft-cited definition of democracy states that it is 'a political method . . . a certain type of institutional arrangements for arriving at political – legislative and administrative – decisions'.[9] Through this institutional arrangement 'individuals acquire the power to decide by means of a competitive struggle for the people's vote'. It is that kind of 'competition for leadership' that defines democracy as 'free competition for a free vote'. This is the paradigmatic 'minimalist' (or 'procedural') definition of democracy that focuses on the electoral process and, when considered institutionalized, describes regimes as democratic, expecting that free and fair elections will necessarily pave the way towards citizens' 'excellence of living under a constitutional rule'.[10] As a result, many new regimes that have displayed signs of such institutional arrangements were treated as democratic and expected to progress towards a liberal form of democracy. According to David Beetham, this was a common error when the meaning of democracy had been equated with its institutional forms, which meant no more than elevating a means into an end, and confusing an instrument with its purpose.[11]

However, Schumpeter also outlined several caveats to his definition, stating first that 'the electoral method is practically the only one available for communities of any size', which should not exclude other, less competitive 'ways of securing leadership ... and we cannot exclude them because if we did we should be left with a completely unrealistic ideal'; and second, the competition for leadership should also be 'implicitly' related to 'the legal and moral principles of the community'.[12] In other words, the famous definition turns out not to be as 'minimalist' as its isolated reading may first suggest, and implies the idea of multiple forms of democracy that may differ from the ideal, as well as the connection with the moral and legal spirit of the community, which is regarded as the cornerstone for building democracy. This, however, has been lineally interpreted with the intention of introducing a common denominator to compare proliferating regimes, failing, nevertheless, to address their individual trajectories as well as their 'non- or not entirely-democratic' properties.

In a similar vein, Huntington refers to democracy as a political system that exists 'to the extent that its most powerful collective decision makers are selected through fair, honest and periodic elections in which candidates freely compete for votes and in which virtually all the adult population is eligible to vote'.[13] Furthermore, he supports the treatment of democracy as a 'continuous variable' that may be deployed to identify degrees of democracy amongst different countries, and this makes his definition of democracy less parsimonious or exclusive than it may have originally seemed.

Larry Diamond, Juan Linz and Seymour Martin Lipset in their assessment of new regimes offer a more extended but similarly parsimonious version of the definition of democracy, that is,

> a system of government that meets three essential conditions: meaningful and extensive *competition* among individuals and organized groups (especially political parties) for all effective positions of governmental power, at regular intervals and excluding the use of force; a 'highly inclusive' level of *political participation* in the selections of leaders and policies, at least through regular and fair elections, such that no major social group is excluded; and a level of *civil and political liberties* – freedom of expression and the press, freedom to form and join organizations – sufficient to ensure the integrity of political competition and participation.[14]

All these definitions appear to be heavily centred on institutionalized elections and surrounding freedoms that are seen as either necessary or sufficient for the fair functioning of elections. However, what the practice of some modern

regimes suggests instead is that, although elections may well be institutionalized and run at constitutionally defined intervals, voters may have the right to
participate and compete for elections, and a regime itself may be sustainable,
nevertheless these features do not make the workings of a system more democratic, and at best it will remain a 'quasi-democracy'. This tendency has
spawned a discussion regarding the nature of hybrid regimes[15] and the rise
of competitive authoritarianism,[16] which in many ways resembles Aristotle's
definition of a demagogical democracy that presumes a certain settlement of
democratic institutions, but legally and 'morally' provides grounds for the
succession or the rise of yet another authoritarian leader.

Robert Dahl's definition of polyarchy – that is, a polity that presupposes
varied forms of realization of an ideal of democracy – is one of the very few
exceptions to the above conceptual parlance. He views democracy as an
opportunity for citizens (i) to formulate, (ii) to signify and (iii) to have preferences weighted equally in the conduct of government.[17] He turns his focus *on
and away from* elections, postulating the significance of the life of the citizenry during the interim periods and, more importantly, the significance of
their awareness, knowledge and 'enlightened understanding' of their rights
and responsibilities.[18]

This is where O'Donnell takes the discussion further by suggesting that the
reason for the lack of conceptual clarity in defining modern democracy lies not
with the numbers or diversification of the new regimes, but with the fact that
citizens, as 'autonomous, reasonable and responsible social beings',[19] were
hitherto excluded from the process of *defining* democracy.

The logic of the new regime is such that, when it imports the institutional
paraphernalia of democracy (elections, constitution, parliament and so on),
it also acquires a legal system that constitutes the rights and responsibilities
of a legal human being. This, however, when *morally* ungrounded, may cause
a severe disjunction 'between these rights and the general texture of society'.
The workings of such a regime are determined not so much by an institutional
or legal framework as by understanding the expectations and behaviour that
citizens of a given country display. The process of building democracy in
these circumstances resembles an impossible process of building a ship at
sea[20] – that is, placing an institutional-cum-legal carcass of an intended democratic polity on the non-existent or deficient social capital[21] of a given society.
The outcome is usually such that new regimes either tend to move in circles
(as in the case of Ukraine) or shift to an authoritarian government (as in the
case of Belarus), inasmuch as the electorate is not prepared to reciprocate mul-
tilaterally with elected governments or to introduce a 'politically responsible'
texture into an imported concept of democracy. Furthermore, in such regimes,
the vigour of political awareness or citizens' 'enlightened understanding' is
further impaired by the general effectiveness of the legal system, which is

often reinforced to serve the rulers rather then the ruled. This is due to the inability of the ruled to negotiate their rights with the appointed government on a mutual basis. Differing levels of citizens' political awareness,[22] therefore, stipulate (i) that democracy may evince differentiation in its forms; (ii) that democracy may not be the only or the best form of a sustainable government; and finally (iii) that citizens are treated by their governments in accordance with the level of their political awareness and readiness to negotiate.

On the Meaning of a Demagogical Democracy

When analysing democracy we generally restrict ourselves to the belief that the prevailing liberal-representative form is pre-eminent, yet in the changing contemporary world this may not be the best means to form strong, stable government. Instead, democratic government as a partnership between the governed and the governors is versatile and sensitive to the needs of such partnership. The form of democracy should, therefore, be defined by the citizenry and in accordance with its aspirations and the level of political engagement. The purpose of the partnership is to achieve 'a life of excellence' for individuals under a constitutional rule, no matter what form of democracy or regime in general this entails.

For much of political history democracy was not seen as an ideal to be achieved. Other forms of government were viewed as more capable of providing order to society. Aristotle, for example, following his teacher Plato, and in that Socrates, saw democracy as a *perversion* of a constitutional form of government. He argued that democracy viewed the interests of the needy as paramount, not the common good of all. In fact, he stated, there may be no ideal form of government. Machiavelli likewise echoes a similar belief that the ideal form would be a *fusion* of the two perversions – democracy and oligarchy:

> In a well attempted polity there should appear to be both elements and yet neither ... They might be equally well-disposed when there is a vicious form of government – but through the general willingness of all classes in the state to maintain the constitution.[23]

Many new regimes have achieved a degree of stability trying to accommodate their citizens' needs through seeking their approval in accordance with the system's legal and institutional potential. Many of them are also cases of a 'lesser democratic presence' – that is, they are less than democratic, although not necessarily authoritarian – but nevertheless should be viewed within the continuum of democracy reflecting the level of 'enlightened' partnership between the governed and their governors.[24] Aristotle, for example, pointed out that of all existing forms of democracy there is one that is particularly vulnerable to oligarchic manipulation and dictate, which he labels a 'demagogical democracy'.

This sort of democracy, he argued, is open to the objection that it is not constitutionally valid because decrees supersede the law. He wrote:

> There are different forms of democracy ... A fifth form of democracy is that in which not the law, but the multitude have the supreme power, and supersede the law by their decrees. This is a state of affairs brought about by the demagogues ... The demagogues make the decrees of the people override the laws, by referring all things to the popular assembly. And therefore they grow great, because the people have all things in their hands, and they hold in their hands the votes of the people, who obey them ...[25]

Nevertheless, Aristotle continued to refer to this regime from its outset as a form of *democracy*.[26] It may be the worst of its kind, but it still remains a democracy by assuming constitutional arrangements that cannot be overruled, but are negotiated with and approved by the citizenry. On a democratic continuum, a demagogical democracy reflects a borderline case, being neither democracy nor dictatorship. It is in a way a 'quasi-democracy', an 'almost' democracy, associated with sustainable government and quasi-democratic workings of the system, which nevertheless keep the citizens (quasi-)content.

This kind of democracy thrives in a legally biased framework that favours the rulers, and is associated with a relatively low level of political awareness on the part of citizens. A demagogical democracy functions to create the perfect illusion of a democratic partnership between those in power and their retinue who elect them to act on their behalf, and to make voters believe that their opinion matters. It allows provisions for elections, the conditions that surround them, and other institutional arrangements, as well as providing grounds for a 'quasi-informed choice' and 'quasi-control' over decision making. It can be viewed as an 'almost' democracy because of its democratic institutional arrangements, which imply that no open alteration of the Constitution is possible without popular consent. The essence of such democracy, however, is *manipulation*, and no matter how quasi-inclusive and competitive the relationship is, it suggests a strong bias towards the rulers – the demagogues – who use the low level of public consciousness to negotiate their benefits from the system legally.

Such partnership may eventually develop into 'a collective monarchy', allowing the citizens to rule as 'many in one'. When 'the many have the power in their hand, not as individuals, but collectively', the regime is no longer under the control of law, and will seek to exercise merciless authority in an attempt to maintain order and to be in control of public disaffection. 'This sort of system in which all things [become] regulated by decrees, is clearly no longer a democracy in a true sense of the word ... for decrees relate only to particulars'.[27] It therefore favours those in power, or as Levitsky and Way put it, 'these are regimes in which democratic rules simply serve as to legitimate an existing autocratic leadership'.[28]

The quintessence of a demagogical democracy, therefore, is the public learning and public bond that exists between the rulers and the ruled, because the ruler can only 'reign' above the law when full legitimacy and the approval of the ruled has been obtained. This public bond includes the process of mutual satisfaction and admiration, and also an understanding that, without each other, both parties will lose the ability and opportunity to govern. The ruler needs 'the mob' to sustain his authority in office. When growing in strength, he will require a collective *aficionado* to appreciate his deeds, which he begins to see as the great 'altruistic' gift to his people as well as an obligation to continue his 'rule'. In return, the ruled need the impression of involvement and influence over government decision making, which also imparts trust and confidence in their choice of the leader. In addition, they need a comrade, and a common man who can understand their needs and represent their views authoritatively. In this, they fall into a 'cursed partnership' when, instead of improving their situation, they live in anticipation of it, achieved through continuous pledges and changes in the Constitution. The temporary winner here is the leader who continues ruling through negotiation and coercion when negotiation ceases to appeal. The longer the partnership lasts, the more likely it is to acquire 'tyrannical' features and eventually outlast its democratic format. Covert coercion, forcible mass mobilization and the introduction of state ideology may become the typical measures of keeping the balance of power in place, until the mob learn ('enlightened understanding') from their experience about the inadequacy of such a partnership.

The gestation period for a demagogical democracy can be lengthy and intricate. It becomes sustainable when a legal system begins to stipulate such a relationship. When a ruler is overthrown the legal framework may continue to function in the same way, thereby harnessing the evolution of the new order. Typifying examples of how a demagogical democracy becomes embedded are indicated in the situation in Ukraine, where negotiations regarding changes to the Constitution have been suggested by the president in the light of the 2004 presidential election, and in Belarus especially, after the alteration of the Constitution in 1996 which ensures governance by decree and presidential omnipotence. Its strength lies with the uninformed mob and their lack of understanding of the workings of democracy.

'Demagogical Democracy' in Belarus and Ukraine: Tentative Conclusions

In the light of the above deliberations about democracy, we now ask whether Belarus and Ukraine are cases of a demagogical democracy. They are neither fully authoritarian, nor fully democratic. They may be typified more as 'quasi-democratic' by having institutionalized elections and certain freedoms, all-level representation and constitutional rule, when formally all are subject to law, and no amendments are possible without popular consent. The legal system, however, works not to protect the agency – that is 'legal, sensible and responsible individuals' – but to legitimize the leadership. It also functions through decrees and constitutional reforms, as well as through the invisible mechanisms of legal control and manipulation. The purpose of enforced control is to reduce the scope for the acquisition of political literacy by the voters, and hence their ability to reciprocate over their rights and duties.

Belarus and Ukraine are two new regimes that seem to fit the criteria of a procedural definition of democracy (in varying degrees), a 'quasi-democracy' that allows for certain institutional arrangements of democracy, but no provisions for appropriate 'moral conduct' on the part of the agency, which is the case in a demagogical democracy. Belarus has steadily mastered its way of 'quasi-negotiation' and 'quasi-partnership' between the leadership and the citizens, which is reflected in the words of the Belarusian president, Alexander Lukashenko, asserting that 'if the people of Belarus ask me to continue my job, or if national circumstances change to instability and chaos, I will consider running for the third term in office, no matter what'.[29] Ukraine, by way of comparison, is currently struggling to realign the needs of the leadership and to curb people's political learning and literacy in order to remain in control.

To understand how both regimes function and what the future of demagogical democracy holds for them, we shall examine the *modus operandi* of the public mind-set – conventionally, a pivot of regime stability or change – which shall include people's understanding of democracy, their attitudes, expectations and reasoning that ensue their voting behaviour and support for current leadership.

National Surveys: From 1998 to 2003[30]

The 2003 surveys in Belarus and Ukraine were designed in such a way as to reflect any change that might have occurred in the public mind-set between 1998 and 2003, a five-year period of cumulative change stimulated and verified by both parliamentary (2000 in Belarus and 2002 in Ukraine) and presidential (2001 in Belarus and 1999 in Ukraine) elections – a third institutionalized electoral cycle between the early 1990s and 2003 that assumes the presence of certain freedoms to allow for free and fair competition.[31] Respondents were asked a similar set of questions to those in 1998 to reflect their understanding of democracy as well as to determine whether their values and trust in various institutions had altered.

After 12 years of the presence of democratic institutions (elections, parliament, relatively free mass media, jurisprudence and so on), the voters were expected to adopt democratic discourse both attitudinally and behaviourally.

This, however, has not been the case. Survey evidence suggests a great deal of inconsistency in people's value orientation and their behaviour. It emerged that 'institutionally' the citizens of both countries are ready to foster democratic foundations, which is not the case with their 'attitudinal' or 'moral' conduct. In other words, the institutional paraphernalia of democracy may seem to have been successfully established and endure in the public mind, whereas their value orientation has remained largely unaltered, or regressed towards more 'authoritarian' judgements over time.

On a positive note, some noticeable changes towards democratic institutions may be observed. The 2003 surveys reveal that people generally oppose direct presidential rule, censorship of the mass media and the abolition of parties. They also deem anti-democratic and inhumane the use of force by police and troops to curb protest marches, the sentencing of protesters by the courts, and laws passed by parliament to ban demonstrations. Furthermore, in both countries elections are seen by a majority of respondents as the best way to obtain democratic government, and parliament as important 'for improving the situation of the country' (see Table 1).

TABLE 1
PUBLIC ATTITUDES TO DEMOCRATIC INSTITUTIONS AND VALUES, 2003

	Belarus (per cent)		Ukraine (per cent)	
Would you approve of . . .?	Entirely or somewhat agree	Entirely or somewhat disagree	Entirely or somewhat agree	Entirely or somewhat disagree
Direct presidential rule	44	43	36	55
Strict censorship of the media	28	61	29	63
Abolition of parties and civil organizations	24	58	28	51
The use of force by police	20	67	9	84
Courts' sentencing	22	64	9	79
Laws to ban protests	10	76	5	87
The use of troops	7	81	3	93

Notes: The above responses are based on the questions, 'Would you agree that in a situation of emergency it would be better if (i) the president introduces direct presidential rule; (ii) there is strict media censorship; (iii) we get rid of political parties and civil organizations; (iv) the police's rights are expanded; (v) the police use force against protestors; (vi) courts use severe sentences to prosecute protestors; (vii) the government passes laws to forbid public protests; and (viii) the government uses troops to stop strikes?' Figures in rows do not add up to 100 per cent because of the existence of other options ('don't know' and 'refused to answer'), which were excluded from the analysis. Percentages are rounded up to the nearest whole number; 0.5 is rounded up.

Source: Author's survey.

These positive patterns of opinion, however, run in contradiction with the fact that a third of each population were still undecided about the role parliament plays, and were certain that democracy was an alien regime to their respective country; about half could find no differences between existing parties, and the majority believed that parties served the interests of their leaders. Moreover, an absolute majority in both countries thought that politicians were not to be trusted, and that they, as always, manipulated public opinion to their advantage. This had risen by ten per cent in Belarus, and 20 per cent in Ukraine, since 1998.

These tendencies have been further escalated in people's cognitive attitudes to democracy. When asked, for example, what democracy means, and what respondents understand under this term, only three per cent in Belarus and, surprisingly, one per cent in Ukraine replied that democracy for them meant 'government by the people'. Only one per cent in Belarus but none in Ukraine responded that 'democracy gives an opportunity for people to affect decision-making in the country' and implies 'personal responsibility, respect for others and more duties'. About one-third of respondents in both countries associated democracy with the provision of freedoms, especially those of expression and association, and in some cases absolute freedom; very few mentioned law, human rights and equality. In Belarus, 'crisis and complete anarchy' came second in respondents' evaluation of their understanding of democracy, and over a fifth of respondents in both countries found the question difficult to comment on. The general diversity of answers, however, was striking, ranging from defining democracy as 'something different from communism', 'dignified living' and 'life without looking back, free of fears', to 'mission impossible' and 'the political regime of the USA' (see Table 2).

If we compare these results with the 1998 record, the *only* positive change one can observe is that of a minor downturn in the number of the 'undecided', which may suggest that people are finally beginning to define their opinions in more categorical terms. It can be noted, however, that during the past five years the people's view of democracy as 'provision of freedoms', often associated with 'total freedom', received little or no clarification over time. In contrast, some essential qualities of democracy seem to have lost their appeal to the populace, as Table 2 conveys.

The comparison between the 1998 and 2003 surveys also reveals a definite increase in the number of subscribers to more 'anti-dissident', uniform and authoritarian tendencies across the board (see Table 3). Disagreements surfaced only when evaluating the role of dissent and the presence of foreigners critical of the government.

Despite some obvious similarities in the patterns of opinion between the two countries, the differences become transparent when analysing people's attitudes

TABLE 2
PUBLIC UNDERSTANDING OF DEMOCRACY, 2003 AND 1998

What does 'democracy' mean to you?	Belarus (per cent)	Ukraine (per cent)
Provision of freedoms (complete freedoms)	30 (−0.9)	23 (−14.7)
Crisis, anarchy, corruption	13	4
Difficult to say	13 (−16.7)	19 (−8.6)
Obedience to law	6 (−0.6)	9 (−1.1)
Protection of human rights	5 (+1)	3 (−8.8)
Total freedom	3	11
Governance by people	3 (−9.9)	1 (−5.5)
Equality	1	9

Notes: Percentage shifts between 1998 and 2003 for repeated definitions of democracy by respondents are reflected in brackets. A positive or a negative sign indicates increase or decline in the number of subscribers to the same opinion. Percentages are rounded up to the nearest whole number. The sums in columns do not round to 100 per cent because of the selection of replies above 1 per cent that are specifically relevant to this discussion.

Source: Author's survey and extracts from 1998 survey 'Understanding Democracy': see note 30 for explanation.

towards politics: 58 per cent in Belarus seem not to care who is in power so long as the situation is improving; by contrast, 76 per cent of Ukrainians are concerned about 'the quality of leadership'. Again, 47 per cent of the Belarusians would rather not interfere in politics, as there might be damaging repercussions, which contrasts with 86 per cent of Ukrainians disagreeing with this sentiment. A majority of the respondents in both countries, nevertheless, agreed that 'common people would always be excluded from power'. Despite their ostensible passivity, a striking 46 per cent of the Belarusians (+27 per cent) believe that participation in politics is 'a duty', which is countervailed by 75 per cent of the Ukrainians deeming it as the opposite.

People's trust in various institutions is another testimony as to whether they are 'morally' ready to reciprocate and negotiate their rights and responsibilities with their governments. It appeared that trust in institutions had on average grown by ten per cent since 1998 in both countries. This, however, was concomitant with the ten per cent fall in trust of the Belarusians in their president (which still remains ten per cent higher than in any other political institution in the country, except for the army, reaching 65 per cent). In Belarus the least trusted institutions are political parties (12 per cent, up by seven per cent), trade unions (23 per cent, up by one per cent), parliament (30 per cent, down by three per cent) and judges (32 per cent, up by five per cent); whereas in Ukraine, these are parties (14 per cent, up by ten per cent), the presidential administration (20 per cent), parliament (up by 13,

TABLE 3
PUBLIC APPRECIATION OF 'AUTHORITARIAN VALUES'

	Belarus (per cent)		Ukraine (per cent)	
Do you believe that...?	Entirely or somewhat agree	Entirely or somewhat disagree	Entirely or somewhat agree	Entirely or somewhat disagree
Society should not tolerate political views radically different from those of the majority	49 (+12)	36	40 (−0.9)	42
Demonstrations and protest marches should be banned for breeding extremism and disorder	46 (+1)	34	48 (−2.1)	35
Freedom of expression can be harmful if it accommodates various extremist views	49 (+4)	28	39 (−0.8)	46
It is better to live in an orderly society than allow for certain freedom to be used to destroy us	47 (−0.2)	33	49 (−13)	40
Those who dislike our way of life must not be given a chance to speak up	20	71 (+8)	19	73 (+12)
Foreigners who criticize our government should be expelled from the country	36 (−0.2)	52 (+7)	38 (−2.1)	50 (+9)

Notes: Percentage shifts between 1998 and 2003 for repeated issues are reflected in brackets. A positive or a negative sign indicates increase or decline in the number of subscribers to the same opinion. Percentages are rounded up to the nearest whole number.

to 21 per cent), and equally the president (23 per cent, up by 12) and government (23 per cent, up by 14).

People's fears differ as well in the two countries. In Belarus, about 86 per cent of the population are concerned about impoverishment and growing state patronage, and by the lack of adequate resources to be able to afford clothes, medicine and food (in descending order). In Ukraine the main worry is corruption and patronage (88 per cent of those polled), along with the growth of inequality and the incompetence of the authorities. The prospect of dictatorship in both countries comes as the least feared future, with just 13 per cent concerned in Belarus and 47 per cent in Ukraine.

In summary, as recent opinion polls indicate, after nearly 15 years of change and the installation of democratic institutions, citizens in both countries continue to display inconsistent views and controversial evaluations of the democratic framework and the principles of democracy. A positive sign is that citizens by now seem to have become used to the idea of having institutional forms of democracy, even though some institutions are still being valued quite low in terms of their activities and impact on the system (for example, parties, parliaments and judges). This perhaps has more to do with their practices than their institutional value.

What remains of great concern is the noticeable discrepancy between people's 'institutional' and 'emotional' acceptance of democracy. They may abide by 'new' institutional settings but simultaneously confess intolerance of dissent and display explicit leniency towards strong leadership and government by decree (particularly in Belarus). They may welcome elections and a multi-party system, but entirely distrust all levels of government and abstain from voting, thereby discarding the assumed partnership between the governed and their governors, and 'delegating' their choices and decisions to *appointed* officials. In other words, the institutional forms of democracy may well be embedded and supported, but are certainly not trusted or engaged with.

The Belarusian population was revealed as more 'institutionally' as well as 'dutifully' ready to serve ideas of democracy, but appeared to be more 'authoritarian' in its judgements and, although well read, it felt more disengaged from the actual process of politics. The Ukrainians were more critical and presented themselves as more knowledgeable, which, however, runs in contradiction with the fact that 75 per cent of respondents believe that 'participation in politics' has nothing to do with citizens' rights and responsibilities.

Focus Groups: 1999 and 2003[32]

Focus groups were designed in such a way as to allow comparison and in-depth evaluation of people's beliefs and convictions. Respondents were asked to define what democracy meant for them, evaluate the state of democracy in their own country, express their value orientations and finally assess their bond with national leaders. The findings appeared to be concomitant with the evidence revealed by national surveys, and aided further desegregation of national data to an individual-level response. The principal findings reflect diverging patterns of understanding and value orientation in people's evaluation of democracy in the two countries, which may shed light on why democracy has not become established in Belarus and why progress towards democracy remains protracted in Ukraine.

The Idea of Democracy

Focus groups in both countries revealed a good understanding of what democracy should presuppose institutionally. This was particularly relevant for

Ukraine, when a few noted that democracy is 'when people's rights are accounted for'; 'the only chance to affect government decision-making is through elections. Hence, we must achieve free and fair elections'; 'it is about the power of idea and supremacy of law'; and finally, 'it is freedom of speech, expression and mass media'. In other words, the institutional paraphernalia of democracy in Ukraine seemed to have endured in people's minds, and respondents would object to the complete abolition of parties, parliament or elections. There were, however, some atypical answers ranging from generalizing democracy as 'absolute freedom' or 'the power of money' to describing it as a state when one is 'not to be beaten' or 'repressed'.

Belarusians revealed a different understanding of democracy. For many it was 'difficult to fathom', and meant 'absolute order', 'compliance with rules', 'discipline, high morals', 'respect for others' and 'equality and education'. To others it was 'a mechanism of subordination of the minority by the majority' as well as 'power of repression', ineffective representation', 'public violence' and 'all-permissiveness'. The prevailing *leitmotif* was about 'order and obedience to rules', and 'duties and responsibilities'.

The Evaluation of National Democracy

Ukraine again was 'leading' in its 'institutional' understanding of the workings of democracy. While describing the real state of affairs as 'criminal democracy', 'shambles democracy', 'clan democracy' and 'a corrupt state', many Ukrainians, nevertheless, believed in the endurance of democracy in the country, and provided sensible explanations regarding its deficiencies. There were claims that 'we need to change laws' and 'the judiciary system, which must be independent and unbiased', and change not the framework but the 'content' of parliament, the presidential administration, and the president – in fact, 'all branches of power' – in order 'to get rid of former communists' impeding democratization. All were united in their opinion that the core problem of a slow progress to democracy actually lay with people's 'Soviet mentality' and their stereotypes of the past.

The majority declared parliament as not 'just important, but very important', but what 'we need to work out is how to make it more efficient and to control it', because in the end 'we feed them'(!). This was counterbalanced, however, by claims that 'because parliament is ineffective, we need one strong leader with a team', and 'we only need MPs to help the president', which suggested that, although the mechanism of representation and legislation is understood as essential, it is still viewed as an auxiliary means to a one-man leadership, and the role of a president is considered to be central.

Belarusians again reveal a different level of understanding of the workings of democracy. First, they failed to describe the current state of affairs in the country, generally commenting that it is like a 'falling-apart *kolkhoz* [collective farm]', a state 'without ideology' which 'has no name'. Some said they 'had never thought on such a grand scale' and should have been given time 'to do some reading and to prepare notes'(!). On the question 'What needs to be done in order to improve national conditions?', respondents quoted 'moral upbringing', 'education of our society' and 'more discipline', along with 'a state body to invigilate the process (as in old times)', 'strong executives' and 'strong leadership'. They also claimed that today's Belarusians lack 'culture', 'a general idea, ideology' and 'welfare'.

When assessing the role of parliament and MPs, many commented that 'we do not need the present MPs', 'they are all corrupt and ineffective', and 'we do not know them'. In fact, 'we do not need them', because 'they will not solve our specific problems, the executive will do it for us'. 'We may need the Supreme Soviet,[33] but not the local MPs'; 'they are all powerless, under this law'.

The difference in views between the respondents in the two countries is remarkable, especially in evaluating the necessity of democratic institutions. In Ukraine, no matter how ineffective or 'big' the parliament is, 'we must never be rid of it, but reform it instead', 'we must be in control', whereas in Belarus one can sense an abyss between the governed and the governors, with the latter reduced to the role of one individual. As evidence suggests, although the Belarusians may well be ready to live with the institutional paraphernalia of democracy, it has not yet become a vital, organic part of their lives. They will not get rid of parliament or parties, not because they are vital for the functioning of democracy, but because they are already in place, and traditionally, old items are kept because one day they may become useful.

Values and Beliefs

Respondents were asked about their view of working relationships between parliament and president, their attitudes towards a single-handed leadership, especially in emergency situations, and ideal leadership. Ukrainians again took the lead in giving a negative response to the question of whether a leader's authority might be extended beyond the law in case of emergency, and commenting that 'nobody can be above the law, in any circumstances', as otherwise it 'would inevitably lead to dictatorship'. In Belarus, by contrast, the majority positively viewed the prospect of transferring powers to the president if a situation of emergency occurred, citing names such as de Gaulle, Hitler, Stalin and George W. Bush as leaders who were hitherto given such powers.

The comments on a single-handed authority were generally split in both countries, with one group arguing that 'one leader is good, but ten minds are better', and 'opposition will necessarily bring control over a leader'

(Ukraine). It was dominated, however, by the opinion of others saying that 'there should be one strong leader', 'obedient to law' (Ukraine and Belarus).

Examples of ideal leaders in Ukraine included Peter I (the Great), John F. Kennedy, Vladimir Putin and Alexander Lukashenko, who was cited as being able 'to keep people under order', 'he does not rely on oligarchs', and, hence, 'has incorrupt government', 'he is generally a good leader'; the Belarusians mentioned Margaret Thatcher, Stalin, Lenin and Alexander Luka- shenko again. One even commented, 'I honestly do not see how there could be any other alternative to our President Lukashenko' (male, 65).

Finally, on the question of whether a retiring president should nominate a successor, opinions were split again. Both Ukrainian and Belarusian respon- dents commented that they would welcome a successor 'if he or she were a normal person, and . . . if in a democratic country'. Others, in a slight majority, noted that 'we must elect our presidents', but 'may welcome recommen- dations from a retiring president'.

This leads us to a conclusion that, 'emotionally', respondents in both countries are not yet ready for democracy, advocating strong and single- handed leadership and being uncertain about the supremacy of law in a crisis. Belarus again has displayed a propensity towards a traditional *tête-à- tête* relationship between the ruler and the ruled, with no other social capital to diversify it.

Intimate Bond Between 'You and Your President'

Finally, the comparison between the 2000 and 2003 focus groups, and national surveys, conveys that the intimate link between the president and his people has not yet been 'touched' by other forms of social capital engagement. Although many were dissatisfied with the outcomes of Kuchma's government in the past eight years, 18 per cent of the Ukrainian respondents confessed that they would vote for him again, and still found him reliable, consistent, trusted and experienced. People's reasoning for supporting the president, however, displayed a different tendency: a shift from 'liking his programme' in 2000 to 'having no better alternative' or him being 'a lesser evil' in 2003.

In Belarus, by contrast, respondents stated that in many cases he still remained an icon for them – open, whole-hearted and to be trusted – whilst recognizing that he failed his voters on many counts. Some noted that their opinions about the president 'had changed . . . for the better', and they continued believing in his pledges: 'He is very caring: he provided us with everything we need' (female, 74).

In general, however, a rise in critical thinking could be observed: 'I am often ashamed to have him as my president', 'especially, when people ask "what is happening in Belarus?", why people are disappearing, and when the Belarus–Russia Union is taking place, I feel ashamed and at a loss to explain' (male, 46); 'I think he has done his best, and burnt out. He won't do any better. Nothing will change' (female, 54). Some, however, supported his 'cautiousness' and incremental steps in reforming the system, especially with regard to the Russia–Belarus Union and the introduction of the Russian rouble. Others noted that 'at present there is no real alternative to the president, and I think we will have to vote for him for a third time' (male, 67). The shift in public opinion has become obvious: respondents moved away from their intimate adulation and passionate defence of their leader, which in 2000 was manifested in terms such as the following:

> I believe that in many cases he is simply misinformed. He cannot control everything himself. And those around him always play dirty tricks on him (female, 53, December 2000);

> Although he [Alexander Lukashenko] is a tyrant, he is our, home-grown [tyrant], and . . . this warms the cockles of our hearts (male, 44, December 2000).

By 2003 he was receiving more critical evaluation, which still has more to do with his 'critical acclamation' than real criticism:

> I understand it is difficult . . . But he did not fulfil what he pledged, we now can see more bureaucracy around, the militia grew by three times, and the cost of housing doubled. I understand he needs a good team, but no one forced him to choose a bad one (male, 65, April 2003);

> I still believe in him, and his promises and statements. However, I do not hope for anything better. It's just the hope that is left, . . . and yourself' (female, 48, April 2003).

In summary, although there may have been some changes towards accepting institutional forms of democracy and limited criticism of government policy-making, this has little altered people's emotional judgements and value orientations. In many cases, however, they still believe in the intimate bond between themselves and their leader, who appears to be their only hope to bring stability and peace to their countries.

This presents favourable conditions for the flourishing of a demagogical form of democracy, which casts an illusion of democracy when voters believe they have established an intimate link with the rulers, which allows for quasi-control over the system by means of elections. In reality, however, the rulers continue to see in people's trust an opportunity to legitimize their autocratic leadership, and do so by way of decrees and manipulation. The quasi-democratic wrapping of their deeds is carefully propagated to keep the voters hopeful, whereas the internal workings of the system, now embedded in the legal system, stipulate nothing other than the power of an authoritarian leader.

Both systems, in Belarus and Ukraine, continue to operate with popular consent and within the framework of a Constitution (for example, the president cannot and will not alter the Constitution unless with a majority vote based on popular deliberation), a method described by a respondent in 2000 as 'democratic authoritarianism', that is, 'a democratic way of electing an authoritarian leader', and is considered here as an illusory form of democracy, a 'demagogical case'. This quasi-democracy formally allows for mass participation and contestation, and survives via manipulation, deceit and, if need be, repression. What happens indeed is that incumbent governments use democratic norms and public approval to engineer a system to their own design. And the best way they see is through maintaining the supremacy of presidential authority over the other institutions of power and to ensure the longevity of the president for the purpose of regime survival. By this token, Lukashenko and Kuchma, for example, become the embodiment of national stability and act as its guarantors, whose removal from office may be interpreted as the subversion of the national interest. As Aristotle originally noted, although democracy is a perversion of a constitutional government, it nevertheless remains the most tolerable form of all, in which the normal role of the government is 'to act in the interests of the citizens but this need not be the same as acting according to their wishes, since those in power may have a better idea of what is in the interest of the citizens than they do themselves'.[34]

Conclusion

In this essay we have revisited the role of agency in our understanding of the workings of democracy, and its application to the practices in new regimes. It was argued that the oft-cited procedural (or minimalist) definitions of democracy focusing on democratic institutional paraphernalia (elections, parliaments, law) were not sufficient to capture the complexity of the functioning of the new regimes, and their ensuing incarnations. These definitions fail to elucidate why in the new regimes, despite their degree of consolidation, the practice of institutionalized elections and the respective behaviour of voters, the expected liberal democracy is not occurring.

In the course of this study it was suggested that there may be other forms of democracy that can offer sustainable government, and a 'demagogical democracy' is one such form that new regimes may acquire. The key to our understanding of the workings of democracy, or indeed any other form of government, should lie less with elections and conditions surrounding them, and more with the evaluation of the role agency plays in shaping new polities – that is 'a moral conception of human beings as autonomous, reasonable and respon-sible individuals' acting in partnership with elected government.

Different forms of democracy are believed to be largely the consequence of differing levels of citizens' political awareness and engagement into the actual process of politics. The greater the moral awareness of their choices and responsibilities, the greater the prospects there will be for 'constitutional rule' to endure.

After 15 years of change, many post-communist regimes may welcome the institutional forms of democracy, but 'morally' and 'emotionally' appear not to be ready to adopt its principles and values. Ukraine and Belarus have revealed a striking discrepancy in their people's behavioural and emotional attitudes, which have caused considerable differentiation in the workings of their systems, despite certain structural and cultural similarities. The citizens of these two countries display little understanding of their rights and respon-sibilities, thereby allowing for manipulation and dictate by their governments. Instead of working in reciprocal partnership, they are forced to resort to a quasi-democracy (if at all), associated with governance by decree and delega-tive leadership, which Aristotle termed a 'demagogical democracy' – the worst of its kind of democracy and one with a propensity to tyranny.

The United Kingdom's New Labour government's motto, 'education, education, education', may not only aid the reduction of 'democratic deficit' in 'old democracies', but also be used to build robust foundations for the new ones, with the aim of achieving an 'enlightened' partnership between the rulers and the ruled.

NOTES

1. For the purposes of our discussion, Belarus and Ukraine may be more suitably viewed as cases of a 'quasi-democracy', offering a democratic façade accompanied by less democratic prac-tices, or, using Aristotle's words, a 'demagogical democracy'. Such an outlook will aid a better understanding of the discrepancies occurring in these systems, which hamper or indeed reverse the process of fostering democracy to authoritarian practices in the above regimes.
2. For more details see Guillermo O'Donnell, 'Illusions about Consolidation', *Journal of Democracy*, Vol.7, No.2 (1996), pp.34–51; Guillermo O'Donnell, *Counterpoints: Selected Essays on Authoritarianism and Democratization* (Notre Dame, IN: Kellogg Institute Series, University of Notre Dame Press, 1999).
3. Richard Sakwa, 'Putin's Politics: Normality, Normalcy or Normalisation?', paper presented at the annual conference of the British Association of Slavonic and East European Studies, Fitz-william College, Cambridge University, 29–31 March 2003.
4. See the useful discussion by David Collier and Steven Levitsky, *Democracy 'With Adjec-tives': Conceptual Innovation in Comparative Research*, working paper No.230 (Notre Dame, IN: Kellogg Institute Series, University of Notre Dame Press, 1996); Larry Diamond, 'Thinking about Hybrid Regimes', *Journal of Democracy*, Vol.13, No.2 (2002), pp.21–35; Steven Levitsky and Lucan Way, 'The Rise of Competitive Authoritarianism', *Journal of Democracy*, Vol.13, No.2 (2002), pp.51–65.

5. The state is deemed here to be a form of government, a 'polis', which is not a place or resource, but a 'partnership of citizens in a constitution': see Aristotle, *The Politics and The Constitution of Athens*, edited by Stephen Everson (Cambridge: Cambridge University Press, 1996), p.65, 1276b1–4 and 6–8. Because each state is differently conceived, thereby reflecting the cultural and structural diversity of its citizens, no two individual states are alike, even when sharing the same Constitution; this presupposes the diversity of democratic forms of government.
6. Guillermo O'Donnell, *Democracy, Law, and Comparative Politics*, working paper No.274 (Notre Dame, IN: Kellogg Institute Series, University of Notre Dame Press, 2000), p.35.
7. Adam Przeworski, *Democracy and the Market: Political and Economic Reforms in Eastern Europe and Latin America* (Cambridge: Cambridge University Press, 1991).
8. Robert Dahl, *On Democracy* (New Haven, CT, and London: Yale University Press, 1998), p.85.
9. Joseph Schumpeter, *Capitalism, Socialism, and Democracy* (New York: Harper, 1975), p.242.
10. Aristotle, *The Politics*, p.65.
11. David Beetham, *Democracy and Human Rights* (Cambridge: Polity Press, 1999), p.3.
12. Schumpeter, *Capitalism, Socialism, and Democracy*, p.271 and n.5.
13. Samuel Huntington, *The Third Wave of Democratization in the Late Twentieth Century* (Norman, OK: University of Oklahoma Press, 1991), p.7.
14. Larry Diamond, Juan Linz, and Seymour Martin Lipset, *Politics in Developing Countries: Comparing Experiences with Democracy* (Boulder, CO: Lynne Rienner, 1990), pp.6–7 (original emphasis).
15. Diamond, 'Thinking About Hybrid Regimes'.
16. Levitsky and Way, 'The Rise of Competitive Authoritarianism'; this theme is developed further by Lucan Way elsewhere in this collection.
17. Robert Dahl, *Polyarchy: Participation and Opposition* (New Haven, CT, and London: Yale University Press, 1971), p.2.
18. See Dahl, *On Democracy*. He argues that 'enlightened understanding' of democracy by citizens is an essential part of fostering democracy, without which its legal-institutional framework will not be operational.
19. O'Donnell, *Democracy, Law, and Comparative Politics*, p.35.
20. Jon Elster, Claus Offe, Ulrich K. Preuss with others, *Institutional Design in Post-Communist Societies: Rebuilding the Ship at Sea* (Cambridge: Cambridge University Press, 1998).
21. Putnam defines 'social capital' as 'connections among individuals – social networks and the norms of reciprocity and trustworthiness that arise from them', in Robert Putnam, *Bowling Alone: The Collapse and Revival of American Community* (New York: Simon & Schuster 2000), p.19.
22. O'Donnell uses the term 'political citizenship', which in this context is similar to political awareness, and implies the knowledge by individuals of their rights and responsibilities as legal social beings: see O'Donnell, *Democracy, Law, and Comparative Politics*, pp.45–52.
23. Aristotle, *The Politics*, p.105, 1294b34–39.
24. It is important to distinguish between 'lesser democratic' and authoritarian regimes. Although there may be many similarities between the two (limited pluralism or mobilization or poorly followed rules, and so forth), and the former may well be deficient in some democratic principles, it nevertheless allows for the presence of law and implies that, no matter how manipulative leadership may be, in order to achieve its legitimacy it will seek popular approval, and will therefore negotiate. From this viewpoint, Belarus will be treated as a demagogical democracy, inasmuch as its leader, Alexander Lukashenko, rules under manipulated but generally defined law: see Juan Linz, *Totalitarian and Authoritarian Regimes* (Boulder, CO, and London: Lynne Rienner, 2000), pp.159–60.
25. Aristotle, *The Politics*, p.99, 1292a4–38.
26. Cited in ibid., pp.31–2.
27. Cited in ibid., p.99, 1292a11–13 & 1292a15–16.
28. Levitsky and Way, 'The Rise of Competitive Authoritarianism', p.54.

29. See full script of Lukashenko's interview to the NTV programme 'Lichnyi vklad', 19 July 2003, at <http://www.president.gov.by/rus/president/speech/2003/vklad.html> (assessed Dec. 2003).
30. National surveys were commissioned by the author in March–April 2003 (BA SG-35130), in Belarus (by the Centre for Social and Political Research, BGU) and in Ukraine (by the SOCIS–Gallup). A nationwide sample included in Belarus 1,000 and in Ukraine 1,250 adults aged 18 and upwards; interviews were face-to face; the confidence interval is 99.47 per cent. The 1998 results are the extracts from the 'Understanding Democracy' survey implemented by the same contractors in Belarus and Ukraine. The results were also corroborated by survey evidence gathered by the author in December 2000–January 2001 under EU–INTAS research (99–0245) in partnership with the above contractors.
31. This is the period associated with relatively free and fair elections; the 1990 elections are not taken into consideration here.
32. In each country focus groups were conducted with a focus on national leaders – that is, Alexander Lukashenko in Belarus and Leonid Kuchma in Ukraine. For the purpose of control, two groups of respondents were interviewed for each chosen politician. The sample of respondents reflected the general socio-demographic profiles of leaders' group loyalties (established from opinion polls). The interview groups included 8–9 persons, selected on the basis of positive answers to the following questions:

    1. Do you support this leader? and
    2. Did you vote for this leader in the recent election?

    The participants were selected by a snowball method. Group interviews lasted for two hours on average, and were both audio-taped and video-recorded.
33. Note the reversion to the old name for the parliament.
34. Aristotle, *The Politics*, p.76, 1281b1–2.

The Sources and Dynamics of Competitive Authoritarianism in Ukraine

LUCAN A. WAY

Introduction

In the 1990s, a large number of hybrid regimes emerged in Africa, the former Soviet Union and East–Central Europe that combine elements of democracy and authoritarianism. In such regimes, elections are regularly held but incumbents consistently abuse civil liberties, harass independent media, bully opposition and manipulate elections. Focusing on Ukraine, this article explores both how to conceptualize such regimes and where they come from.

In line with Levitsky and Way,[1] I argue that we need to stop treating these regimes as merely transitional. Such regimes have existed over several electoral cycles and generate a set of key questions ignored in studies of either fully democratic or fully authoritarian regimes. *Competitive authoritarianism* represents one important form of hybrid that is extremely widespread in the world today.[2] In competitive authoritarian regimes, elections are both competitive and also the primary means of gaining and keeping political power. Yet, regular abuses of civil and political liberties make it impossible to call these regimes democratic. After the Cold War, such regimes existed in at least 25 countries located in East Asia (Cambodia, Malaysia and Taiwan), the Americas (Dominican Republic, Nicaragua, Haiti, Mexico and Peru), Central Europe (Albania, Croatia, Macedonia, Romania, Serbia and Slovakia), the former Soviet Union (Armenia, Belarus, Georgia, Russia and Ukraine), and sub-Saharan Africa (Cameroon, Ghana, Kenya, Senegal, Tanzania, Zambia and Zimbabwe).

This essay examines the dynamics of competitive authoritarianism in post-Soviet Ukraine – focusing on the extent of incumbent power over elections, the legislature and the media. Over the course of the 1990s, the Ukrainian political system suffered from increasingly systematic incumbent abuses of power but still remains highly competitive.

The failure of democracy and the emergence of hybrid rule in Ukraine cannot simply be reduced to poor elite decision-making, and it has little relationship to institutional design. Instead, Ukraine's competitive authoritarian regime has been the outgrowth of structural legacies of the Soviet era that have facilitated incumbent abuses of civil and political liberties. I argue for a 'supply side' rather than 'demand side' conceptualization of Soviet structural legacies. The most important legacies of the Soviet era have very little to do with the degree of popular support for democracy. Instead, a weak rule of law, weak civil society and a weakly developed market economy, inherited from the Soviet Union, have made it easier for incumbents to use state resources to undermine potential sources of opposition.

A supply-side approach to understanding the role of structural factors gives us a better understanding of the particular mechanisms that reproduce non-democratic rule over time than do standard demand-side approaches that focus on popular support for democracy. Furthermore, such an approach to structure avoids the determinism of some other accounts. A precise understanding of how Soviet legacies function reveals ways in which they may be overcome.

Conceptualizing Hybrids: Between the Pessimists and the Optimists

Despite (or because of) the fact that democracy has been studied so intensively in political science,[3] there remain important disagreements about what it takes for a country to be called 'democratic'. Recent students of regime transition can generally be separated into 'optimists' and 'pessimists'. The core disagreement in studies today is whether the term 'democracy' should be broadly applied to any countries with regular and at least semi-competitive elections, or only to those countries that meet the standard criteria advanced by Dahl, including fully free and fair elections, respect for civil liberties and free media. The pessimists are very sensitive to non- or partial fulfilment of democratic norms. In the post-communist context, pessimists such as Ken Jowitt have viewed liberal or democratic institutions simply as façade and not meaningful.[4] Other observers such as Marina Ottaway take partial political freedom in hybrids seriously, but implicitly assume that the presence of serious and regular violations of civil and political rights make democratic political competition a 'fiction'. She seems to suggest that, even in countries such as Venezuela, Croatia and Senegal, commitment to liberal democracy is simply 'rhetorical' and 'elections are not the source of the government's power'.[5]

Yet the 1990s witnessed the emergence of numerous regimes in the world in which free speech is severely limited and civil rights regularly violated, but in which elections *remain competitive*. Post-Cold War elections in Ukraine, Russia, Serbia, Peru, Zambia and Zimbabwe, among others, have been marked by severe restrictions on opposition access to media, arrest and harassment of opposition leaders, and moderate vote stealing. In these cases, the field of competition is heavily tilted in favour of the incumbent. However, in contrast to fully authoritarian countries, *there is still a meaningful electoral playing field*. Elections, while unfair, create uncertainty yet are still considered the primary means of gaining and keeping power. In some cases – as in Ukraine in 1994, Zambia in 1991, and Peru and Serbia in 2000 – incumbents have actually lost. At the same time, victories by incumbents are not simply the outgrowth of administrative fiat but result from either the popularity of the incumbent or a relatively unpopular, fragmented or outmanoeuvred opposition.

Other observers have viewed hybrid regimes quite differently. In contrast to the pessimists, the optimists have treated the existence of even semi-competitive elections as signs of democracy.[6] This is the view that dominates the Western media, including the *New York Times*, which continues to call Russia a 'democracy' despite widespread media censorship and harassment of opposition.[7] According to this view, countries are democratic even if there are regular violations of civil and political liberties. Often, such a view has been justified by an assumption that the flaws in the democratic process are temporary or transitional – rather than more permanent – features of the regime. Especially in early analyses of elections in the former Soviet Union, election violations were often described as residual remnants of the old order likely to fade with time.[8]

There are four important problems with this broad application of the word 'democracy' to countries that have regular and competitive elections but suffer persistent violations of civil liberties. First, as many have stressed, it is obviously highly problematic to assume that countries are necessarily going to become democratic.[9] Second, such regimes are not simply transitional but have existed over long periods of time and several election cycles – over a quarter of a century in Malaysia, close to 20 years in Mexico and over ten years in Russia and Ukraine.

Third and most critically, these regimes raise a series of key empirical and theoretical questions that are totally ignored in studies of either fully democratic or fully authoritarian regimes. Studies of democracy have typically focused on such issues as the structure of party competition, presidential popularity and constitutional design. Such topics can certainly be important in hybrid regimes. Yet the study of hybrid regimes also involves other questions and institutions that are totally ignored in most studies of democracy. For example, a central question in hybrid regimes is whether and under what conditions incumbents will abide by the results of elections that they lose. Studies of democracy obviously take this for granted. Similarly, the fate of many autocrats in hybrid regimes in the past 10 years has hinged on whether they could successfully crack down on opposition protests or rebellious institutions – as in Russia in 1993, Serbia in 1996 and 2000, or Zimbabwe in 2002. In such cases, the autocrat's relations with the military are often a key to the outcome of crises. Autocrats in hybrid regimes must also develop informal mechanisms of censorship and control over the media. Such issues and processes are essential in hybrid regimes but totally ignored in studies of democracy.

A fourth and related reason to be more restrictive in the use of the term 'democracy' is that the oppositions in regimes with poor human rights records face very different challenges from those in full democracies even when elections are competitive. Restricted access to media and harassment by police, tax officials and other government agencies all make it much more difficult – but often not impossible – for the opposition to win an election. In Africa and the former Soviet Union, where civil society is extremely weak, such obstacles have meant that the most serious opposition has come mostly from within the ranks of former government leaders who have benefited from disproportionate access to media and other state resources, rather than from the ranks of civil society or regional leaders. Thus, in Kenya, Moldova, Russia, Tanzania, Ukraine and to a lesser extent Zambia, incumbents have been most seriously threatened by former high-level ministers, parliamentary leaders or vice-presidents[10] – Rutskoi and Primakov in Russia, and Sangheli and Lucinschi in Moldova.[11] This has been especially true in Ukraine, where Prime Minister Kuchma defeated President Kravchuk in 1994, and Kuchma in turn has been threatened by Prime Ministers Evhen Marchuk, Pavlo Lazarenko and most recently Viktor Yushchenko.

In sum, distinguishing between democratic and hybrid regimes is not simply a question of whether you view the progress of democratization as 'half empty or half full'. Rather, the study of hybrids involves a focus on qualitatively different and broader sets of questions and institutions than do studies of fully democratic or fully authoritarian regimes. For this reason, they deserve to be treated as separate regime types.

Competitive Authoritarian Regimes after the Cold War

Over the past ten years, numerous conceptions of hybrid regimes have emerged, each drawing attention to different democratic deficits.[12] Some have focused on restrictions of citizenship according to ethnic criteria,[13] while others have drawn attention to the weakness of horizontal checks on presidential power.[14] More recent conceptions have focused – as we do – on the regular abuse of civil and political liberties. 'Electoral authoritarianism' describes countries that have regular elections but that suffer from significant abuses of civil and political liberties.[15] This concept does not distinguish between countries with elections that are merely façade and countries where elections effectively determine who has power. Similarly, Ottaway describes 'semi-authoritarian' regimes that – as noted above – respect some civil and political liberties but have elections that are merely 'fiction'. Finally, our conception of 'competitive authoritarianism' describes regimes in which elections are the primary means of gaining and keeping power.[16] However, regular abuses of civil and political liberties by incumbent political leaders make it impossible to call these regimes democratic.

Given so many other conceptions of hybrid rule, why add yet another? The main reason is that our concept makes a clearer and more analytically useful distinction between hybrid and fully authoritarian regimes. Many concepts – most notably 'electoral authoritarianism' – put a great deal of emphasis on the presence or absence of regular elections, be they effective or façade. Yet it is not at all clear that the mere presence of formal electoral institutions in the absence of real political competition is a sufficiently important marker to distinguish regimes. After all, many highly closed regimes – including the USSR – had regular and highly ritualized elections. The presence or absence of purely legitimating and symbolic elections would seem to tell us very little about the character of the regime.[17]

Elections in Competitive Authoritarian Regimes

The core distinction between competitive authoritarian regimes and fully authoritarian ones is the presence of effective electoral competition for the top executive position. In contrast to elections in fully authoritarian regimes, elections in competitive authoritarian regimes – even if highly unfair – generate genuine uncertainty. Opposition in competitive authoritarian regimes can – by gaining enough electoral support – win an election and take power from the incumbent. By contrast, in fully authoritarian regimes such as Azerbaijan, Kazakhstan or Egypt, possibilities of power alternation rest primarily outside of elections, and lie with the leader's health, choice of successor, conflicts within the inner circle, or a combination of these. In such regimes, extreme lack of popular support for the incumbent may threaten political stability or undermine policy implementation but rarely leads directly to loss of power.

Given the high degree of fraud in many competitive authoritarian elections, it is not always easy to distinguish between effective and façade elections. The central point of distinction lies in how votes are counted. If the vote count is mostly fraudulent then the elections lose their meaning and countries can be considered fully authoritarian. Generally speaking, competitive authoritarian incumbents win by no more than 70 per cent in elections. Margins of victory greater than that suggest extremely extensive vote theft. By contrast, in competitive authoritarian elections, electoral observers and parallel vote counts keep the share of purely fraudulent votes to no more than five–ten per cent of the total vote. Thus, in the most recent Ukrainian elections in 2002, President Kuchma successfully manipulated the vote in 'closed' election precincts such as prisons, hospitals and military bases, where his supporters very often gained 100 per cent of the vote. Yet, intensive monitoring and high international attention made it impossible for him to manipulate the total nationwide count severely. As a result, overt manipulation appears to have accounted for no more than two per cent of the vote and several strongly anti-presidential forces made it into parliament.[18]

The most recent presidential elections in fully authoritarian Azerbaijan provide useful contrast. Officially, the incumbent Heydar Aliev's son won 77 per cent of the vote. Yet the process of vote counting and tabulation left serious doubt about the actual results. OSCE observers reported widespread ballot stuffing, pre-marked voting papers, multiple voting and 'significant' problems counting votes in most precincts – including falsification of the number of votes in a precinct and the bribery of precinct commission members to sign protocols they considered fraudulent. Observers also noted serious problems in vote tabulation in 90 per cent of the sites visited. Finally, the electoral commission arbitrarily excluded the results of 694 precincts before announcing the final results.[19] All of this makes it impossible to know how the population actually voted. As a result, the elections cannot be called competitive and instead seem designed primarily to legitimize the existing power structure. This is quite different from truly competitive elections in Russia, Ukraine and other competitive authoritarian regimes, where only a limited number of votes are stolen outright.

While elections are the most important sites of political contestation in competitive authoritarian regimes, parliament and the media also represent important sources of opposition that the executive is able only partially to control.

The Legislature

In fully authoritarian regimes, legislatures are generally either non-existent or completely subordinated to the will of the executive. By contrast, in competitive authoritarian regimes, legislatures are often weak but nevertheless represent important centres of opposition to the regime. While the impact of the laws passed is often uncertain, the legislature provides key resources to regime opponents – including immunity from prosecution, access to media and funds for staff.[20] These advantages combined with international legitimacy can make the legislature difficult to ignore. In Ukraine, the legislature used its resources most effectively in the early 1990s when President Kravchuk was relatively weak. The legislature consistently rebuffed Kravchuk's decisions[21] and forced early presidential elections. The legislature was also strong enough at this point to dictate Kuchma's choice of prime minister in 1994.

After 1994, however, the legislature ceased to take a strong proactive role – but instead acted to thwart various presidential initiatives. Between 1994 and 2001, the legislative leadership was backed by a strong and oppositionist

Communist Party. As in Russia, it provided one of the few serious counter-weights to executive authority. Since 2000, the legislature has successfully thwarted efforts by the president to strengthen executive rule and extend Kuchma's tenure beyond 2004. Furthermore, it has acted as an important stage for opposition activity. In late 2000, the oppositionist Oleksandr Moroz used parliament to reveal secret tapes made of President Kuchma that seemed to implicate him in the murder of the journalist Georgii Gongadze. More recently, parliamentary deputies have used parliament to draw attention to problems of media censorship.

The Media

Like other democratic institutions in competitive authoritarian regimes, the media have suffered regular harassment and abuse – but still represent important source of opposition to the government. In Ukraine, the most serious criticism of the government has come from newspapers such as *Sil'ski visti, Dzerkalo tizhnya* and *Vichirni visti.*

In contrast to some fully authoritarian governments, the Ukrainian government lacks the ability completely to control journalists and prevent criticism from being aired. Especially in the 1990s, political pressure and censorship was very often sporadic or reactive – resembling a game of cat and mouse between the authorities and certain maverick editors and journalists.

Such 'cat and mouse' behaviour by regime incumbents is evident in the widespread use of libel laws to stifle dissent – a practice prevalent in other competitive authoritarian regimes.[22] Officials in Ukraine have made extensive use of very open-ended libel laws. Until very recently in Ukraine, public officials could use civil suits or criminal libel cases against journalists who had damaged their 'honour and integrity'. In 1998, journalists suffered 123 libel convictions and four imprisonments for libel. The Union of Journalists claimed that journalists lost two out of three such cases on average.[23]

Problems with the media have been most acute in television, which has fallen under increasing monopolistic incumbent control since the mid-1990s. Early on, in the years immediately following the collapse of the Soviet Union, there existed what one close observer of Ukrainian television called a 'plurality of media dependencies'.[24] Under this system, journalists faced political pressures – but had a pluralism of forces to choose from. In the 1994 presidential election, for example, the Ukrainian state media were heavily biased in favour of the incumbent Leonid Kravchuk, while the very popular Russian station Ostankino heavily favoured Kravchuk's opponent Leonid Kuchma.[25] Simultaneously, during non-election time, the state media included some important criticism of the government.[26]

In 1995–97, the privatization of TV stations and investment from the United States and Germany generated several new stations – such as Studio

$1+1$, ICTV and STB. During this period, the production of electronic news was relatively decentralized. News programme anchors, journalists and editors all played a significant role in determining the content of news programming.[27] As a result, criticism of the government appeared sporadically in certain news broadcasts or on certain weekly news programmes, such as 'Pislyamova' (Postscript) or 'Vikna' (Windows), that were broadcast in the 1990s.

Until the very end of the 1990s, direct executive interference into television programming was relatively sporadic and tended to be felt most acutely during elections. For example, just before the 1998 parliamentary elections, the authorities attacked and ultimately took off the air programmes such as 'Pislyamova' that became too controversial.[28] Political pressure also became especially intense during the 1999 presidential election. The STB station, one of the smaller private TV stations in the 1990s, was targeted by the government authorities because of its *relatively* unbiased coverage of the elections.[29] In the months preceding the election, STB was harassed by the state tax authorities, the licensing inspectorate, the environmental health inspectorate, the district tax administration, the city tax administration, the district tax militia, the government control commission, and the Ukrainian Frequency Supervision Agency, which ordered the station to discontinue its satellite uplink. The station's commercial director was also attacked by unknown assailants in his home.[30] Finally, in October 1999, several weeks before the election, STB relented and changed the composition of its Administrative Council – after which coverage of the president became markedly more positive.[31]

In 1999–2002, Kuchma gained increasingly central and direct control over both state and private television. Pressure took on a progressively more active character as administrative officials increasingly sought to dictate the character of media coverage on a regular basis between elections. Kuchma's son-in-law, Viktor Pinchuk, took control over STB TV and also Dnipropetrovsk's Channel 11, which had broadcast anti-Kuchma programming in the 1998 parliamentary elections.[32] In the summer of 2002, the government began dictating how news should be covered on all television stations by distributing *temniki* (from the Russian abbreviation for 'themes of the week') – extensive instructions about how certain events should be covered and what the media should ignore. For example, discussions of the opposition were supposed to emphasize infighting between leaders and to portray them as supporting extremist ethnic demands. Certain figures such as Yulia Timoshenko, a former deputy prime minister who became a major opposition leader in 2001, were not supposed to be mentioned at all. Simultaneously, the media also reduced live talk shows and restricted guests to certain individuals trusted by the administration.[33]

At the same time, though, the government is still constrained in the extent to which it can overtly censor. Thus, journalists interviewed by Human Rights Watch report that directives are sometimes ignored and that there is a reluctance to fire journalists because such an action may create scandal. Sometimes, journalists are punished by transfer to less desirable posts or by having unreported pay reduced. However, many face no consequences at all.

In sum, competitive authoritarian regimes are defined by the uneasy coexistence of effective democratic institutions and authoritarian practice. Elections are unfair but remain competitive. The legislature is weak but is an important source of opposition. Finally, the media face constant harassment but can be highly critical of the government.

Structural Explanations and the Sources of Competitive Authoritarianism in Ukraine

How do we explain the emergence of competitive authoritarianism in Ukraine and other post-Soviet countries? Initially, the collapse of the Soviet Union and democratization in East Central Europe and Latin America convinced many observers that democracy was not limited by structural conditions but instead was the product of 'elite decisions and institutional design'.[34] In particular, discussions in the early and mid-1990s focused on constitutional crafting and the 'perils of presidentialism'.[35] Yet failures to democratize fully, such as those described above, have led many to move away from a focus on crafting. Indeed, in countries where democracy has faced problems, constitutions and laws have often been very fluid.[36] Often institutional design is a *reflection* rather than a *cause* of democratic decline.[37]

Simultaneously, there are clear geographic patterns in the distribution of democracies and non-democracies that have led many to focus less on relatively contingent factors such as institutional design and more on long-term structural factors.[38] Outside the Baltic states, post-Soviet countries are significantly less democratic than their East and Central European counterparts.[39] Cultural approaches centring on differences of religion have often been raised to explain divergent outcomes. Indeed, Eastern, Muslim and Orthodox countries are more likely to be authoritarian than Western, Protestant and Catholic ones.[40]

Yet many of these structural explanations rarely go beyond correlational analysis. The exact mechanisms of causality are often totally unclear. For example, it is not obvious how Eastern Orthodoxy or Mongol invasions several hundred years ago translate into more vote stealing today. Structural accounts need to provide a better description of the means by which undemocratic regimes are reproduced over time.

Demand-Side Approaches to Structure

To get a better understanding of the causal logic underlying many structural accounts it is useful to distinguish between demand-side and supply-side causal mechanisms. Demand-side mechanisms, the core of most cultural approaches, focus on the strength of popular support for either democracy or authoritarianism. Demand-side structural explanations for authoritarianism became particularly prevalent in the early scholarly interpretations of the Nazi rise to power, which was seen as an outgrowth of social atomization and alienation in Germany.[41] These accounts centred on the ways in which fascism answered certain broadly-based psychological needs.

In studies of post-communism, demand-side structural approaches have focused on popular attitudes towards democracy and political participation. Thus, Jowitt has argued that communism generated a 'ghetto political culture' characterized by an extreme absence of trust.[42] Similarly, Charles Gati has traced the decline of democracy in the former Soviet Union to popular disillusion with democratic rule.[43] Others have focused less on popular opinion *per se* and more on the dangers of extremist parties and ideologies.[44] Communist and proto-fascist parties in the 1990s were often seen as the main threat to democratic rule in the former Soviet Union. Domestic democratic activists in countries such as Russia and Ukraine feared the communists to such an extent that they readily allied themselves with former *nomenklatura* officials in order to prevent the election of communist parties and candidates.

Yet, Nazism aside, democracy has rarely died at the hands of popularly elected and explicitly anti-democratic or extremist parties or leaders. Much more common causes have been foreign invasion, military coup or the use of anti-democratic methods by 'democratic' leaders such as Boris Yeltsin in Russia, Levon Ter-Petrossian in Armenia, Frederick Chiluba in Zambia, or Sali Berisha in Albania. Power has a way of diminishing the attractiveness of a free press and free and fair elections. Indeed, the main lesson of the 1990s in the former Soviet Union is that the non-ideological, ex-*nomenklatura* 'centrists' who gained power were much more serious threats to democracy than the self-proclaimed communists, who lacked the resources and support to seize control.[45]

Moreover, many studies suggest that support for democracy in the region is relatively high.[46] A recent poll in Ukraine showed that 74 per cent of Ukrainians in both eastern and western parts of the country support the election of governors.[47] Support for democratic institutions has been further demonstrated by the relatively high (by North American standards, at least) voter turnout in Ukraine and the rest of the former communist bloc.[48] Finally, existing distrust of some democratic institutions is likely to be a *reflection* rather than a *cause* of poorly performing democratic failure.[49] In sum, there is little evidence that problems with democracy in Ukraine or most of the rest of the former Soviet Union have anything to do with extremist parties, a lack of popular support for democratic norms or an active desire for autocratic rule.

Supply-Side Approaches to Structure

An alternative supply-side structural approach focuses on the existence or absence of opportunities for leaders to use extra-legal means to stay in power rather than the demand for authoritarianism *per se*. The shape of these opportunities has been determined by the post-Cold War international environment and Soviet institutional and economic legacies. While post-Cold War international liberal hegemony has increased the costs of maintaining authoritarian rule, the institutional and economic legacies of Soviet rule generated critical mechanisms and opportunities for leaders to harass opposition and manipulate elections.

The end of the Cold War created serious obstacles for autocratic leaders. The loss of non-Western external patronage, the demonstration effect created by other democratic transitions, the proliferation of international non-governmental organizations and some state-to-state pressure have forced most leaders to permit regular elections and give at least rhetorical support for democratic norms. At the same time, most observers agree that, with the exception of the European Union conditionality, Western pressure alone is insufficient to create democratic rule. Pressure for democracy tends to be highly sporadic and inconsistently applied, and to focus almost exclusively on elections to the exclusion of civil liberties.[50] Thus, for most countries in the former Soviet Union and elsewhere, the success of democracy hinges on domestic politics.

The Soviet Union left three important institutional and economic legacies that have facilitated the imposition of autocratic rule. First, the Soviet system left behind weak rule of law that has multiplied the institutional mechanisms that incumbent leaders may use to thwart opposition challenges. In the Soviet period, law was used strictly as a means of state domination and did little to constrain the arbitrary exercise of power.[51] The Communist Party was generally considered above the law, and laws were very often selectively enforced. In the post-Soviet context, the weak rule of law has translated into a pervasive use of state institutions by incumbents to hold on to power and undermine opposition. Legally non-partisan state agencies such as the law enforcement agencies, state tax administration and regional state administrations are widely used to assist the incumbent by harassing opposition and manipulating elections. Law enforcement has widely been used to enforce laws selectively against opposition figures. Keith Darden has forcefully argued that in fact state leaders in Ukraine have both encouraged and monitored violations of the law in order to facilitate the use of blackmail and keep lower level officials in line.[52]

In Ukraine, as in other post-Soviet states, the tax administration has also become a key mechanism of central state control over dissent. The arbitrary ways in which tax laws are enforced and penalties determined give incumbents tremendous opportunities to punish sources of opposition.[53] Accusations of tax evasion have been widely used against opposition newspapers such as *Pravda Ukrainy, Vseukrainskie vedomosti* and *Polityka* in 1998, and *Sil'ski visti*.[54] More recently, publishers such as *Tak Spravi*, which produced the biography of oppositionist leader Yulia Timoshenko, have been targeted by tax authorities.[55] Similarly, STB TV, which partially resisted Kuchma's efforts to slant coverage during the 1999 presidential election, was visited constantly by tax inspectors and had its bank accounts frozen.[56]

In addition, tax evasion charges were widely used against prominent opposition leaders such as Yulia Timoshenko and representatives from the opposition party *Hromada* in the late 1990s.[57] Finally, the tax administration appears to have been a weapon to coerce local leaders to support Kuchma during the presidential elections. As Keith Darden cogently shows, the tax administration became a key means of blackmailing officials to obtain their compliance. Illicitly recorded tapes of the president, released in 2000–01, show Kuchma ordering tax officials to threaten local officials in order to get their electoral support:

> It's necessary for a tax worker to go to every collective-farm head in every village and say: 'Dear friend, you understand clearly how much material we have on you so that you could find yourself in jail tomorrow.' ... And there is probably more than enough material on every collective-farm head. Yes or no? Probably yes. That's why the militia, ... that is, the services ... they all have to, that is, take to [the task] and have a serious talk with every collective farm head.[58]

Regional state administrations have also been used extensively to secure the power of incumbent politicians. Regional leaders' importance during elections arises from their control over the regional press and budget distribution, plus their *de facto* influence over regional tax and other officials.[59] In the early 1990s, under President Leonid Kravchuk, the government in Kiev had only weak control over many regional governments in eastern and southern Ukraine. As a result, many local leaders actively undermined Kravchuk's campaign for the presidency in 1994.[60] Learning from this experience, Kuchma established firm central control over regional governments. Despite being elected on a platform calling for greater regional autonomy, Kuchma successfully resolved regional problems and re-established vertical political control. Regions ceased demanding greater autonomy. Simultaneously, maintaining the Kuchma regime through electoral manipulation and other means has become an informal but core competency for the heads of regional state administrations. Those who have failed have quickly been fired. Within two months of the 1998 parliamentary elections, Kuchma dismissed 14 governors and 18 district state administration chairmen in areas where his supporters had not done well. Similarly, days after the 1999 presidential elections, Kuchma fired governors in regions where the communists did well.[61]

Next, the weakly developed market economy and concentration of resources in state hands – legacies of Soviet rule – have further increased the capacity of the government to thwart opposition. More so than its East European neighbours, the Soviet-era economy was deeply embedded in communist institutions and isolated from the West.[62] Partly as a result, the post-Soviet business class has been tightly tied to the state. Ukrainian oligarchs, like their Russian counterparts, have made most of their money through arbitrage,[63] distribution of budgetary resources in private banks, and access to energy monopolies.[64] As in Russia, the result has been a business class that is highly reluctant to criticize executive power. Those who have broken with Kuchma, such as Pavlo Lazarenko and Yulia Timoshenko, have suffered loss of income, state harassment, exile or a combination of these.

In the absence of a developed market economy and independent business class, it has been extraordinarily difficult for a strong and autonomous media to develop. Media outlets cannot rely on advertising for survival and most of their potential sponsors have made their money through government connections. This has been particularly problematic for the development of independent television, since that requires substantial funds.[65]

Finally, as in many other post-communist countries, civil society or non-state voluntary organizations are relatively weak in Ukraine.[66] Soviet totalitarianism successfully atomized the population and eliminated virtually all forms of autonomous non-state social organization. Institutions such as the Church, which provided an important source of opposition in Poland, were strongly implicated in Soviet power structures. As a result, civil society groups in the post-Soviet era have tended to be small and highly dependent on foreign financing. This has hampered opposition efforts to mobilize the population. In the face of extreme economic decline, unpaid wages and an extremely unpopular president supported by just five per cent of the population, the opposition has been unable to sustain mass protest. Efforts at mass mobilization that achieved some success with demonstrations of close to 50,000 in the spring of 2001 and autumn of 2002 quickly petered out. There has been nothing close to the massive and sustained demonstrations of approaching half-a-million in Serbia in 1996–97 and 2000.

Existing evidence suggests that failures of mass mobilization have more to do with the lack of opportunity created by a predominance of highly fragmented and inexperienced opposition organizations rather than any particular distaste for political participation. Thus, respectably high turnout rates of around 70 per cent in Ukraine show that the population is not resistant to political participation *per se*.[67]

In sum, I have argued for a supply-side conceptualization of structural obstacles to democracy in the post-Soviet context. The central forces in the former Soviet Union undermining democracy have not been entrenched popular disaffection with democracy, support for extremist groups or generalized distrust – factors emphasized by many observers in the early 1990s – but institutional opportunities for abuse by incumbents, created by Soviet economic and institutional legacies. The weak rule of law, the absence of a strong independent business class and the underdeveloped civil society all give incumbents a wide range of opportunities to use extra-legal mechanisms to stay in power. As noted above, one result is that the most viable opposition has come from former ministers in government who have directly benefited from the state leaders' uneven access to media and other resources. Thus, by late 2003, Kuchma's former prime minister, Viktor Yushchenko, had become the favourite to succeed him in the 2004 presidential elections.

A supply-side approach focusing on Soviet institutional and economic legacies by itself cannot account for all regime outcomes in the former Soviet Union. Other factors, such as state weakness, EU policy and ethnic nationalism also play important roles. Nevertheless, Soviet institutional and economic legacies have clearly been important forces behind the failure of democracy in much of the former Soviet Union.

Furthermore, a supply-side conceptualization of structural legacies has two main advantages over some other structural accounts. The first is that this perspective focuses on concrete causal mechanisms linking historical legacies to undemocratic outcomes. Second, this approach is not deterministic. Weak rule of law, civil society and the market economy are structural in the sense that they are difficult for any single individual to change. Yet they only create problems for democracy if leaders are willing to use non-democratic means to stay in power. Unfortunately, such willingness may not be so rare. While most politicians probably do not strive for total power in the manner of Saparmurat Niyazov in Turkmenistan, many leaders do not give up power easily. Thus, it does not seem far-fetched to suppose that many Western politicians, if placed in Russia or Ukraine, would suppress media criticism and manipulate elections in a manner similar to that attempted by Kravchuk, Yeltsin and Kuchma.

At the same time, one can envisage two situations that might in the medium term create democracy in the post-Soviet structural context. First, leaders sometimes *do appear* who have the vision to submit themselves willingly to weakly institutionalized democratic institutions and give up power despite the having the capacity to hang on, in a manner similar to that of

George Washington in the United States. However, in the absence of other factors, the appearance of such a leader might lead at best to a kind of 'contingent democracy'[68] that would collapse should a less self-restrained politician come to power.

Second, the real prospect of full integration into the European Union would be likely to discourage leaders from making use of anti-democratic measures available to them. EU conditionality differs fundamentally from other less successful forms of international pressure discussed above. Unlike all other Western states or transnational agencies, the EU demands full compliance with democratic norms and uses extensive and highly institutionalized monitoring. Perhaps most importantly, in contrast to standard political conditionality, the (real and perceived) benefits of EU membership are sufficiently large as to induce far-reaching concessions on the part of broad groups of the elite.[69] The result is that countries such as Romania, with an equally troublesome post-communist legacy, have democratized to a remarkable extent.[70] To date, the EU has not seriously considered Ukraine for membership.[71] However, if this were to change, the prospects for democracy would improve dramatically.

Conclusion

This essay has explored the sources and dynamics of hybrid or competitive authoritarian rule in post-Soviet Ukraine. The concept of competitive authoritarianism captures an important set of regimes that emerged after the Cold War that are both non-democratic and competitive. Such regimes need to be treated on their own terms. They have both existed in countries for long periods of time and raise a set of questions untouched in the study of full democracies. In the post-Soviet context, competitive authoritarianism has been the outgrowth of a democratic international environment, on the one side, and a strongly anti-democratic structural environment created by Soviet institutional legacies, on the other. This structural legacy has often been understood in terms of popular disaffection with democracy. However, regime trajectories in the former Soviet Union suggest that structurally created opportunities for abuse by incumbent office-holders have been much more important forces undermining democratic rule than extremism or support for authoritarianism.

NOTES

1. The conceptual discussion of hybrids in this article draws heavily from a joint research project with Steven Levitsky on competitive authoritarian regimes after the Cold War. For some

   conclusions, see Steven Levitsky and Lucan A. Way, 'The Rise of Competitive Authoritarianism', *Journal of Democracy*, Vol.13, No.2 (2002), pp.51–65.
2. Korosteleva, in this collection, refers to these regimes as 'demagogical democracies'.
3. Despite the fact that the vast majority of the world's modern regimes have been undemocratic, the field of political science over the last 100 years has overwhelmingly focused on democracy. A May 2002 JSTOR search of political science journals going back to about 1900 found 2,690 references in titles of articles and book reviews to pluralism and democracy, compared with 681 references to virtually all types of non-democracies (including autocracy, authoritarianism and subtypes of authoritarianism, dictatorship, fascism, monarchy, one-party and single-party regimes, patrimonialism, sultanism, totalitarianism and tyranny). Since 1990, the imbalance has been even more extreme: 881 references to democracy or pluralism, compared with 84 references to different types of non-democracy.
4. Ken Jowitt, 'Dizzy with Democracy', *Problems of Post-Communism*, Vol.43, No.1 (1996), pp.3–8.
5. Marina Ottaway, *Democracy Challenged: The Rise of Semi-Authoritarianism* (Washington, DC: Carnegie, 2003), pp.3 and 15. She puts these countries, which have all had recent alternations of power, in the same category as Egypt and Kazakhstan that have had no recent alternations.
6. Compare Marco Bojcun, 'The Ukrainian Parliamentary Elections in March–April 1994', *Europe–Asia Studies*, Vol.47, No.2 (1995), pp.229–49; Stephen Sestanovich, 'Russia Turns the Corner', *Foreign Affairs*, Vol.73, No.1 (1994), pp.83–99; Michael Bratton and Nicolas van de Walle, *Democratic Experiments in Africa: Regime Transitions in Comparative Perspective* (Cambridge: Cambridge University Press, 1997). For a similarly broad definition of democracy that focuses on alternation, see Adam Przeworski, Michael E. Alvarez, Jose Antonio Cheibub and Fernando Limongi, *Democracy and Development: Political Institutions and Well-Being in the World, 1950–1990* (Cambridge: Cambridge University Press, 2000).
7. See, for example, articles on Russia in the *New York Times*, 9 Nov. 2003.
8. *Local and Presidential Elections in Ukraine* (Kiev: Democratic Elections in Ukraine Observation and Coordination Centre, 1994); Bojcun, 'The Ukrainian Parliamentary Elections'.
9. See Thomas Carothers, 'The End of the Transition Paradigm', *Journal of Democracy*, Vol.13, No.1 (2002), pp.5–21; Levitsky and Way, 'Rise of Competitive Authoritarianism'.
10. In Russia, the Communist Party leader Gennadii Zyuganov, who challenged Yeltsin in the 1996 elections, was an exception to this rule in large part because the Communist Party was almost the only non-governmental organization that could draw on extensive organizational experience.
11. In 1993, in Russia Vice-President Alexander Rutskoi attempted to overthrow the Yeltsin government. In 1999, many felt the Russian Prime Minister Yevegenii Primakov presented the most serious challenge to Yeltsin. In Moldova in 1996, Prime Minister Andrei Sangheli and the head of parliament, Petru Lucinschi, ran for the presidency against the incumbent Mircea Snegur.
12. For a complete list, see David Collier and Steven Levitsky, 'Democracy with Adjectives: Conceptual Innovation in Comparative Research', *World Politics*, Vol.49, No.3 (1997), pp.430–51; Levitsky and Way 'Competitive Authoritarianism'; Ottaway, *Democracy Challenged*.
13. Philip Roeder, 'Varieties of Post-Soviet Authoritarian Regimes', *Post-Soviet Affairs*, Vol.10, No.1 (1994), pp.61–101.
14. Guillermo O'Donnell, 'Delegative Democracy', *Journal of Democracy*, Vol.5, No.1 (1994), pp.55–69.
15. Andreas Schedler, 'The Menu of Manipulation', *Journal of Democracy*, Vol.13, No.2 (2002), pp.36–50; Jason Brownlee, 'Double Edged Institutions: Electoral Authoritarianism in Egypt and Iran', paper presented to the 2001 Annual Meeting of the American Political Science Association (APSA), San Francisco, 30 Aug.–2 Sept. 2001; Steven Fish, 'Authoritarianism Despite Elections: Russia in Light of Democratic Theory', paper presented to the Annual Meeting of APSA, San Francisco, 30 Aug.–2 Sept. 2001.
16. Levitsky and Way 'Competitive Authoritarianism'.

17. Such elections in the Soviet Union seem to have generated disproportionately high turnout among the poor in the early post-Soviet period, but did absolutely nothing to create greater pluralism before Gorbachev came to power: Donna Bahry and Lucan Way, 'Civic Activism in the Russian Transition', *Post-Soviet Affairs*, Vol.10, No.4 (1994), pp.330–66.

18. Andrew Wilson, 'Ukraine's 2002 Elections: Less Fraud, More Virtuality', *East European Constitutional Review*, Vol.11, No.3 (2002), available at <http://www.law.nyu.edu/eecr/vol11num3/focus/wilson.html> (accessed in Nov. 2003); Erik Herron and Paul E. Johnson, 'It Doesn't Matter Who Votes, But Who Counts the Votes: Assessing Election Fraud in Ukraine's 2002 Parliamentary Elections', unpublished manuscript, University of Kansas, available at <http://www.ku.edu/ ~ herron/elections/papers/fraud.pdf> (accessed 15 Oct. 2003).

19. Organization for Security and Co-operation in Europe (OSCE), *Republic of Azerbaijan Presidential Election, 15 October 2003: OSCE/ODIHR Election Observation Mission Report* (Warsaw: OSCE, 2003), pp.17–18 and 20–25, available at <http://www.osce.org/documents/odihr/2003/11/1151_en.pdf> (accessed 30 Nov. 2003).

20. The communist parties in both Russia and Ukraine have relied extensively on parliamentary funds to staff their parties: see Luke March, *The Communist Party in Post-Soviet Russia* (Manchester: Manchester University Press, 2002). In the 1999 presidential election in Ukraine, the parliamentary paper *Holos Ukrainy* was one of the few major papers to come out against Kuchma.

21. For examples of when parliament thwarted Kravchuk's initiatives in late 1993, see FBIS-SOV, 29 Nov. 1993, p.61; FBIS-SOV, 26 Nov. 1993, p.53; FBIS-SOV, 10 Nov. 1993, pp.77–8; FBIS-SOV, 15 Nov. 1993, p.68.

22. See Levitsky and Way, 'Competitive Authoritarianism'.

23. See 'Ukraine', *Communications Law in Transition Newsletter*, Vol.1, No.7 (2000), available at <http://pcmlp.socleg.ox.ac.uk/transition/issue07/ukraine.htm> (accessed 15 Nov. 2003).

24. Andrei Tychina, 'Pressa: Rabota pod pressom', *Zerkalo nedeli*, No.37, 28 Sept.–5 Oct. 2002.

25. European Institute for the Media, *The 1994 Parliamentary and Presidential Elections in Ukraine: Monitoring of the Election Coverage in the Ukrainian Mass Media* (Düsseldorf: EIM, 1994), pp.189–91.

26. Bohdan Nahaylo, 'After Glasnost: Ukraine', *RFE/RL Research Report*, 2 Oct. 1992, pp.10–17; idem, 'Media in the Countries of the Former Soviet Union: Ukraine', *RFE/RL Research Report*, 2 July 1993, pp.5–6.

27. Human Rights Watch, *Ukraine: Negotiating the News: Informal State Censorship of Ukrainian Television* (New York: Human Rights Watch, 2003), available at <http://hrw.org/reports/2003/ukraine0303> (accessed 1 Nov. 2003).

28. Internews, *Report on Internews Activities for the Fourth Quarter, 1997* (Kiev: Internews, 1998).

29. OSCE, *Ukraine Presidential Elections, 31 October and 14 November 1999: Final Report* (Warsaw: OSCE/ODIHR, 2000), available at <http://www.osce.org/odihr/documents/reports/election_reports/ua/ukr99-1-final.pdf> (accessed 30 Nov. 2002); 'Ukraine', *Communications Law in Transition Newsletter*.

30. *Internews Report*, 1998.

31. OSCE, *Ukraine Presidential Elections*, 1999.

32. *Internews Report*, 1998, p.7.

33. Human Rights Watch, *Ukraine: Negotiating the News*, pp.21–2.

34. Robert Moser, 'Introduction', in Zoltan Barany and Robert Moser (eds.), *Russian Politics: Challenges of Democratization* (Cambridge, Cambridge University Press, 2001), pp.1–19 (p.10).

35. Juan J. Linz, and Arturo Valenzuela (eds.), *The Failure of Presidential Democracy* (Baltimore, MD: Johns Hopkins University Press, 1994).

36. Steven Levitsky and Lucan A. Way, 'Autocracy by Democratic Rules: The Dynamics of Competitive Authoritarianism in the Post-Cold War Era', paper presented to the Annual Meeting of APSA, Boston, MA, 19 Aug.–2 Sept. 2002.

37. Gerald Easter, 'Preference for Presidentialism: Postcommunist Regime Change in Russia and the NIS', *World Politics*, Vol.49, No.2 (1997), pp.184–211.

38. Zbigniew Brzezinski, 'Ten Years After the Soviet Breakup: The Primacy of History and Culture', *Journal of Democracy*, Vol.12, No.4 (2001), pp.20–26.

39. Ilya Prizel, 'Assessing a Decade: Eastern Europe and the FSU after the Fall of the Berlin Wall', *SAIS Review*, Vol.19, No.2 (1999), pp.1–15; Laurence Whitehead, 'Geography and Democratic Destiny: Eastern Europe a Decade Later', *Journal of Democracy*, Vol.10, No.1 (1999), pp.74–9; Jeffrey S. Kopstein and David A. Reilly, 'Geographic Diffusion and the Transformation of the Postcommunist World', *World Politics*, Vol.53, No.1 (2000), pp.1–37.

40. Prizel, 'Assessing a Decade'; Andrew Janos, *East Central Europe in the Modern World: The Politics of Borderlands from Pre- to Post-Communism* (Stanford, CA: Stanford University Press, 2000); Kopstein and Reilly, 'Geographic Diffusion'.

41. Cf. William Kornhauser, *The Politics of Mass Society* (Glencoe, IL: Free Press, 1959).

42. Jowitt, *New World Disorder*, p.288.

43. Charles Gati, 'Mirage of Democracy', *Transition*, Vol.2, No.6 (1996), pp.6–12.

44. Cf. Stephen Shenfield, 'The Weimar/Russia Comparison: Reflections on Hanson and Kopstein', *Post-Soviet Affairs*, Vol.14, No.4 (1998), pp.355–68.

45. This is not to say that extremist ideology played no role in regime outcomes in the post-communist world: Gamsakhurdia in Georgia and Milošević and Tudjman in Yugoslavia are obvious examples. However, in many other countries, including Belarus, Russia and Ukraine, such factors have played a minor role in the decline of democracy.

46. Timothy J. Colton and Michael McFaul, 'Are Russians Undemocratic?', *Post-Soviet Affairs*, Vol.18, No.2 (2002), pp.91–121.

47. *Dzerkalo tizhnya*, No.26, 12–25 July 2003.

48. For comparative voter turnouts, see <http://www.idea.int/Voter_turnout/othereurope> (accessed 15 Nov. 2003).

49. Ellen Carnaghan, 'Thinking about Democracy: Interviews with Russian Citizens', *Slavic Review*, Vol.60, No.2 (2001), pp.336–66.

50. Joan M. Nelson and Stephanie J. Eglinton, *Encouraging Democracy: What Role for Conditioned Aid?* (Washington, DC: Overseas Development Council, 1992); Olav Stokke, 'Aid and Political Conditionality: Core Issues and the State of the Art', in Olav Stokke (ed.), *Aid and Political Conditionality* (London: Cass/EADI, 1995); Gordon Crawford, *Foreign Aid and Political Reform: A Comparative Analysis of Democracy Assistance and Political Conditionality* (New York: Palgrave, 2001); Ottaway, *Democracy Challenged*. For an in-depth discussion of the role of international factors, see Steven Levitsky and Lucan Way, 'Ties that Bind? International Linkage and Competitive Authoritarian Regime Change in Africa, Latin America, and Postcommunist Eurasia', paper presented at the Annual Meeting of APSA, Philadelphia, PA, 27–30 Aug. 2003.

51. Kathryn Hendley, *Trying to Make Law Matter: Labor Law and Legal Reform in Russia* (Ann Arbor, MI: University of Michigan Press, 1996).

52. Keith A. Darden, 'Blackmail as a Tool of State Domination: Ukraine under Kuchma', *East European Constitutional Review*, Vol.10, Nos.2–3 (2001), available at <http://www.law.nyu.edu/eecr/vol10num2_3/focus/darden.html> (accessed 1 Oct. 2003).

53. Thus, it is probably not coincidental that in L'viv in 1991 a new building initially intended for the Communist Party was handed over to the tax administration following the collapse. In many ways, the tax administration fulfils the party functions of vertical control.

54. *RFE-RL Newsline*, 18 June 1998 and 18 Oct. 2000.

55. Human Rights Watch, *Ukraine: Negotiating the News*.

56. *RFE/RL Newsline*, 9 June 2000 and 30 Aug. 1999.

57. Ibid., 18 Sept. 1998.

58. Darden, 'Blackmail'.

59. Lucan Way, 'The Dilemmas of Reform in Weak States: The Case of Post-Soviet Fiscal Reform', *Politics and Society*, Vol.30, No.4 (2002), pp.579–98.

60. Lucan Way, *Pluralism by Default: Challenges of Authoritarian State-Building in Belarus, Moldova, and Ukraine*, working paper No.375 (Glasgow: Centre for Studies of Public Policy, 2003).

61. *RFE/RL Newsline*, 9 and 24 Nov. 1999.

62. Lucan Way, 'Understanding the Role of Historical Constraint in Post-Communist Development', *Studies in Comparative and International Development*, Vol.37, No.2 (2002), pp.97–8.
63. In the very early 1990s, like many others Yulia Timoshenko used government contacts to buy raw materials at state-controlled prices and resell them for a huge profit on the international market.
64. Lazarenko and Timoshenko became very rich through access to gas monopolies. Viktor Medvedchuk has made substantial money through control of electricity distribution.
65. While just nine per cent of media outlets in Ukraine are state-owned, the president has *de facto* control over television through informal networks (see discussion above).
66. Marc Morjé Howard, 'The Weakness of Postcommunist Civil Society', *Journal of Democracy*, Vol.13, No.1 (2002), pp.157–69; Adrian Karatnycky *et al., Nations in Transit 2001* (New York: Freedom House, 2001).
67. For comparable discussion about the connection between turnout and political engagement in Russia, see the contributions in this collection by White and McAllister, and Hutcheson.
68. Steven Levitsky, personal communication.
69. Steven Levitsky and Lucan Way, 'Ties that Bind?'. For further discussion of the impact of EU accession on 'democracy' in Eastern and Central Europe, see McManus-Czubińska *et al.* in this collection.
70. Melanie Ram, 'Romania's Reform through European Integration: The Domestic Effects of European Union Law', Kokkalis Program on South-Eastern and East-Central European studies, available at <http://www.ksg.harvard.edu/kokkalis/GSW1/GSW1/20%20Ram.pdf> (accessed 20 Oct. 2003).
71. Paul Kubicek (ed.), *The European Union and Democratization* (London: Routledge, 2003).

Conclusion: Democracy in Post-Communist Europe: Fifteen Years On

PAUL G. LEWIS

As the foregoing contributions have shown, democracy in post-communist Europe can be evaluated in both its quantitative and its qualitative aspects. The quantitative dimension can be defined more easily – and here the pattern established during the early post-communist years has tended to survive and strengthen. In 1991 only nine out of the 19 countries concerned (more accurately, eight before the dissolution of the Czechoslovak republic) were judged free – and effectively democratic – on the basis of Freedom House country scores. All of these maintained or improved on their score by 2000 – thus suggesting a general extension or deepening of the democratization process in this group of countries. The other ten states, rated unfree or partially free in 1991, mostly stayed in those categories. The general picture, in quantitative terms, is thus of a certain progress in democratization through the decade, accompanied nevertheless by continuing regional diversity.[1]

Qualitatively, however, there has been an underlying condition of stasis or arrested development that characterizes much of post-communist democratization, and this is a specific aspect of political change – or the lack of it – that needs to be accounted for. It is a task that raises particular questions and, as Bunce[2] points out, provides an outcome that suits regional conditions rather well, in that the hybrid regime is often one particularly acceptable to its rulers and also promises a substantial degree of legitimacy. Deficient democracy thus characterizes much of the region, while democratic quality remains problematic even in the more advanced countries.

Different reasons have been identified that might help explain this phenomenon. From one point of view, it is the weak development of the rule of law and the consequent failure to build an adequate constitutional order that is the problem. From another, what is missing in many third-wave democracies are its basic institutions – the fundamental problem being that the new regimes have been installed in contexts that lack the framework of the modern state, the precondition of most first-wave democracies and a necessary political basis to which too little explicit attention has been paid. Many post-communist democracies, like others in the 'third wave' of democracy, have therefore 'started democratization backwards' and failed to progress far beyond the forms of electoral democracy.[3] It has often not been realized, either, that many post-communist states have faced not just the double transition of political and economic transformation, nor even a triple change that combines these with state formation, but a yet more complex challenge of a quadruple transition in which the processes of nation-building and state construction are quite distinct.

Combined with this are obvious weaknesses in the basic features of the democratic process identified here in Morlino's model of the subversion of democracy, and further developed in Berg-Schlosser's article in this collection. The development of *civil liberties* is clearly reflected in the Freedom House country scores reported above, and these at least are relatively well established in the leading democracies of Central Europe that are now joining the European Union. The quality of democracy may further be gauged by reference to the level of *participation*, thoroughly investigated by White and McAllister and by Hutcheson here. With respect to electoral turnout and membership of political parties, for example, such indices are generally quite low (particularly in Poland and Hungary), although not greatly out of line with trends in Western Europe.[4] The establishment of patterns of *contestation* is also problematic, not least in terms of the development and consolidation of effective party systems.

It is, therefore, increasingly realized that the process of post-communist democratization is a complex one in which a range of critical factors is highly interdependent. How the body politic is constituted and the basic form taken by the newly emerged post-communist states was a matter of primary significance. Constitutionalism is of great importance for the development of post-communist democracy, not just because of its association with the development of a *Rechtsstaat*, accountable democratic processes and a legal basis for the conduct of democratic politics, but also because of the functions it performs in serving to constitute the body politic and form an inclusive political identity. This dimension is not far removed from the much discussed (but often loosely defined) issues of political culture that have also been seen as so central to the process of post-communist democratization, and which have been addressed by White and McAllister, Way and Korosteleva in this volume to emphasize the importance of social learning in forming the patterns of political participation. Furthermore, democratic development is often identified with Europeanization in this sense – the assumption of a consciously (West) European identity – and is in practice intimately associated with both the structures and processes that are designed to lead to formal EU membership. The major problem from this perspective is that any contemporary European identity is remarkably difficult to define. 'Europe' has come to represent values that are largely instrumental ('deals rather than ideals'), while the close link between material wealth and democratic achievement confirms a self-reinforcing dynamic of European integration and a view of politics that is essentially technocratic, as demonstrated by McManus-Czubińska and her collaborators in their comparative review of Poland.

The democratic deficit much deplored in the institutions and processes of the EU is thus also reflected in the ambiguities of post-communist democratization, and in the sharp division drawn between the more wealthy democratic countries close to EU membership and the second division of those slower in the democratization process. The process of democratization has not always been strengthened nor the cause of democracy necessarily invariably well served by the strengthening of West European links. The top-down approaches often adopted have not been particularly effective in strengthening processes of democratic consolidation or in tackling the weaknesses of civil society so often identified as one of the major problems of post-communist political development. Democratic conditionality has been a blunt instrument that is disproportionately harsh on states less advanced on the path of economic and political development.[5] Recent analysis confirms that post-communist democracy has been to a significant extent 'foreign made' and 'imported', and that democratization has been externally facilitated and indeed threatened by external agencies. This has had major implication for the quality of democracy. As McManus-Czubińska *et al.* confirmed, for many accession countries EU membership has been a forced, economically driven rather than a civilizational choice. In a similar vein, Korosteleva detected an obvious discrepancy between the 'imported' institutions of democracy and the lack of citizens' emotional attachment to them in the former Soviet states that seem to impede their progress towards full democracy. There is certainly evidence to suggest that the neo-liberal economic formula underlying the 'Washington consensus' has been indifferent to – or even in conflict with – democratic ideals, while Western pressures have imposed strict restraints on the exercise of self-rule by East European 'democratic' governments.

The above-mentioned observations point to important areas of conflict between the dominant conceptions of economic and political change which produce further areas of tension in the problematic process of post-communist democratization. Unfortunately, too, such problems are likely to be more acute in the more disadvantaged countries, which are both poorer and less advanced in terms of democratic development. Recent research confirms earlier insights concerning the politically beneficial consequences of socio-economic development – that once a reasonably wealthy country has become democratic it is likely to remain so.[6]

As is seen, post-communist Europe – previously associated with monolithic Soviet rule – is now rapidly diversifying in its move towards more democratic government. The new post-communist states display varying progress and achieve a differing quality of democracy. As shown in this collection, significant problems are still to be overcome, but some progress has been made, and many states now seem to be better placed to cope with their democratic shortcomings.

NOTES

1. Paul G. Lewis, 'Central and Eastern Europe', in Peter Burnell (ed.), *Democratization Through the Looking-Glass* (Manchester: Manchester University Press, 2003), pp.153–68 (pp.155–8). The eight countries that were free in 1991 were Bulgaria, Czechoslovakia, Estonia, Hungary, Latvia, Lithuania, Poland and Slovenia. Unfree or partially countries were Albania, Belarus, Bosnia, Croatia, Macedonia, Moldova, Romania, Russia, Ukraine and the rump Yugoslavia (Serbia and Montenegro).
2. Valerie Bunce, 'Comparative Democratization: Big and Bounded Generalizations', *Comparative Political Studies*, Vol.33, No.6 (2000), pp.703–34.
3. Richard Rose and Doh Chull Shin, 'Democratization Backwards: The Problem of Third-Wave Democracies', *British Journal of Political Science*, Vol.31, No.2 (2001), pp.331–54 (pp.332–40).
4. Paul G. Lewis, 'Political Parties', in Stephen White, Judy Batt and Paul G. Lewis (eds.), *Developments in Central and East European Politics 3* (Basingstoke: Palgrave, 2003), pp.153–72 (pp.166–7).
5. Karen Smith, 'Western Actors and The Promotion of Democracy', in Jan Zielonka and Alex Pravda (eds.), *Democratic Consolidation in Eastern Europe, Volume 2: Institutional and Transnational Factors* (Oxford: Oxford University Press, 2001), pp.31–58 (pp.55–6).
6. Adam Przeworski and Fernando P. Limongi Neto, 'Modernization: Theories and Facts', *World Politics*, Vol.49, No.2 (1997), pp.155–83 (p.177).

INDEX

Please note that page references to Tables or other non-textual material are in *italic* print